Plays for a New Millennium

New Work from Padua

Introduction by Steven Leigh Morris

T0151465

Produced by Sideshow Media LLC, New York, NY

Editorial director: Dan Tucker
Editorial assistants: Kathryn Williams, Catherine Grace Hannibal
Cover and interior design: CoDe. New York Inc., Jenny 8 del Corte Hirschfeld and
Mischa Leiner
Supervising Padua editor: Guy Zimmerman

Guy Zimmerman
Padua Playwrights Productions
964 Tularosa Drive
Los Angeles, CA 90026

Printed in the United States of America

Distributed in the United States and Canada by Theatre Communications Group,
520 Eighth Avenue, 24th Floor, New York, NY 10018-4156.
ISBN: 0-9630126-6-5

Contents

The plays collected here were produced by
Guy Zimmerman between 1996 and 2006 in Los Angeles.

This book is dedicated to the playwrights and actors
who made those productions possible, and, most of all,
to Murray Mednick.

The Sound of Los Angeles
by Steven Leigh Morris

Pictures generally tell the stories in this film and TV town. The words are mere decoration to the subtext behind, say, Chris Rock's smirk, or Danny Glover's bluster, or Sandra Bullock's giggle or Bruce Willis's gentle stoicism. Words are the sounds tucked between and around the explosions and car crashes and peekaboo sex scenes and crusading armies depicting legends of medieval vengeance and karmic justice that show up in video stores from Beijing to Timbuktu. These kinds of films reflect American optimism, where corrupt cops eventually feel the blowback of their misdeeds, as do corporate miscreants and serial killers slashing throats with the de rigueur explanation of having been molested as kids. Might eventually makes things right in Hollywood, and God is on His throne, most of the time. Such are the superstitions being so effectively marketed from Los Angeles and distributed whole-sale, mostly through pandering violent images tailored to maximize profits. So powerful are the visual pictures, you can watch an American action movie in Moscow or Tokyo with a local language voice-over and, understanding not a word, find the story barely diminished.

If Hollywood movies present to the world a picture of Los Angeles—of America, even—then the Padua playwrights (many of them working in television and film) present an anti-picture. They are a collective of wordsmiths who represent one of the city's most authentic, legitimate theater voices.

Their dissident vision starts with their motives of creation, which start with founder Murray Mednick—a Brooklynite transplanted to Los

Angeles. In 1978, Mednick founded his outdoor Whitmanesque summer camp for playwrights (The Padua Hills Playwrights Festival) in the foothills of the San Gabriel Mountains, near Claremont, about fifty miles east of downtown L.A.

Mednick's dedication both to his own writing and to the nurturing of colleague scribes has been described as "singular" by the playwright Jon Robin Baitz, who floated through Padua Hills as a student for a couple of seasons in his youth. The singularity Baitz describes has to do with the Paduans creating theater "as a reaction to the toxicity of living in a company town" and their uncompromising pursuit of despondent literary truths, based on observation laced with wit, rather than superstition laced with balm.

Mednick's plays, and those of other Padua writers, start with the primacy of words and sounds. On stage, the characters are positioned rather than blocked. Standing at points of stasis, they deliver leanly constructed quips, and jazzy riffs and arias from a place where Jack Kerouac meets Samuel Beckett. Behind words that are sometimes earnest, sometimes sardonic, most of the subtext comes from sarcasm, or some variant of it.

The commitment of these writers is to the refinement of a language that delivers insights rather than bromides. The Padua endeavor was never for commerce. Nor was it particularly popular. It still has a devoted following that one might reluctantly call a market, but that market was never mass, and will never be.

Nonetheless, the Padua playwrights embody as much a true voice of L.A. as Steppenwolf embodies a voice of Chicago. The mythology Padua, as a group, conjures starts with Los Angeles as an emblem of vanity, hubris and celebrity. The invariable comedy comes, of course, from L.A.'s larger context in the scorching, blinding Mojave Desert, a no-man's-land with a grandeur that belittles equally would-be kings and actors with ferocious apathy. If God is indeed on His throne, as Hollywood implies, He shows a profound disinterest in the fates of the characters in these Padua plays, people largely bloated by a self-importance that slowly evaporates with the travails of time and of living on a desert oasis.

In Padua's latest collection, this aesthetic is perhaps best expressed by a character in Sarah Koskoff's *The Apple Juice Man*—a soliloquy by Dan Sackiss, a former stage actor-turned-TV producer:

> And the sun it burns my eyes first thing. I remember. (*Beat*) And I raise my arm like this to cover my eyes like this (*Pause. He demonstrates and looks around. Pause*) And I have my own space, you know, too. I have my own space. So it's not like I have to, I have to wander in some big lot, or some big parking structure. Nah, I have my own, my own space. It has my name on it too. Painted on the cement block or whatever that thing is. And it makes me feel, I don't know... good. To see that. You know? Everyday. I feel good to see my name like that. Feels like I've accomplished something... 'Cause people, 'cause in Hollywood—not everybody gets a name on a space. I mean with all those cars, all those cars, it's lawless to think of them circling and circling and searching and limited spaces and swarming the roads and the freeways and all looking for a place, looking for a place to park. And to know every day my car not only has a place, but my name on it. My name is on that fucking spot. You know? (*Pause*) That means some-

thing for fuck's sake (*Pause*)... So anyway, I'm walking to my car and and and... And the great vastness of the desert. I never noticed it. And the cars. The noise of them. The cars. (*Pause*) The sky suddenly—the desert (*Pause*) The vastness of it suddenly. I feel myself walking... How do I? Uh. Just the, uh, the sky over my head. Just... And I'm suddenly it's like I'm... I feel a pain in my chest. I feel a pounding in my chest...

The Padua playwrights aren't writing so much about Hollywood's moral vacuity, as in, say, David Rabe's *Hurlyburly*, as about its metaphysical vacuity, with a poeticism akin to that of Nathanael West's, via James Joyce.

The desert looms large in John Steppling's *Dog Mouth*, a study of ego and fame as seen through petty criminals scavenging along the rails that traverse the desert. Calamity—and elliptical memories of it—informs Guy Zimmerman's *Vagrant* and Mednick's *G-Nome*, where instead of people moving through time, time moves through them, leaving behind impressions from quasi-real atrocities. Surrealism also abounds in Wesley Walker's *Wilfredo*, set in a Mexican bar visited by Americans and filled with a toxic brew that provokes ethereal conflicts.

The most striking departure from the Padua form comes in John O'Keefe's *Times Like These*, an episodic story of two actors in a Weimar German theater, one of them Jewish, as the Third Reich begins its crusade. This is O'Keefe's response to post-9/11 domestic policies in America that, in the intervening years, have become intermingled with the theology of extreme evangelical Christians—their strategy for world domination so clearly outlined in the Project for a New American Century. In conjunction with this movement, the United

States government doggedly refuses to reduce its mind-boggling nuclear arsenal, as though the Soviet Union were still a force to be reckoned with. America is not the Fourth Reich, though some patterns of her global ambition and persecution are alarmingly similar to imperialist empires throughout history.

Literature's twentieth-century existential writings and theater's absurdist movement grew, respectively, from the horrors of World War I and the nuclear detonations over Hiroshima and Nagasaki. How could God be on His throne with such cataclysms occurring under His nose? This question was implied in a generation of theatrical and metaphysical writings, of which the Padua playwrights are one obvious legacy. The driving debate of mid-twentieth-century literature was between a Catholic philosophy upholding the comforting idea of death paving the way for rebirth, versus that of secularists, who believed that death paved the way to the grave, and oblivion.

Curiously, in this fledgling century, as our government tries to justify the use of "bunker buster" nuclear devices as a legitimate military strategy, our Evangelicals speak of the Rapture, and how an impending nuclear apocalypse will open the door to salvation, and is further proof of God's majesty.

In the twentieth-century, the horrors of self-destruction could be lamented through poetical meditations. This has been the scope of the Padua playwrights, with their internal dreamscapes and imploding characters. Today, the prospect of Armageddon actually has to be argued against as a matter of policy. Even just twenty years ago, all of the plays in this collection would have been received as lamentations. In 2006, they're part of a political debate, which is really a debate with the devil.

Baby, Jesus!

by Murray Mednick

Baby, Jesus! *was first produced at The Lost Studio by Circus Minimus in 1996, under the direction of Guy Zimmerman, with the following cast:*

Jennifer: Dawn Howard
Chrystal: Roxanne Rogers
Margaret/Dorothy: Cinda Jackson
Paul: John Steppling
Mordecai: Murray Mednick

Characters

Jennifer *A pregnant teen.*

Chrystal *Jennifer's friend, older.*

Margaret/Dorothy

Paul

Mordecai

A room with a Christmas tree, lit from inside, a plastic Baby Jesus, a Madonna and Child, a phone. JENNIFER listens in as CHRYSTAL speaks with MARGARET on the phone.

Margaret	*(Phone voice)* I'm sorry, dear, what did you say your last name was?
Chrystal	*(Spells it)* Kimmineu.
Margaret	My, what kind of a name is that, dear?
Chrystal	German. I'm part German, part Irish.
Margaret	Ramsey Kimmineu. I'm very glad to meet you, Ramsey. Are you calling from Las Vegas?
Chrystal	Yes, Ma'am. It's 6:00 here now. What time is it there?
Margaret	Oh, it's 7:00, Ramsey, in Chicago. You can call me Margaret. Have you decided that adoption is the best plan for the future of your baby, Ramsey?
Chrystal	Oh, for sure.
Margaret	Why?
Chrystal	Well, I don't know how to say this, but I'm too young. I want to party. I want to go back to drinking beer and partying.
Margaret	Oh. Have you been taking care of yourself, dear?
Chrystal	That's what I'm saying. I've been living like a nun, taking care of myself, what's inside me. But I can't, um, you know... become a mother right now. I have to face that, come to terms with that, and I have, so I'm calling, and this is my first call.
Margaret	The very first one?
Chrystal	Yes, Ma'am. I don't want to string out a whole bunch of people. Who want to be parents. I want to take them one at a time. When I find, you know, the right situation, then I'm ready to make a commitment.

Margaret	I see. Sounds good. Do you smoke, Ramsey?
Chrystal	No, Ma'am. Margaret. I haven't had a smoke and I haven't had a drink... in eight months.
Margaret	Well, that's fine, Ramsey. Can you tell me something about the father?
Chrystal	He's a blonde, like me. About six-two. Blue eyes. Very good looking. He's a first-generation American, part Swiss, part Finnish.
Margaret	What does he like to do?
Chrystal	Oh, he's a college boy. He wants to be a musician, I think. But he doesn't know what he wants, really. He writes poetry and songs. Then he wants to be a painter. He paints a lot. I don't know. I don't know and he don't know.
Margaret	My, my. When is the baby due?
Chrystal	January fifteenth.
Margaret	Oh, my.
Chrystal	Yeah. *(Big sigh)*
Margaret	That's in less than a month, Ramsey.
Chrystal	I know it. And it's twins.
Margaret	Oh, my goodness!
Chrystal	I'm a moral person, really. But I'm not ready for that, and neither is he, Michael. That's the father. I'm moral, though, and I want them to have a good home.
Margaret	Oh, my.
Chrystal	Most people adopt again, you know. They adopt, and then they adopt again. This way you can do it all at once. Get the entire family. And everything is fine. They'll be five or six pounds when they're born, which is good for twins.
Margaret	Do you know... uh...?
Chrystal	It's either two boys or two girls, identical. They're facing

	each other with their arms around each other. Isn't that sweet? They're in one water bag, so you can't see the genitalia. So we don't know what sex. I only gained twenty-six pounds.
Margaret	Ramsey?
Chrystal	Michael's a kid. He just wants attention. He'll sign papers. It's easy here in Vegas. So we can do our thing.
Margaret	What is your thing?
Chrystal	I'm a cocktail waitress. *(Pause)* What I want to do right now. *(Pause)* I quit, I had to, after the first six weeks, I had to quit, I haven't worked. Now I want to go back to work.
Margaret	Is this bogus? Is this a bogus call? Ramsey? *(CHRYSTAL hangs up, laughs)*
Chrystal	Margaret. I called her last night, as a person named Lisa. Fifteen years old. I had a totally different voice. We talked for forty minutes. Mrs. Margaret Harrington, of Chicago, an artiste. She wants an artistic child. Caucasian.
Jennifer	That was... Jesus, Chrystal, incredible.
Chrystal	You want to try it? Get a lady on the phone?
Jennifer	We could do that.
Chrystal	Talk to one? You get these women on the phone, they're dying to take your baby, whatever, they'll listen to your story.
Jennifer	It could be triplets. *(Laughs)*
Chrystal	No, you have to make up a good story. You be believable. It's like acting. It's just like acting, only nobody can tell because it's your voice, it's only your voice, it's so cool. It was the water bag that blew it with Margaret.
Jennifer	You're really good, though.
Chrystal	Triplets sound funny. They'll get alarmed. They'll hand up the phone, like with the water bag. You want to keep them on the phone, and, you know, explore.

16

Jennifer	I'm seven months, and who's the father?
Chrystal	You make him up. Some jerk. They don't know. They can't tell anything.
Jennifer	I have ideas for that.
Chrystal	They don't see your body. They don't see you. They just hear this voice, this lost soul, this little teenage girl, if you want. It's an 800 number, so they even pay for it, these people. You have a *TV Guide*? Where's my *TV Guide*?
Jennifer	Here's a *TV Guide*.
Chrystal	Not the paper, the regular one, from the store.
Jennifer	It's so cool, because you could be another person. You become another person, on the phone.
Chrystal	Here it is. What would be your name?
Jennifer	What's a good name?
Chrystal	Oh, you know, like a teenage name, like a good American name, a Protestant name, like Kimberly. Or Jennifer.
Jennifer	And who are you?
Chrystal	Well, I don't have to be here.
Jennifer	In case you're here.
Chrystal	I'm your best friend, and my name is Mary. How old are you?
Jennifer	Twenty-three.
Chrystal	Say nineteen. They expect that. Nice little voice. Little teenager. Fucked a guy. Whatever. Do not like abortions. Poor thing. Like that. Thing is, don't know too much ahead of time, because that's the fun part, making it up. You know, you have to be ready. Who the person is, what's their angle. And you never know with these people, but be careful about money, don't say anything about money.
Jennifer	Don't ask for money.

Chrystal	No, they get suspicious. The thing is to keep them on the line, get their hopes up. I had one for an hour and 35 minutes. Tabetha and a lady named Rachel, in New York City. I was Tabetha, from a little town in Arkansas... Rockingport.
Jennifer	What area code?
Chrystal	Any area code.
Jennifer	If they ask for a number.
Chrystal	What difference does it make? Pick a number. And now is a good time. Now is the perfect time. The day before Christmas, because they're lonely, they're thinking about it, see what I'm saying?
Jennifer	Why?
Chrystal	I have my reasons. Las Vegas is good, because they can get a quick relinquishment there.
Jennifer	I mean, why do you do it?
Chrystal	I don't know why. I like the acting. I hate these people. You know, what kind of world is this? Advertising for babies.
Jennifer	It's different.
Chrystal	I feel like doing another one. You want to do it?
Jennifer	I should get my act together.
Chrystal	Not too much.
Jennifer	No, I mean to start off. You have to start somewhere.
Chrystal	Me and Rachel, we had a whole relationship. Not me, Tabetha. Tabetha and Rachel. New York City in Queens. I learned a lot, believe me. All about Queens, all about Rachel and Morty. The Sterns. What they do, how they live, the sad tale, the many woes.
Jennifer	What was with them?
Chrystal	Infertility. Right? No baby. Want a baby. Jesus. He was a film professor in a college. And she was an editorial assistant,

	Rachel, for a magazine. What do you think, did they want a smart kid, or what?
Jennifer	A genius intellectual.
Chrystal	I could tell by the sound. You got a Rachel and a Morty in the city of New York, or Queens. Guy is fifty, and she is thirty-nine, which I'm not so sure is the truth, and they're so vain. So, I could hear that. They want to be nice to a Gentile birth mother. You know how the Jews are, they're insecure. They got a Tabetha in Arkansas, the poor thing, she never saw a Jew in her life probably, maybe they're gonna get a bright little Gentile out of Arkansas to bring up, so I said the father was a computer programmer who was engaged to a pre-med student.
Jennifer	What were you?
Chrystal	I was Tabetha. Seventeen. In Arkansas. Tabetha had memorized the complete New Testament.
Jennifer	Oh, that was clever!
Chrystal	Yeah, and then I said some quotes.
Jennifer	You can do that. You're knowledgeable.
Chrystal	And you know what she lets slip? Rachel? We're making conversation. She says, "We don't say that, because for us it is not the Old Testament, it is the Bible. There is not a new and an old, there is only the Bible." So I make a long silence. Silences really get them. They think it's all gone wrong. "Tabetha? Are you there? I didn't mean anything by that, Tabetha. We are not prejudiced people, my husband and I." So I reassure her, and I explain that even though I'm young, I have the church. I have the church in my life. I believe in Jesus. I believe in the baby Jesus. And that is why I'm against abortion. I'm against abortion because of

my religious beliefs. And so is the father, who is now my ex-boyfriend.

Jennifer   That's a good story.

Chrystal   Anything partly true will work. Because it's easier. You become. I became Tabetha. That's the thing. That's the kick. That and the way you can twist them around. These people. Then I asked the big one, right? I go, "How will the child be raised? Because religion is very important to me. Religion is the most important thing, because I was raised a Mormon. Otherwise they get confused." And Rachel goes, "This would be an open adoption, Tabetha." I called myself Tabetha. "That's how it works in the contemporary world of adoption. Therefore the child would know, he would know what he was and he could choose, he could have a choice."

Jennifer   Do the Mormons believe in Jesus?

Chrystal   I don't know. I don't know a thing about Mormons. And neither did Rachel.

Jennifer   Tell me, how did you get pregnant?

Chrystal   They don't care.

Jennifer   I would care.

Chrystal   You wouldn't care. You want a baby. Jesus, what do you care? But not a rapist, and not an unknown. That they don't like. It makes a bad impression. And not a black guy, either. Unless, you know, you get that hit, you get a feeling they might go for that, you hear what I'm saying? Then you say, "I think maybe his father could be black." Like, a tantalizing half-breed, with hazel eyes. Some people, you don't know. And it's a performance. You could make up a whole romance, a tragedy. On the phone, on the spot.

Jennifer   How did I get pregnant?

Chrystal	Come on, you and your boyfriend, who is a very nice guy, a sweetheart, but immature, he's not ready for a relationship, you were out, your I.U.D. slipped. An accident. Whatever. You had a steady, one time he overlooked precautions. You get pregnant easily. You could throw that in. That always gets them. To get pregnant easy.
Jennifer	I'm healthy. I have healthy desires.
Chrystal	Hey.
Jennifer	This is the modern world.
Chrystal	Exactly.
Jennifer	I can't have an abortion, my parents are serious Mormons.
Chrystal	You ready to try?
Jennifer	What address?
Chrystal	You make one up, but you hold back. You're shy and confused. You don't want to be a teenage mom. But it's very difficult to give up a baby, remember that. If I had one, I could never give it up. A baby? Jesus. Could you?
Jennifer	Never.
Chrystal	I couldn't give one up, and I couldn't take one from some-body else, either. Okay, let's look in the ads.
Jennifer	Where am I?
Chrystal	I don't know. Say Utah.
Jennifer	Why Utah?
Chrystal	Mormons. Where's the magazine? Here we go. Adoption.
Jennifer	Okay.
Chrystal	Now remember one thing, which is that you want to know them, right? You don't just give your baby away, right? Your own flesh and blood. You want to know what kind of home, what's her expectations, like that. Remember, you're the birth mother.

Jennifer	This is exciting.
Chrystal	It's okay to be nervous. *(Reads)* Richard and Malvina. Florida. Sounds Black. You want to do Black? No. Middle class couple, California. Paul and Dorothy. Will cherish your child. Dorothy. You want to do Dorothy? What time is it in California?
Jennifer	It's early there yet. Is there money in this? There could be money in this. People might send checks.
Chrystal	No.
Jennifer	But I should ask. Because you just don't give your baby away.
Chrystal	You do. You give it away.
Jennifer	In return.
Chrystal	No, they don't want to buy a baby, because baby-buying is illegal. But maybe you never know, because they stretch. They stretch it as far as they can, these people out there in phoneland, in 800-number-land.
Jennifer	Give me the number.
Chrystal	If a guy answers, hang up. You don't want to talk to a guy.
Jennifer	Why not?
Chrystal	They don't want to talk. It's no fun. They're not interested in baby shit and lost teenagers. They don't talk. Ready? 1-800-876-5890. *(Dials)* It's in California. *(Phone rings)*
Dorothy	*(Phone voice)* Hello?
Jennifer	Hello, Dorothy?
Dorothy	This is Dorothy.
Jennifer	Hi, I'm Jennifer. Uh. Is this *TV Guide?* No, I mean, I saw your ad in *TV Guide.*
Dorothy	Of course, Jennifer. Thanks so much for calling.
Jennifer	You're welcome. Uh. Well, I...

Dorothy	That's all right. I'm nervous, too. This is a whole new... uh... experience for me, ha, ha. I mean, it's difficult. This must be difficult for you, too.
Jennifer	It is, yes.
Dorothy	But I'm so glad you called. I really am. I know how hard it is to call a number in a magazine, a total stranger, about something so important, as important as this must be for you.
Jennifer	Yes, it is.
Dorothy	How old are you? *(Pause)* Do you mind my asking?
Jennifer	Nineteen.
Dorothy	Nineteen?
Jennifer	Yeah. Do I sound young?
Dorothy	You sound very young.
Jennifer	Is that all right?
Dorothy	Yes, of course it's all right, it's perfectly fine. Please don't think I meant anything at all by that. It's fine. *(Silence)* Jennifer? Are you there?
Jennifer	Yes.
Dorothy	It's fine to be young. *(Pause)* It's wonderful. Nineteen. It's great, it's the best age, ha, ha.
Jennifer	It's okay.
Dorothy	Of course, this is a hard time for you, isn't it? Jennifer?
Jennifer	Yes, it is, uh...
Dorothy	Dorothy.
Jennifer	Yes, it is, Dorothy.
Dorothy	Well, I take it that you have decided that adoption is the best plan for your baby.
Jennifer	Yes.
Dorothy	When is the baby due?
Jennifer	Uh, I think it's due on... February twenty-fifth.

Dorothy	Oh! So you're in your seventh month?
Jennifer	Yeah, it's seven months.
Dorothy	Oh! Do you have a doctor? Jennifer?
Jennifer	Yes.
Dorothy	I should have asked you, I'm sorry, I'm excited about this, but did you have a confirmed pregnancy test?
Jennifer	Do I need one? *(Looks to* CHRYSTAL*)* I don't think I need one. I mean, I know I'm pregnant.
Dorothy	Of course, you do. I meant from the doctor. *(*CHRYSTAL *nods)* Officially.
Jennifer	Yes, I did.
Dorothy	So you're almost in your seventh month. God. I have so many questions. It's a little overwhelming. This is my first call. Is this your first call?
Jennifer	Yes.
Dorothy	Do you have questions? *(Silence)* Well, if you don't, that's all right, Jennifer. Maybe you will later. Do you mind if I ask you a couple of things now?
Jennifer	No.
Dorothy	Well, where are you? I know this sounds silly, but where are you? *(Pause)* I mean, where are you calling from?
Jennifer	Nevada.
Dorothy	Nevada. Whereabouts in Nevada?
Jennifer	It's a little town. It's near Salt Lake, I mean Las Vegas. Rockingport.
Dorothy	Las Vegas.
Jennifer	It's near there.
Dorothy	Is it snowing?
Jennifer	It's not snowing.
Dorothy	Oh. Too bad, I love the snow. I miss it.

Jennifer	It doesn't snow there?
Dorothy	I'm in Los Angeles.
Jennifer	Oh. Okay.
Dorothy	It never snows here. And I'm originally from Pennsylvania. Stroudsburg, P-A, where it snowed in the winter. We had beautiful Christmases. So that's why I'm saying... Anyway, Merry Christmas, Jennifer.
Jennifer	Thank you. Are you hanging up now?
Dorothy	No. I just thought, I don't want to press you. I'd love to keep talking, if you would like that, Jennifer. *(Silence)* Are your parents there? Jennifer?
Jennifer	They're here, but I'm not staying with them. I'm not stay-ing with them because they don't like the idea.
Dorothy	Of you being pregnant?
Jennifer	They don't like the idea of anything.
Dorothy	You mean?
Jennifer	Not anything.
Dorothy	They don't like you being pregnant, and they don't approve of abortion either, is that what you mean?
Jennifer	Yes.
Dorothy	But they know about adoption?
Jennifer	Excuse me?
Dorothy	They know you want to give the child up for adoption?
Jennifer	Oh, yes.
Dorothy	I'm glad, Jennifer. Where are you staying?
Jennifer	I'm staying at a friend's house. They're Greeks. They're all in there now eating fish, and videotaping. They videotape everything. *(CHRYSTAL cracks up silently)*
Dorothy	Is there a number there where you can be reached?
Jennifer	Excuse me?

Dorothy	A phone number.
Jennifer	Yes. Uh, 619-885—uh—9076.
Dorothy	And what's your friend's name, Jennifer?
Jennifer	Ask for Mary.
Dorothy	Mary. Okay. Thanks. I don't mean to ask so many questions, but I'm serious about this. Can I ask you something else important?
Jennifer	Sure.
Dorothy	Do you have medical insurance?
Jennifer	Uh, maybe my parent... I don't know... no.
Dorothy	No?
Jennifer	Uh, no.
Dorothy	Have you applied for Medicaid?
Jennifer	Medicaid? *(CHRYSTAL nods vigorously)* Yes, I have. Because my parents, you know, they won't.
Dorothy	They won't pay for it.
Jennifer	They won't and my boyfriend won't. So, how else?
Dorothy	You're very brave, Jennifer.
Jennifer	I don't have any money.
Dorothy	What's he like, your boyfriend?
Jennifer	He's a jerk.
Dorothy	Oh.
Jennifer	You know, he's not stupid or anything. He's just a jerk. He is immature. *(CHRYSTAL is cracking up)* Carl. I can't stand him.
Dorothy	Why not?
Jennifer	He's like, he's not in the picture, like he doesn't get it.
Dorothy	How old is he?
Jennifer	He's twenty.
Dorothy	Well, he's still a kid, Jennifer.
Jennifer	I can hardly talk to him. Because he doesn't pay any

	attention. He can't deal with my problems because he has too many problems of his own.
Dorothy	That's quite common, Jennifer.
Jennifer	He's a total mess now. I mean, it's Christmas, and he's spending all of his time in the library. He won't even talk to me. And the reason is, he's there with his ex-girlfriend, the one before me. So he doesn't have time for me. And the reason she's there is, she's a deaf-mute. Actually, she died. Today.
Dorothy	Wait a second, Jennifer.
Jennifer	I know this sounds weird. I know this sounds strange. His ex-girlfriend, she's Myra, she had problems, because of her condition, and Carl had to be there. It's a medical condition. And today she died, so now he has to do that. You know, the funeral and stuff. I hope he spends the rest of his life in jail.
Dorothy	Carl?
Jennifer	Not Carl. Carl is a sweetie-pie, really. He's the nicest guy. He is harmless. He's just, you know, inexperienced. I mean the... I can't explain it. But not Carl.
Dorothy	What's Carl like?
Jennifer	Uh, he's very good-looking. (CHRYSTAL *nods vigorously*) Carl ain't ugly. He's a grey-eyed ladykiller, that boy. Because he's sweet. It's not just looks. And he's very smart, like me. I think I am, you know, smart. But I think he's young for his age.
Dorothy	How tall is Carl?
Jennifer	Five-ten, maybe. He's a bit taller than me.
Dorothy	How tall are you?
Jennifer	I'm five-nine-and-a-half.

Dorothy	Oh.
Jennifer	Is that okay?
Dorothy	Of course it's okay.
Jennifer	Because if that's a problem.
Dorothy	It's not a problem. My husband is short. But if it's not a problem for you, it's not a problem for us. You sound... wonderful, Jennifer.
Jennifer	He could be short, your husband. Is it Paul?
Dorothy	Paul.
Jennifer	He could be short. I only would want, you know, a good upbringing. I would want... it... to have morals. Because I'm a very moral person. Otherwise, short's okay.
Dorothy	If we were to go on, Jennifer, if we were to go further with this, then you would get to know us. We would all get to know each other. Would you want that? *(Pause)* My husband, Paul, is an absolutely wonderful man. You could talk to him if you want to. Would you like to say hello to Paul? Hear his voice? He's right here.
Jennifer	Okay.
Dorothy	Say hello to Paul. Paul?
Paul	*(Phone Voice)* Hello? Jennifer?
Jennifer	Hi.
Paul	Hi, Jennifer. This is Paul. I'm very glad to meet you. How are you?
Jennifer	Fine.
Paul	How are things in, where is it, Utah? No, Nevada. How are things in Nevada?
Jennifer	They're fine.
Paul	That's good, Jennifer. Are you feeling okay?
Jennifer	I feel fine. I mean, I'm big.

Paul	Well, of course you are.
Jennifer	I bang into things. At night, I can't turn over. But... I'm not sick, or anything.
Paul	Good, Jennifer. Uh, let's see. Are you having a nice Christmas holiday so far?
Jennifer	Fine.
Paul	Good, Jennifer. Well, this is very exciting for us. I hope it is for you, too.
Jennifer	Okay.
Paul	I hope we can get to know each other. I'm sure we will.
Jennifer	Okay.
Paul	Well, I've about shot my load, ha, ha, Jennifer. I guess I'll give you back to my wife. I think you'll be more comfortable with her. Dorothy? Here's Dorothy. 'Bye, now.

(DOROTHY comes back on the line)

Dorothy	*(Phone Voice)* Jennifer? Are you there?
Jennifer	Hi.
Dorothy	That was Paul. *(Silence)* He's shy. As I feel you are. And it's perfectly understandable. So if you want to get off the line now, that would be all right with us. *(Pause)* And we could speak again soon. What do you think? *(Pause)* Just a few more things maybe you should know, if you want.
Jennifer	Okay.
Dorothy	Well, we live fifteen minutes from the beach in a nice house with plenty of room. Paul is in the motion picture business, so he's pretty busy, but I plan to be a stay-at-home mom. I'm sure that's probably important to you, that your child have a stay-at-home mom.

Jennifer	Does he know people?
Dorothy	You mean, in the business?
Jennifer	Paul. Like stars? Does he know stars?
Dorothy	Movie stars? Well, yes, a few.
Jennifer	Who does he know?
Dorothy	Can I tell you next time, Jennifer? Can we talk again soon? Can I call you at that number? Meanwhile, I could send you photos if you want. I could send you photos of us, and the house, and stuff. And you could send some photos, too, if you want. Do you want to continue with this? We would like to...
Jennifer	It could be twins.
Dorothy	I'm sorry?
Jennifer	It could be twins.
Dorothy	Twins!
Jennifer	I was afraid to say, but it could be.
Dorothy	Oh, my God.
Jennifer	Yeah.
Dorothy	You had an ultrasound?
Jennifer	I guess so.
Dorothy	You guess so?
Jennifer	I mean, yeah. I had one.
Dorothy	Oh, my God.
Jennifer	They thought there might be another head in there. Behind. Another head. Is that okay?
Dorothy	I don't know. It's a shock to me right now.
Jennifer	Because it could be two. Identical.
Dorothy	I'm in shock.
Jennifer	They would be really good-looking. Their father is like a movie star with his looks.
Dorothy	I don't know what to say.

Jennifer	And I guess I'm pretty.
Dorothy	I believe you, Jennifer. Um...
Jennifer	I know I am. I'm popular.
Dorothy	Let me just ask you, Jennifer, uh—
Jennifer	It really gets me, you know, about that mother who drowned her kids?
Dorothy	Yes?
Jennifer	Why did she do that? She could have done so many things, and that's what she did. Like, who did it? You know what I'm saying?
Dorothy	I'm not sure, Jennifer.
Jennifer	Like, who committed the crime? *(CHRYSTAL starts waving at her)* Because she herself didn't do it. She couldn't have done it herself. It wasn't herself who did it. Not the mother. Like, I didn't do it. But it happened. It's just weird. Because you can't take it back, even though. They're dead, they're drowned. Because, you know, time. How could it happen? It's like with, uh, Carl.
Dorothy	What?
Jennifer	I mean, his ex. She had a medical condition. Why didn't they do something? And she does. *(Pause)* And now America is in shock. Like on TV.
Dorothy	Me too, Jennifer. Let me just ask you. Would he sign papers? Carl. Would he sign a relinquishment? *(CHRYSTAL nods frantically)*
Jennifer	Don't worry about that, uh, Dorothy.
Dorothy	You're sure he's the father? *(Silence)* Well, I have to think about this, if you don't mind, Jennifer. *(CHRYSTAL hands her a slip of paper)*
Jennifer	Why do you want to adopt?

Dorothy	That's a good question. That's a fair question, Jennifer. My husband and I, Paul and I, we tried for seven years. We tried and tried. *(Pause)* It was awful. We went to these doctors, to a clinic, here in Southern California, a fertility clinic. These people. I have so much rage. They have all these photographs on the wall... of babies... they could have been adopted, for all I know... *(Sobs)*... Babies, Jesus... I took all these drugs... and the only time... we conceived... we did it on our own. And we lost it. It didn't take. We did that on our own. But these doctors, they string you along. We did inseminations, we did everything, and nothing worked. And finally... finally, they said, "That's it. You have to quit. You will never have children." Do you know what that's like? Do you have any idea how that feels? For a woman? To be barren? I'm sorry. It's not your fault. But that's why. That's the answer to your question. These people. My husband told me, it becomes a business. That's what happens. The fertility business. So we decided. We had to give up, and we decided to adopt. Jennifer? Are you there? *(Pause)*
Jennifer	You deserve it, Dorothy.
Dorothy	I'm sorry.
Jennifer	You deserve to have a child and be parents, Dorothy, you and Paul.
Dorothy	Thank you. I'll call you. Can I? Would you like our address? I'll give you my home number, if you want, not the 800 number.
Jennifer	No, you call me.
Dorothy	Would you like my lawyer's number?
Jennifer	Uh, the lawyer? *(Chrystal shakes her head)* No, could we

	talk more first? I'd like to get to know you guys, like your expectations and your ideas of parenting. Okay?
Dorothy	Of course. Can I give her your number?
Jennifer	Yes, she could call me, your lawyer.
Dorothy	Good. Let me just check the number. 619-885-9076. Is that correct?
Jennifer	Yes.
Dorothy	We'll call you.
Jennifer	I'll be here.
Dorothy	And we'll continue. Okay? Meanwhile, I'm so glad you had the courage, Jennifer, to do this.
Jennifer	Thank you, Dorothy.
Dorothy	It was good talking to you, and we'll talk soon. Okay?
Jennifer	Yes.
Dorothy	We'll talk soon. Bye-bye.
Jennifer	'Bye. *(Hangs up. Pause)* Whoa.
Chrystal	I told you.
Jennifer	That was an experience!
Chrystal	Really. You were funny! *(The phone rings.* CHRYSTAL *answers it)* Hello?
Mordecai	*(Phone voice)* Hello, who am I speaking with?
Chrystal	This is Chrystal.
Mordecai	Ah, Chrystal. Chrystal. Life as you have known it is over, Chrystal.
Chrystal	Who is this?
Mordecai	This is Mordecai, Chrystal. Mordecai Stern. New York. The bill for the 800 number, Chrystal. It lists the calls and the origin of the calls. So I've got your number, Chrystal, and I know where you are. And I'm coming. I'm coming. I will track you down, and I will smite you.

CHRYSTAL hangs up the phone as she gasps and covers her mouth.

BLACKOUT.

The End

4 Way Mars
by Murray Mednick

4 Way Mars *was originally produced at Glaxa Studios by Empire Red Lip in 1998, under the direction of Wesley Walker, with the following cast:*

Chris Kelly
Rick Dean
Lisa Joffrey
Dawn Howard

4 Way Mars is the first in a series of plays in which the playwright, Murray Mednick, strips away character attributions in order to heighten the dynamic quality of his theater texts. Listening closely to each other during the rehearsal process, performers and directors must uncover who says what.

After 4 Way Mars, Mednick continued to explore and refine this approach in his late plays **Tirade For Three, Gary's Walk, Girl on a Bed, G-Nome** *and* **Clown Show for Bruno,** *reinventing the classical Chorus in a modern context.*

I never knew anything about women. As a boy, my desire was so over-whelming a force that I felt it as an abstraction, an absolute, a form of worship. The actual taste of a girl's mouth—her breath, her smell—came as a shock.

(Off) A woman's mouth—it's a wonderful thing. The taste, I mean. If her breath is sweet. Where I grew up, you know, you could run into some mouth problems.

I hated to hurt their feelings, to see them weep, to feel the consequences of my actions, to feel my actions, to feel. In those days, I was at War. I was fighting, or I was preparing to fight, or I was recovering from battle, nursing my wounds, staunching the blood.

Is that so?

Yes.

You were in the military?

No. Psychologically speaking.

Did you rehearse?

What?

Did you rehearse these lines?

Well, that's interesting.

(Off) Mouth disease. Odor disability.

Why?

(Off) You were mean.

Why is it interesting?

Yes.

Well, it sounds like a made-up story, doesn't it?

Yes.

Tonally.

(Off) No, you worshipped them as objects. The actual taste was another story.

I too can remember some unfortunate consequences.

There was one, she comes to mind, she had skin like the softest satin, and, uh, warm velvet were her private parts, in the city of Philadelphia, when I was young. After the sex, she said she expected us to get married now, and I said, "Who do you think you are?"

(Aside) An actress.

"Who do you think you are?"

(Off) That's why you failed at reproduction.

"Who do you think you are to want to marry me."

(Off) I never gave it a thought. I wasn't entitled. It was out of the question. The only possibility was a life of crime.

Sick.

(Off) Addiction, humiliation.

Your ego talking. That's your idea of the Self. That's what you think a self is. Historical/meaningful.

That's really interesting.

Thought you were an ace, but you're nothing but a gene transmitter, a cell, a blip on the event horizon.

Very interesting.

(Off) Enjoyed myself, though, with Suzanne.

(Off) You don't know, you could have been happy with her. You don't know. Suzanne. Could have flashed a leaf on the tree of life with her.

(Off) Flashed a leaf?

She wanted to be married. I had no idea what marriage was.

(Off) What is that?

Domesticity? Enough money to live on? Regularity?

(Off) Flashed a leaf?

The right to a family, love, the right to a life. A job, a career. Who knows what could have transpired? But it didn't.

Because you're neurotic and deformed.

I was doing something else at the time.

What?

God knows. I was hallucinating. What love is, what a woman is.

Insecure.

I think there are levels. There is the procreative function and the creative function.

(Off) What has neither beginning nor end?

(Off) A riddle?

(Off) Yes. Two things.

(Off) And the answer?

(Off) Love and Time.

Say again?

Levels. Functions.

Meaning?

Well, that's interesting, because I don't remember what I was going for there.

It's an attitude. You want their attention but you don't want them too close.

Who are they?

(Off) Anger and Fear.

Who are they?

You heard me.

(Off) Yes?

(Off) Is the answer to what question?

They're your superiors.

Oh. Is it a class issue, then?

(Off) Okay, I give up.

(Off) Question: What are the twin attitudes of the Lower Man?

You never get over that. An idea and an attitude. Harboring resentments. Offended. Without human rights.

(Off) We all breathe the same air.

Is it a class thing? Is it the venom of the underclass?

What? Venom of the underclass that what?

That, uh, I lost the thought there.

You've got to do something about that. Your mind is like a sieve.

I meant with an attitude.

Well, isn't that what I said?

You were emphasizing the class issue here.

I don't want to talk about issues. I don't want to hear about another fucking issue.

(Off) Is fear an attitude? Is anger an attitude?

(Off) I really don't give a shit. Do you?

Marx was an idiot, thinking as he did, deep in thought, that you could fix the moral nature of man. That man could be improved through a mechanism of the state. It's idiotic. But must we capitalize upon the misfortunes of others?

The misfortunes of others? What does that mean?

The weakness of others. The stupidity of others.

Not misfortune. Inferiority. They don't work, it's too bad. The jerks on the street, they get sick and die, that's how you get rid of them. Even the gamblers have to work.

They work?

They work with numbers, they bet on work.

On somebody else's work.

It takes balls, it takes nerve.

But somebody has to work, somebody has to work in the first place, somebody has to work.

That's right.

(Off) What is the "creative function"?

(Off) Is this a test?

(Off) I'm asking.

(Off) "Imagine, death, imagine."

It's an adaptation, the gambling. It's adaptive behavior.

That's why guys like to fuck around.

They didn't have stock exchanges on the rolling savannahs. The hunter-gatherers. No Bourse, no NASDAQ, no City of London. Do you believe in an invisible world?

(Off) Beckett?

(Off) Yes.

(Off) Sublimation?

(Off) Yes.

Most of the world is invisible, pal.

Then what is evolution?

The five senses. Various tubes, bone and cartilage, a pump, a nervous system, reproductive facilities, and off she goes.

Push a button and the thing reacts.

Of course, we want 'em young. Virginal. In white.

(Off) We're confusing levels here.

(Off) They'll never be able to follow this.

(Off) We're confusing levels. The divine and the creative. Creative is not divine. Procreative is not divine.

(Off) You like that idea, don't you?

(Off) What idea?

(Off) That they can't follow this. Why?

(Off) Because it's incomprehensible, that's why.

You gotta admit. Virginal is nice. White is nice. Young is nice.

(Off) Divine love flows endlessly. Time flows endlessly.

What's not to admit?

(Off) Isn't joy the force of life itself?

(Off) Is that a real question?

The ordinary pleasures of the moment, the thing itself in the moment. I love it. I really do. I can have an attitude, or no attitude at all.

Can you?

(Off) There you have a theory of time.

(Off) Where?

(Off) Here, now.

Yes. Because positive is silly and negative is worse.

I see. You have these creatures smashing the brains of children and feeling justified and all right about it. It's a mechanism with no remorse. It makes me mad. They shot mothers and their babies, shot them together and threw them in a ditch. I can't get over that. I want revenge for that.

(Off) According to that theory, divine love is the love of God for Himself.

(Off) So what?

(Off) No beginning nor end. It is the knit and the knitting.

What would you do?

I want to go there and push people in front of trains.

Then you'll feel better?

And I hope there is a Hell.

Maybe Hell is another planet.

Maybe we're on it.

Maybe it's Mars. No, Mars is War.

I'm a volatile person. An emotional person. And I have a right. I have rights. I have fucking rights.

(Off) It's impossible to understand reality. I don't think we can take it in.

(Off) People want to make money, raise their kids.

(Off) See the babies? See the babies in the picture? See, in this one, they're alive. They're crying, probably. Hysterical. And in this one, it's a moment later, they're all dead. See how white they look, the women? And this schmuck over there is finishing them off, and that prick is standing there watching. He's dreaming about his dinner. He's thinking, "Soon I'll be home with my little dearie."

(Off) Ah, here we are on Mars.

This reminds me so much of something.

Oh, what's that?

A winter afternoon, dusk coming early, front door open, cooking and washing sounds from the kitchen, people, voices, a tricycle, toys, patches of snow and ice, brown grass, mud in the driveway.

(Off) Red earth, with a red horizon.

(Off) Not Earth. Mars.

(Off) Soil, ground. Rocks.

(Off) Exactly. Red sunset on the horizon. It's fucking weird. Isn't it? It's weird. From the point of view of being? Isn't it weird?

Inside, a man. A charismatic figure. A master, unchained to the state.

What are they doing in the house?

They are interested in learning. They are interested in the art of learning for free.

Unbelievable.

Incomprehensible.

What is he saying?

He says: The state is helpless against the real forces of life.

(Off) The moral life of man cannot evolve without effort.

(Off) Whose effort?

(Off) His own effort.

(Off) Arbitrarily. I'm going to push them under trains and throw them off of bridges. Total strangers. What do you think of that?

The forces are big, much too big. Try the surf sometime, see what you can do with it.

Ride it.

Yeah, ride it. But you can't do anything to it.

Okay, I know.

(Off) I don't think anything about it.

We are a species, which means a specific program. Which includes marriage, and the simple delights. Do you follow? You have to sign up as a member, finally, of the species.

I think she's beautiful. I think she's absolutely beautiful. And sweet. And innocent. And loving. And I will cherish her forever. Bring her on, my friend.

They're all different, but the same. I guess that's the point.

Let there be union, let there be dancing!

(Off) It is an idea of the absolute as the whole, or all, or everything in the universe at once.

I guess that's what life is all about.

(Off) Well, I'm aware of that.

(Off) Why does anything have to be said at all?

It's a love story.

(Off) I fly tonight. Tomorrow they begin to die at random.

BLACKOUT.

The End

Dog Mouth

by John Steppling

Dog Mouth *was produced at Evidence Room in Los Angeles by Padua Playwrights in January 2002, under the playwright's direction. The set was designed by Jason Adams, with lights by Rand Ryan, and original music and sound design by Carl Lundberg. The cast:*

Dog Mouth: Steve Davies
Nyah: Nyah Gwynne
Becker: James Storm
Weeks: Hugh Dane

Characters

Dog Mouth

Nyah

Becker

Voices

Weeks

Act One

Scene 1

*Lights up on an open area in the desert. A railroad track
runs down the center of the stage. The track disappears into
the distance. Standing and looking off into the distance is
a man of about fifty or fifty-five. This is DOG MOUTH. He
looks grizzled and may be missing a couple teeth. He wears
jeans, and a jail issue denim jacket. Silence. A long silence.*

Dog Mouth   I have changed. *(Pause)* I am a changed man. I am a man
changed.

*After a pause a woman's voice is heard. This is the voice of
NYAH.*

Nyah   *(Off)* Is it true, what they say?

Dog Mouth   I am not the man I was.

Nyah   *(Off)* No, no you're not. You're not the same man as
before.

Dog Mouth   That man, the man I was, the man I used to be... can you
tell me who he was?

Nyah   *(Off)* I didn't know him, I didn't know that other man.

Dog Mouth	Nobody knew him, I don't know if he existed, if he was real. *(Pause)* You ask me is it true?
Nyah	*(Off)* What they say, I asked if what they say is true?
Dog Mouth	Well, what do they say? Tell me what they say.
Nyah	*(Off)* They say you killed someone.
Dog Mouth	They say that? They say I killed someone? I wonder who they think I killed?
Nyah	*(Off)* They say you killed a man, pushed him from a moving train, beat him with a crow bar and stole his money and pushed him from a moving train.
Dog Mouth	*(Silence)* What man, what man died in this fall from a train?
Nyah	*(Off)* Denver Red, it was Denver Red, and it was in Salinas.
Dog Mouth	I knew a man named Denver Red and I've been to Salinas. Been to Salinas more than once.
Nyah	*(Off)* They say you killed him, pushed him from a moving train. *(Silence)* Tell me if it's true, will you, tell me if you've killed before.

Pause.

Dog Mouth	They say it's true. *(Pause)* Do you think it's true? You think I killed Denver Red in Salinas?

Silence.

Dog Mouth	People have said things about me for a hundred years, do you know that?

Pause.

Dog Mouth	Men change, and become other than who they were. Some men die, they fall from trains and people think they were pushed. The world continues to turn, slowly and without fail. Denver Red was born Richard Crowly, and his father was a soldier who died in the penitentiary and never but saw his son Richard once before he was sent away for the rape and robbery of someone in Albuquerque, New Mexico. *(Pause)* I know the story of Richard Crowly, of Denver Red, and I know he was hardly ever in his life in Denver but was called Denver Red all the same. *(Pause)* You ask me if it's true what they say. You want to know if I've killed men, you want to know if I beat Red, if I killed him pushing him from a train in Salinas?
Nyah	*(Off)* I know you are a new man, I know this.
Dog Mouth	Ask me again.
Nyah	*(Off)* I don't need to ask anymore.
Dog Mouth	Go ahead, ask me again, ask me what I've done.

Pause.

| Nyah | *(Off)* Is it true that you've killed before? |

Pause. Dog Mouth *turns around, he smiles just a little, he turns and looks up the tracks into the distance.*

| Dog Mouth | What do you believe? What is important is what you believe. The answer can only be about what you believe, because people will say anything, people will say things because they are ignorant and know nothing and because their lives are empty and stupid and what people say isn't worth pissing |

on. What matters is what you think, the question here is what do you believe, deep in your heart, way down underneath all the bullshit and newspapers and TV and gossip is your heart which is pure and which contains the truth. Tell me, what is in your heart?

Silence. Lights fade out.

*

Scene 2

Lights up slowly. NYAH *sits on railroad tracks. She is anywhere between eighteen and twenty-five; it's hard to tell. She is around six or seven months pregnant. She wears overalls and a bandana around her head. She is beautiful, wears no makeup and looks just a bit dusty.* DOG MOUTH *stands as before.*

Nyah   Where does this train end up? *(Beats)* Where is it's final stop, the place it's going, the place they want it to go?

Dog Mouth   This train used to go to Seattle. That's what it once did, when I thought about such things.

Nyah   And now? It doesn't go to Seattle anymore?

Dog Mouth   I believe it goes to northern California. I'm not sure, it could still go to Seattle, could still go to Seattle.

Pause.

Nyah   Was it different when it went to Seattle?

Dog Mouth What the hell are you asking? *(Pause)* It's a train, it went to Seattle, and now, now it may not go to Seattle, or, or it may still go there, or it may go to Spokane or to Stockton, but all the same it's a train, it's always gonna be a fucking train, is what I think.

NYAH nods. Silence.

Nyah Did you ever ride it all the way to Seattle?

Dog Mouth I rode it to Seattle, once or twice. I was a young man then.

Nyah They tell me the baby will start kicking soon and I'll be able to feel it. *(Pause)* Did you ever feel the baby kick, Shirley's baby, when she was pregnant?

Dog Mouth I don't recall that.

Nyah I believe them, that I'll be able to feel it kick, but I haven't felt anything yet. *(Beats)* Do you remember when Henry was born? Tell me about that.

Dog Mouth I wasn't there when Henry was born, and I wasn't there when Henry died.

Silence.

Nyah Shirley has told me that it was a difficult birth. She was in labor for I guess she said twenty hours. *(Beats)* Shirley seems so old, she seems too old to have been your wife. Is that mean?

Dog Mouth I don't care if it is mean. I have nothing to do with Shirley, and I don't talk to Shirley.

Nyah When does the train come?

Dog Mouth Does being pregnant make you unable to shut up? Is that part of what happens, you just can't stop talking? I'll have to look that up, the talking problem with pregnant women.

Silence.

Nyah   I wanted to talk to you about the baby, and it is your baby too. But you never want to talk about it, never want to say anything unless someone else is around. Someone's around then you'll talk. *(Pause)* TV reporter, then you talked, then you patted me on the belly and said this was your new life. TV reporter smiled, nodding his head, and smiling at me.

Silence. Sound of a train whistle.

Dog Mouth   Sometimes when I'll be walking, just be a city, walking down a street. I'll see a certain kind of woman, a mother, with her children. Maybe it's only one, but I'll see her with her child, her son, her daughter, and the child will be in the most expensive of strollers... strollers, a new expensive stroller it'll be, and the mother will have stopped wearing makeup, and will be wearing comfortable clothes, expensive clothes of course, but comfortable now, and she'll be newly laundered, clean and fresh, and the child will be even cleaner and fresher, and I'll have to step off the sidewalk for this woman because this new expensive stroller is big, it's bigger than it needs to be, and it's big and I step off into the gutter usually, and there are times that as she passes the child will turn its head while seated in the stroller, turn its little head and look at me and then I'll make a terrible face, the most awful hideous face I know how to make and my tongue will come out and flap at this child and usually it happens that the child will start to cry. *(Pause. Sound of distant train whistle)* I think then how this child might be affected by how I looked at it, by the horrible and monstrous face I made and how my flapping tongue will invade his or her dreams for years, for years I hope, a long and ugly tongue that flaps like the wings of a vulture, and stirs the air like birds of prey circling their dinner... and I've even tried to imagine how the dreams would be but that I cannot do.

Another train whistle. Lights fade out.

*

Scene 3

DOG MOUTH *stands. Sitting near him is* BECKER, *about forty-five or fifty, a more slender and less robust man than* DOG MOUTH. *He is dressed in cheap clothes that are none too clean.*

Dog Mouth You can tell, you can tell even at ten weeks, at twelve weeks. *(Pause)* Watch 'em, if you've got ten in the litter, say, if you watch, one or two will behave in a special way.

Becker What I'm going to do.

Dog Mouth What you're going to do.

Becker We've talked about it, and I've thought about it.

Dog Mouth Good.

Pause.

Dog Mouth A puppy, ten weeks old, I've seen them run right into a wall, charge the wall, head down, dipping their head down but still aiming it at the wall, and charging right for it and they'll crash right fucking into the fucking wall. Like that. That's all. Nothing else matters when you're examining young dogs. All that matters is what is there, at the beginning, when you look to see what you have.

Pause.

Becker You were on television. *(Beats)* I know you been told this, but the reporter said you were like Attila the Hun. *(Laughs)* I looked the motherfucker up and he's right.

BECKER laughs. DOG MOUTH does not.

Becker I seen where this reporter has spoken to the cop in Oregon.
Dog Mouth I know that cop.
Becker Well, the cop is doing a book, or like a book thing, and it's about riding the rails and about the crime and violence. *(Laughs)*
Dog Mouth What are you laughing at?
Becker This cop, he's retired now, just last week, took an early retirement. He is now a writer, and he's writing a book.
Dog Mouth I'll be in that book. You were going to talk to me about that, you were going to talk to me about Sam.

Becker	Sam is doing twenty-five years.
Dog Mouth	Sam is doing his twenty-five years in Florida. Indian River, which is where someone else famous was kept.
Becker	Who was famous at Indian River?
Dog Mouth	*(Pause)* They'll charge into the wall and do you know what you can see after they've hit that wall full tilt? *(Beats)* One will shake himself and do it again. Another will stumble back to find its mother. Which one is the better dog? It's the one went back to his mother. Does that surprise you?
Becker	Nothing surprises me. Am I supposed to be surprised?
Dog Mouth	Sam is about possibly the stupidest man I've ever met.
Becker	My dad raised bulldogs. I remember the pit man—the man, Jack something, weighed three hundred pounds and had a heart attack in my dad's back yard, in our backyard and almost died. You think I don't know about dogs?
Dog Mouth	Crooked Dice is a Registry of Merit bitch and I saw her, always she would work the front end, pull 'em by the nose, and she'd like to make 'em panic, and always at the front end which is where she made them look at her at her face and in her eyes was flame and she was a six time winner. She beat two other four time winners, she beat that Cajun dog right down in Bogalusa or where the fuck that town is, whatever they call it, and niggers handled the first four time winner, a big nigger named Curly. Big, big nigger.

Silence. BECKER *paces.*

Becker	I was going to ask not to do it, Dog Mouth. *(Beats)* But you give me the place, tell me where, and I'll do it. I'll do it.

Dog Mouth Jim and I both owned Crooked Dice and she produced very little because she died. She did have a litter, and in it was Banjo and he's a good dog, but she died, and Jim buried her in his yard, under where the kennel is now. Registry of Merit is not bullshit. I took her to three different states and anyone called us out, we went, that bitch couldn't be beat. I won't ever have another dog like that.

Becker So tell me place, show me when and where, and I'll do it. Fuck all this, and just tell me where, tell me the place.

DOG MOUTH is nodding to himself. Lights fade out.

*

Scene 4

Lights up slowly. DOG MOUTH and NYAH are exactly as in Scene 1. The light is dimmer, suggesting evening.

Nyah And she said that to me. This is what Lindy said she said, why is Nyah going to live with that man, he's mentally ill. Why is she going to have a baby for Christ sake, have that man's baby when he has been in prison and is mentally ill. *(Beats)* I thought Marie was my friend, and I feel like going right over to her where she lives. If she lived here... well, if we were near where she lived I would go right over to her house so it's a good thing we're where we are. *(Pause)* Marie is nobody to be calling anyone else a name, I think she's spread her legs for enough.

Dog Mouth	Is Lindy your friend?
Nyah	I think she is.
Dog Mouth	I wonder why she told you this.
Nyah	*(Beats)* She tells me everything. You think she shouldn't have told me?
Dog Mouth	I think it's made you upset.
Nyah	I love you, Terry. Is it OK, do you mind if I call you Terry?
Dog Mouth	That's my name, one of my names.
Nyah	I know that but do you mind if I call you that, when we're alone, it makes me feel different and special to call you by the name you were born with and a name almost nobody else knows.
Dog Mouth	I think a lot of people know my name is Terry.
Nyah	I love you, though.

Pause.

Nyah	Do you feel good that I am so young?
Dog Mouth	Should I feel good that you're young?
Nyah	I am a lot younger than you.
Dog Mouth	*(Laughs)* Lots of people are younger than me.
Nyah	But they don't love you and I do. I love you and I will always love you. *(Pause)* You don't like to talk about these things, do you?
Dog Mouth	What is it we're talking about do you think?
Nyah	*(Beats)* My mother said I was sick and must have a disease and my father spit at me.

DOG MOUTH nods. Silence.

Nyah	Have you looked at the newspaper I gave you? Have you looked at the picture?
Dog Mouth	The picture of that boy with his head cut off. That boy was stupid, thinking he knew about hoppin' trains, and he was young and immortal wasn't he? *(Pause)* I never seen him before and now he's in God's country isn't he, damn fool. Fuck that boy, fuck him throwing his life away.
Nyah	He was just a young boy.
Dog Mouth	Remember when that bird you had died? Little canary or something?
Nyah	Parakeet.
Dog Mouth	You said the same thing, said, "it was only a little bird, just a little bird," and you were crying.
Nyah	Yes.
Dog Mouth	Just a little bird, just a young boy. *(Beats)* And you cried over that bird, and I felt bad for you, Nyah, I felt terrible.
Nyah	You didn't seem to feel bad.
Dog Mouth	No. *(Pause)* I can't stand to think on that, I just stop, I look away and go on with what I have to do. *(Pause)* Because its unbearable, the death of a bird, unbearable, unbearable. *(Beats)* I saw that young boy was wearing Nike shoes, you could see it in the picture, the photograph, see his shoes and they looked new and they were Nikes. And right next to his fucking Nikes was his fucking head. Like the head was looking at his Nikes, admiring his brand new expensive Nikes. Almost no blood, just a little, seeping away from the head, the neck, cut clean off, and sitting there, like a basketball or... or, like a cantaloupe. Which was a head, was his head a minute ago, talking and saying dumb shit, and probably screamed too, for an instant, and then got cut off, when he fell, fell right

under a wheel, and got sliced right off and bounced I'd guess, bounced and landed right side up, right side up so he'd get a look, a good view of his Nikes. *(Pause)* I look away when a bird dies, I don't cry about it, because if I started to cry over that bird, that parakeet, I would lose myself forever.

Silence.

Dog Mouth   There's another thing about that newspaper and that picture. A newspaper printing a photograph of a boy with his head cut off.

Nyah   No, they shouldn't have done that.

Dog Mouth   The story in that newspaper says something about the murders, about the hobos getting murdered in the western states.

Nyah   They didn't mention you or anything about Denver Red or...

Dog Mouth   ... but you looked for me didn't you?

Silence.

Nyah   I was worried.

Dog Mouth   I was worried too. But nothing was said so it was alright.

Nyah   I love you.

Dog Mouth   'Course you do. You love me and you're just a young girl and people think you're nuts, but you don't care.

Nyah   I don't care, I don't care what anyone thinks, or what anyone says.

Silence. Lights fade out.

*

Scene 5

Lights up slowly on BECKER *and* DOG MOUTH *squatting down. They watch and listen as the beam from a flashlight coming offstage right is moved back and forth across the upstage area only feet from where they are sitting silently. Men's* VOICES *are heard offstage right.*

Voice 1 ... fucking Arnel... fucking turd licker...

Voice 2 Faggot motherfucker. *(Beat)* The fuck is that?

Voice 1 Old bottles...

Voice 3 ... someone was...

Voice 1 someone sure.

Voice 3 ... here, someone's been around here.

Voice 2 Arnel isn't...

Voice 1 ... fuck Arnel, Janie said something....

Voice 2 Faggot motherfucker, I'd just...

Voice 3 What's that there?

The beam holds on something far upstage.

Voice 2 Like a candy wrapper.

Voice 3 Go get it.

Voice 2 Suck my dick, go get it yourself.

Voice 1 Come on... I want to go see Wilmer's trailer.

Beam moves away, VOICES *fade out.* DOG MOUTH *and* BECKER *slowly stand and now speak in whispers.*

Becker That was Hudson.

Dog Mouth	Hudson and Browning and that fat kraut, that fat fuck likes to stare at your balls when you shower and likes to make big eyes at you.
Becker	I don't know him, don't know him yet.
Dog Mouth	Fat fuck, big fat fucker with a gut hangs over his belt and he smells like garlic and he stares at your nuts and makes fish eyes at you. Big fat German or something, Dutch, German, Swede, I think he's with the railroad, but he's at the jail anyway, and his breath is bad and his teeth stink, his gut sticking out and shuffling when he walks, shuffling his feet and looking at everyone's dick and licking his lips, and he always cuts himself shaving and has little pieces of paper stuck to his neck, stuck to his fat neck with moles and thick hair growing out of each mole. Fuck him, I hate the cocksucker, fuck him, kraut prick. Benji the Mexican tried to hit him last time I was in jail there, tried to hit him through the bars.
Becker	They got those bars.
Dog Mouth	Bars you can punch through. The man wants to get down on his knees and lick your balls that's what, fat kraut prick.
Becker	Right now it's cold, damn it's cold now.
Dog Mouth	One a.m. What are they doing out at one a.m.?
Becker	When it's cold, damn.
Dog Mouth	Looking for crack heads, looking for "narcotics," looking, looking, looking, looking for dope fiend crack heads, one a.m. *(Beats)* Three of them out here, Hudson and Browning and that fat kraut all out together, all driving around in the one Ford Bronco, smoking cigarettes and breathing in the garlic air of the kraut and they don't care, they're enjoying themselves and if they find the crack heads then everything is good, everything is good like a motherfucker.

Becker	Better if they found you, better even than a crack head. Dog Mouth is his nickname, right? Picked up Dog Mouth, wanted to ask him some questions, yeah, sure, that'd be great.
Dog Mouth	*(Pause)* I hardly sleep anymore. Do you know that? I hardly get tired. *(Beats)* It's a sickness, the sickness of no sleep. It's a sickness that I have now, that I have acquired and I never hardly get tired anymore. *(Beats)* It's something that has happened to me, it's not nothing. I sat awake one night and after that I stopped sleeping. I sat awake thinking of how I was going to die, how it would be when I was going to die, and all night I thought about it, and I thought about it until morning, until it was light and now I can't sleep anymore. *(Pause)* How're you gonna die, Becker? *(Beat)* I think, I sit, when it's quiet, and I think slowly about getting old, and how death is coming closer. I think, think about being old and losing my teeth and how death will get closer and closer and how I'll feel different about it, how I will be able to concentrate on it and sense that moment of death and get a sense of that being the end, of not having to think after that moment, not having to concentrate after that moment, how after that moment there won't be anymore moments or anymore, there won't be anymore. I won't be and I won't have been, and I won't be here to think about that, how I won't be so nothing matters, nothing of me, I won't be looking back the way I was looking forward... I won't look back at that moment, I won't be and then I think about when I was a little boy and I'd think of death, because I did all the time, I thought of death, and I think of that little boy who was me who thought of death all the time and that's who will have stopped being, that little boy called

Terry, or Groucho, they called me that, Groucho, and I'd go someplace to be alone, to be away from Eldon, my father, and be alone and think about dying, and think about how far in the future that was, way, way, far in the future when I'd die. That same little boy who thought that shit will be the same one that dies, same as Dog Mouth, and that little boy Terry, Groucho, will not be able to think back to being a boy, he won't be so he won't be looking back. There are no memories after you die. All of that, all of that time between that small boy and that toothless nasty old fuck, all of that is just wiped out, wiped clean away and all of that thinking will be gone, disappeared, and only nothing is left... see, not emptiness or... "I" won't be left, "I" won't be, and all that "being" between the small boy, and even before, between that and the old dirty mean toothless fuck, all of it is gone.

Pause. Sound of the men's VOICES again offstage, returning. DOG MOUTH and BECKER crouch down again. The flashlight beams appear again, crisscrossing the stage.

Voice 1   ...tell him he smells.

Voice 2   He says you smell.

Voice 1   Tell him to quit farting.

Voice 2   Stop that ugly farting.

Sound of all of them laughing.

Voice 3   Damn, I won't touch him. You can't make me touch him.

More laughs. The VOICES gradually fade so that we hear

them but can't make out any of what is being said.
DOG MOUTH and BECKER come up from their squatting
slowly, hesitantly...

Becker   That was Wilmer... *(Pause)* that was Wilmer.

Dog Mouth   Wilmer'll try to tell them where I am.

Becker   They have Wilmer. He'll try to tell them how to find you, that's true.

Dog Mouth   They'll release him tomorrow.

Becker   He will have told them what he knows. Fuck him, should we kill him?

Dog Mouth   You can't talk like that. Becker?

Becker   Yeah.

Dog Mouth   You can't talk like that.

Becker   Alright, alright, I won't.

Dog Mouth   It doesn't matter if they picked up Wilmer.

Becker   Wilmer. *(Beats)* Wilmer. Fuck.

Dog Mouth   It doesn't matter what Wilmer says, he could say anything, and tell them whatever he wants, I don't care. Wilmer knows nothing about anything, nothing about nothing. See; Wilmer is a man, he's a fucking idiot who lives in a trailer and listens to a radio all day.

Becker   No, he doesn't have a TV, that's true.

Dog Mouth   That's right, he doesn't, and he's a... *(Pause)* I know some shit about Wilmer, so when I tell you he's nothing, a man worth nothing, who knows nothing, I am basing this on facts I know, OK?! *(Pause)* Christ, hiding here, hiding like schoolchildren, I am disgusted with myself, but that's the way it is.

Silence.

Becker   You have a new wife, and a baby coming. *(Beats)* She is a good looking girl too, a young good looking girl.

Dog Mouth   My father, Eldon, he was a sailor, a sailor, and he died at sea. You ever hear of DOHSA? *(Beats)* Death on the High Seas Act and the government created this law so that if a seaman dies while at sea the owner of the ship must pay the family of the dead seaman all of his wages as if he had lived a normal full life. My mother collected forty one thousand dollars, a lot of money back then, and the ship owners paid her too, paid her right away, no bullshit. So Marianne, Marianne took that money and married a half nigger named Kincaid, half white and half island nigger... from somewhere, from an island off South America. Kincaid sure as fuck wasn't gonna take me along, and he sent me to live with people he knew, people in Bakersfield. Marianne and Kincaid left for his island, left to live among the islanders. And so I grew up in Bakersfield, where I lived with the Taylor family. I stayed with the Taylors for about a year and then left.

Becker   How old when you left? You never told me this.

Dog Mouth   Fifteen. I was fifteen. I set out to find Marianne and Kincaid but I only got to San Diego, as far as I got. I am fifty-five now, same age as Eldon, as my father when he died. Eldon was a fifty-five-year-old chief mate on a private luxury boat... private pleasure boat that was often rented by movie stars and the like. John Wayne, he rented it lots of times and Eldon talked with John Wayne more than once. He knew some things about John Wayne, after all, chief mate on a pleasure boat, people do some funny things and Eldon would know what was going on, he'd watch and he never told anyone what he'd see, but the big shots, they knew Eldon had seen and so people like John Wayne, they'd buy my father gifts, at Christmas especially, packages would come in the mail, or people would deliver things. One Christmas someone, might have been John Wayne, could have been I don't know, they showed up with a genuine bear skin rug and a case of scotch. A case of thirty-year-old scotch and a bear rug. The bear rug had the bear's head on it still and I remember playing on that rug, playing with the bear's head, playing soldiers on the head as if it were a big mountain.

Silence.

Becker   So who else, who else famous rented the boat?

Dog Mouth   Lots of different people. Billy Sol Estes rented it once. One time Oscar Levant played piano at a party onboard. One time Mamie Van Doren was on that boat, stayed for the whole cruise. Eldon said he fucked her, but I don't believe him. *(Beats)* Course you never know, but I doubt it, I doubt he fucked Mamie Van Doren.

Long silence.

Becker   Women have always liked you, that's what you hear. *(Beat)* Maybe your dad was like that too, so maybe, right? You don't know.

Dog Mouth   *(Pause)* I like to think he did, I've always liked to think that he did, think that he fucked someone like Mamie Van Doren.

Lights slowly begin to cross fade. NYAH *appears, standing on railroad tracks. The light suggests morning now, the lifting of darkness.* DOG MOUTH *moves over toward her,* BECKER *following. They all speak quietly, looking around a bit nervously as if afraid someone is coming.*

Nyah   You want to feel it kick? *(Beat)* Terry?

Dog Mouth I don't want to feel anything.

Nyah   It's your baby, you don't want to feel it?

DOG MOUTH, *with unexpected suddenness, hits her in the face. She stumbles back and goes down on one knee holding her face. A long silence.*

Nyah   What do you think that will do? *(Beats)* I've been hit before.

Becker Maybe I should leave. Should I leave?

Silence. DOG MOUTH *walks away, looking out at the horizon.*

Dog Mouth They've outlawed dog fights. Officially now, they passed a law. *(Beats)* The way you get a good dog is breeding good dogs. You find out what's a good dog by fighting them. I would cry sometimes when one of my dogs was hurt or killed. I loved all my dogs. But I knew if one was killed, if one fought badly, stupidly, and lost, then that wasn't a dog that I should breed. That dog, it may as well have been killed. Sometimes you can lose and still show gameness, that's fine, I had a game bitch lost twice and I bred her four times just for her gameness 'cause she didn't have much else, no mouth, no endurance, but a lot of heart. The bitch would not back away, wouldn't ever turn. That bitch was happy to die, didn't matter to her. I went out and bred her, bred her straight to some Jeep/Redboy blood. We got two winners from her, one of whom, Pablo, was a five-time winner and a Registry of Merit dog. I later bred him to a bitch who's pedigree we didn't know. Indian Sonny had a bitch, didn't even really know if she was a pitbull, she might'a been something else mixed with bulldog but who cared, she was a winner and you could see looking at her what she would throw. *(Pause)* Centuries of breeding winners and now there is a law says you can't do that. Says it's cruel to fight dogs. Because what they want is a boring, obsequious dog... a boring dog to fetch the ball for you. Such dogs, such useless fucking dogs will not remind them of how fucking useless they are. A real dog, a game fighting dog is a reminder of a life they tell themselves doesn't exist. I believe they know it exists but they lie to themselves, lie and lie and lie and pretty soon... well, it takes some time, it has taken some time, but at some point they start to almost believe that the world is a place where all you have to do is fetch balls.

He slowly turns back and looks at them both. Pause.

Dog Mouth I've had dogs so noble it causes you to suffer just to gaze upon them. You suffer in the presence of such courage and it makes it impossible to flee the hidden world inside us...

you see? And if you stop running away from that hell, that Devil's kingdom that is inside and that is the only real thing there is in life, and if you stop running and if you can't hide from it then you must take that elevator and push down. Ride down inside until you get to where the sin is, and the filth and pain. Then you become someone worth knowing. But if you stay in the lobby, then all your gonna do is fetch rubber balls all your life.

Pause. BECKER kneels down next to NYAH. DOG MOUTH looks at them and then wanders further upstage.

Nyah   Think I haven't been hit? I been hit and I've been kicked.

Becker   You're pregnant. *(Beat)* People can have episodes, you know?

Nyah   Is that what that was? An "episode?"

Becker   People can attack things, I seen a man once attack a city bus, stood in front of it and waited and when it stopped he started hitting it and kicking it and screaming and all.

Nyah   I've been kicked, and I've seen other women kicked and hit with sticks and shit.

Becker   He's not what you would call a good man.

Nyah   I know.

Becker   I don't ask other people's business, though, that isn't a good idea and I don't do it.

Nyah   I love him and I know he isn't a good man but I never wanted a good man.

Becker   Are you alright?

Nyah   I don't know what good men are, and I don't know what good women are either but I've heard people talk about good men since I was little. It was as though they were talking of a rare bird unbodied seen in generations but they still figured it existed, somewhere.

Becker   So you're alright then?

Nyah   *(Pause)* I know what you're supposed to do. I know what Terry told you to do. I wonder why the fuck you're doing it though.

BECKER stands up. Pause.

Becker   First, you don't know what I'm going to do. Second, you don't know a lot of things.

Nyah   Because it's some low life speed freak it's OK? Is that how you think, Becker?

Becker   Are we talking about something here?

Nyah   Asshole.

Becker   Maybe I should kick you, hit you, what do you think? Bitch pops off the way you are, man is fucking obligated to put a fist in her mouth. *(Beats)* Dumb cunt, how old are you? You twenty, twenty-three, some shit like that, and think you can talk to me, think you can call me a name and not get knocked on your ass. Becker is just a broken down nothin', isn't that it? *(Beats)* Bitch, I have *sold* better pussy than you, shit, I was trying to be nice to you. *(Beat)* You are way too fucking young to have any idea what is going on out there.

Silence.

Nyah   *(Quietly)* Tell me about this guy, the one... hell is the name, Muehler, Muehler. *(Beat)* Muehler.

BECKER kneels down again.

Becker   Once, in Oregon, there was a cop. A railroad cop, worked
          for Northern Pacific, and he got this little guy, little old
          fucker, caught him just outside the yard, and he set him on
          fire. *(Beats)* A cop did this. Watched him burn for a minute
          or so and then left and went and had breakfast. *(Beat)* I
          have always wondered what it was he ate for breakfast that
          day. You know? Don't you wonder?

Silence. Lights fade out.

*

Scene 6

*Lights up very slowly but high to suggest the bright heat
of midday in the desert. DOG MOUTH is seated, cross-
legged, on the ground. A sleeping bag is wrapped around
his legs. He has on only a T-shirt and some worn boxer
shorts. BECKER stands nearby smoking a cigarette.*

Becker   At one time, trains had names. The Pan-American Flyer,
          the City of New Orleans. Must mean I am fucking old.
Dog Mouth You're not old. You just want me to say that, huh?
Becker   Those were eastern trains, or southern. Nothin's got a
          name out here, not even trains got names west of
          the Rockies.
Dog Mouth Toss me a cigarette.

He does.

Becker   New Lebanon, in Ohio, city named New Lebanon. You know it?

Dog Mouth You Mr. Geography now?

Becker   My uncle said he liked the name of it, that's why he moved us there. In school they spent a whole week explaining why we're called New Lebanon and how it didn't really have shit to do with Lebanon the country, except it did a little, but they didn't want us thinking we were Lebanese or something.

Dog Mouth *(Beats)* The girl said to me last night, whispered, in the middle of the night, why you want to do this to Muehler? Why is he getting killed?

Silence.

Becker   She said that to me too.

Dog Mouth I am wondering to myself, how's this bitch know his name is Muehler? I barely know his name is Muehler.

Becker   She's a smart girl, and all that.

Dog Mouth This doesn't bother you?

BECKER shrugs. Pause.

Dog Mouth She'd snitch you off, give you up faster than it took to book her.

Becker   I'm doing this. However long it takes, it's going to get done.

Dog Mouth However long.

Silence. DOG MOUTH stands, stretches.

Becker	However long it takes. I'll find Muehler and I'll fucking kill him, like you said.
	DOG MOUTH *steps over next to him.*

Dog Mouth	I know you aren't going to kill him. You wouldn't kill him now, with people knowing about it especially. You're not stupid, I don't think you are, and I know you aren't going to do it.

BECKER stares at him then walks away. Silence.

Dog Mouth	I might start to worry, a man I am in a partnership with, and this man seems too eager, and nothin' bothers him. I might start to worry.

BECKER turns around. Pause.

Becker	I'm not the one with an almost teenage girl hanging around me.
Dog Mouth	She could make a lot of money, telling the story to a newspaper. Tipping off the police and then selling the story. She might make quite a bit of money on something like that.
Becker	Well then, ah, are you... I mean, what is it you're... ah, what is your opinion then?
Dog Mouth	I'm just thinking out loud.
Becker	Just thinking out loud.
Dog Mouth	That's all, that's all I'm doing.
Becker	Uh-huh, that's all, and... well, alright. Alright.

Silence.

Dog Mouth	I started something. *(Beats)* Do you agree with that?
Becker	That you started something. *(Beats)* Yeah, yes, I agree that you started things, started something.
Dog Mouth	What did I start? I can answer that, and this is me, I think that when you join, anything, when you join a group you have responsibilities.

BECKER nods. Pause.

Dog Mouth	We've been, all of us, through a lot of shit and we aren't young, not any of us, and we aren't kids and none of us hasn't been called names and spit on. So together we shared something when we joined and we became something where we had some angle, we had some advantage. We could play the angles a little, have a bit of leverage. *(Beats)* I got nothing to lose anymore. None of us got anything really worth caring about. *(Laughs)* We don't have a good name or a family to care about. We don't have a business or, hell, or, we don't have anyone to answer to. That was the fucking point of coming together.
Becker	All men who carry nothing with them. And Vietnam, all of us were in Vietnam. Except Buddy, Buddy wasn't in 'Nam.
Dog Mouth	Buddy was in prison. *(Laughs)*
Becker	And what we are, we scare people.
Dog Mouth	Everyone, yes. Everyone is scared.

Both laugh.

Dog Mouth	So, I think that the train people, the railroad authorities, they worry that the public will stop wanting to use the

trains, stop paying because the security must not be so good if these lousy hobo bums can go around throwing people off trains and robbing them and doing whatever they want, anywhere, everywhere they want.

Becker   Okay, that's right. That is right.

Dog Mouth   And I wonder, I have to believe, Becker, that when someone is out of line, and you're sure about it, sure they were out of line, then you fucking take their life.

Becker   Otherwise...

Dog Mouth   ... Otherwise everyone will know your just blowing smoke, just a bunch of punks pretending. *(Beats)* And I never pretend, not anything not ever.

Becker   Okay, that's right, that is right.

Dog Mouth   Muehler, who I never even met, not face to face. Muehler is wrong.

Becker   'Course he is.

Dog Mouth   Muehler is wrong.

Becker   No, the man is fucked up, and there isn't any question about it.

Dog Mouth   No.

Becker   I wouldn't say he could be seen except as wrong. Fuck him, the guy is fucking crazy maybe, but he is wrong.

Dog Mouth   *(Pause)* I started this, I started it and we've all benefited, right? We've all done okay on this, with this. And I see no reason to let Muehler fuck with us. I don't care, you know, how it gets done.

Becker   I told you.

Dog Mouth   I know.

Becker   I told you I would take care of Muehler. I know where he lives, most of the time, I know where he is most of the

	time and I told you I would take care of it.
Dog Mouth	Take care of the problem.
Becker	I told you and I'm going to do it, and Muehler is crazy maybe, but Muehler is, Muehler will be sorry, because he made a mistake but that's his problem, not mine.
Dog Mouth	And Nyah, see, Nyah, you just have to trust me. Nyah is my problem. So you just come to me, and that was all you had to do, just come say, Dog Mouth, the bitch is, she talked to me about a thing she shouldn't even know about. Shouldn't even know let alone talk about and fuck with people. She's fucking with you and now I know and so I will handle Nyah.
Becker	Alright.
Dog Mouth	And now I know and you and I have talked and we're straight about it.
Becker	Alright.

Pause.

| **Dog Mouth** | Because this is something which I began. It started with me and that's how, for all time that is how it will be, and that's how it will end. |

Lights fade out.

*

Scene 7

Lights up slowly. DOG MOUTH *and* NYAH *are crouching near the tracks, waiting, listening. Early morning light.*

Nyah So, so Phoenix? *(Beats)* Valley of the Sun. I had a cousin went to Arizona State, the Sun Devils, she was a cheerleader and she loved it there. I was about twelve, and I visited her during spring break and I remember it was really hot and she was fucking just everyone, about the entire football team but she wasn't happy because it was mostly players from the practice squad and not the starters and well, shit, she was so damn ugly I'm surprised anyone fucked her. I remember a lot of pawn shops in Phoenix. All on the highway running out of town, away from the Valley of the Sun, and it's like lined with pawn shops. She fucked this one guy, big black guy, about three hundred pounds, and had a head so big they had to build a special helmet for him 'cause the regular ones wouldn't fit him. She called him "Watermelon Head." He would laugh, he was a nice guy, just big, and he had no idea what he was doing at a university. He and I would talk. We would watch TV and talk. He liked game shows a lot and so that was what we would watch. My cousin was troubled, you know.

Dog Mouth I don't like Phoenix much, not so much, but I don't want to stay here. It's only ten hours, or maybe more, a bit more, to Phoenix. I am going to see a man about a dog there.

Nyah We gonna get a dog?

Dog Mouth I am going to see a man about a dog, not a pet, but a dog.

Silence.

Nyah	What man?
Dog Mouth	A man with a dog. *(Pause)* If it's a good dog, the right dog, then I'll take him down to Matamoros, and we'll see what we can see.
Nyah	So who is this man?
Dog Mouth	His name is Weeks. Supposed to be a nigger, speaking of niggers, and he's supposed to be the shit. Supposed to have the top Redboy-Jeep stock in the country. Outcrossed to Cajun dogs, and Corvino dogs too. Indian Sonny told me so and Indian Sonny never makes mistakes on this stuff.
Nyah	And Weeks is in Phoenix?

DOG MOUTH nods.

The baby is due in August. What's that? *(Beats)* Is that... what? Is that a Leo? Be just like you, have a baby that's a Leo. *(Beats)* Do you think it will be a boy? Can we talk about a name now?

Dog Mouth	What do you want to call it?
Nyah	Terry Junior if its a boy and if it's a girl, then Rosa after my Aunt Rosa.
Dog Mouth	I already have a son named Terry.
Nyah	That's OK, you don't know where he is, you never seen him, hell, I still want to call him Terry. *(Beats)* August isn't very long, and maybe we'll still be in Phoenix. I can't travel the last few weeks you know?!
Dog Mouth	I know. *(Beats)* I don't like Phoenix though.
Nyah	Alright, but it's nice and hot in Phoenix and I sort of like it when it's hot. *(Beats)* Tell me about the dog, Terry.

Dog Mouth Weeks is a man with a name. I keep hearing Weeks, and how that was a Weeks dog, and this one, this one here is out of a Weeks bitch, or about Candy, four-time winner, beat a ROM dog last time, in a match, the match was in New Mexico and Candy goes right out and goes for the rear leg and this ROM dog is game and I heard different things, but it's a Southern Hill Combine dog, but it went on for forty minutes until the ROM couldn't make it, couldn't walk to the line, his legs, both front legs damaged and Bo, Little Bo, he picks him up and Candy wins, and Weeks wasn't there, it was a guy named Racer, and that match was made for a lot of people wanting a Weeks dog. So Weeks is being talked about. And I know Weeks has heard of me, that's what Sonny said, said sure Weeks knows you, knows about you, knows all about the Dog Mouth Man and even knows I have some young bitch knocked up and I been on TV, and Sonny said Weeks asked about the story about Denver Red, and about that man going to jail in Mississippi.

Nyah Everyone likes to talk about the TV story, about the journalist and about the guy going to jail in Mississippi.

Dog Mouth Sure, television, everyone would want to talk about a television story.

Nyah I haven't told anyone we're going. I thought it was best not to.

Dog Mouth They'll know. Doesn't matter, either way. Tell 'em, don't tell 'em.

Nyah I'm glad you're taking me with you.

Sound of a train in the distance. It gradually gets louder and closer throughout the rest of the scene. Both pause, hearing the train.

Dog Mouth	That child is yours. *(Beats)* That child, you'll take care of that child, that has nothing... *(Pause)* That child is yours, and I'm not, don't expect fucking anything from me where the child is concerned.
Nyah	Welfare, I can get welfare. I've been told all how to do that. Plus they give you food stamps, which I already get, but I guess now they'll give me more. *(Pause)* What I want, when the baby comes, is for you, you know, to keep in touch. Only that, and then I'll know, when the baby is old enough to travel, I'll know where to meet up with you.

DOG MOUTH looks at her. Silence.

Dog Mouth	Fine, alright. I can do that.
Nyah	Is Becker coming to Phoenix? *(Beats)* I mean I know he isn't right now, but is he later, and then come hang with us.
Dog Mouth	Becker.
Nyah	I know he isn't coming right away.
Dog Mouth	No. No, he's not.
Nyah	But later, is he coming later?
Dog Mouth	Where do you think Becker is going first?
Nyah	I don't know.
Dog Mouth	Yes you do. You told Becker you knew.
Nyah	I know what he's doing, I don't know where he's going.
Dog Mouth	*(Beats)* Tell me what he's doing.
Nyah	Didn't you want me to know?
Dog Mouth	What's he doing? Tell me what he's doing.
Nyah	He is going to kill someone.

Pause.

Dog Mouth   You think Becker is going to kill someone? *(Beats)* You think that is something should be talked about? If someone were going someplace to kill someone, if that were the case, and if you knew about it, then how would you feel? That's not just an everyday thing, is it? Going to kill someone, that is not an everyday activity. How would you feel about someone getting killed?

Nyah   This... these, these are people I don't know. I don't feel anything.

DOG MOUTH nods, pause, turns away. Silence. The sound of the train suggests it is getting close.

Nyah   I can't help it, I'm curious. *(Pause)* I've always been curious, I can't help it.

DOG MOUTH waves to her to follow him upstage, crouching along the track. The sound is very loud now, and the lights flicker, as though the train is shaking everything, even the ground. NYAH follows closely behind DOG MOUTH as lights fade out.

End of Act One

Act Two

Scene 8

Sound of train whistle. It fades as lights come up slowly.

A man of about fifty stands center stage. The set is the same as before, except now we are in the outskirts of Phoenix. The man is black, his hair graying, and he wears denim overalls. Slung over his shoulder are several leather dog leashes, one attached to a heavy metal obedience collar.

This is WEEKS. *A long silence during which* WEEKS *hardly moves at all. Finally* NYAH *enters. She is even more pregnant and looks ready to deliver any moment.*

Nyah	Tell me, tell me about Phoenix.
Weeks	Phoenix is in Arizona and Phoenix is hot.
Nyah	Do blacks, you know, have it better in Phoenix? Is that why you came here?
Weeks	What makes you think I came here? Maybe I was born here.
Nyah	Were you?
Weeks	Niggers do okay in Phoenix. But it's hot in Phoenix. It's winter now, but in summer, you don't know how hot it can be.

Nyah	Tell me more about Phoenix though. What's it like in the city?
Weeks	*(Beats)* It's low, building aren't tall there, and everything looks like it's been bleached. It has been bleached you see, the sun has taken everything it can from everything that's there. *(Pause)* I always have this sort of dream when I'm here. I am waiting for someone to step over those mountains, a giant, and all we could see would be his boots almost, and he will step on Phoenix. And then there won't be a Phoenix.
Nyah	*(Beat)* What the hell.
Weeks	That's how those mountains seem to me. But when you get right up next to them, then you find that they're real mountains, that they're as big as they need to be and that they're real mountains. You understand?
Nyah	*(Beats)* What about the city, are there lots of malls and shops? And I know that Arizona State is there and there is a football stadium.
Weeks	Sun Devil Stadium. *(Beats)* I've worked selling ice cream at that stadium.
Nyah	You sell a lot, huh? Because it's so hot, right?
Weeks	I would bet that the people in Phoenix eat more ice cream than just about anywhere. *(Beats)* I had a vending license and I had people working for me and I would work the entire season, the five games the Sun Devils played each year. Then there were concerts, revivals, all kind of shit. I sold fucking ice cream at every motherfucking event.

NYAH *nods. She looks around as if expecting someone. Pause.*

Weeks	And now we wait—for the Dog Mouth.
Nyah	No, he is here, I mean, somewhere.
Weeks	I saw you both on TV.
Nyah	Yeah?
Weeks	I know about Dog Mouth, and then later I saw you both on TV. I saw that show, that interview.
Nyah	You like it?
Weeks	I didn't think about what to like. I just watched it.
Nyah	Lots of people watched it, they played it all over the country.
Weeks	Television. Color television. Hell of a thing, and I remember when television wasn't no color.
Nyah	Uh-huh.
Weeks	I had heard about Dog Mouth, heard about his dogs, at one time his dogs were very well known. He had two ROMs, and that little boy, he was a great producer. I had heard of him, I know my business. My business isn't ice cream, and I had known of Dog Mouth.
Nyah	I never saw any of his dogs, you know.
Weeks	You ever gone to a match, seen two dogs?

She shakes her head no. Pause.

Weeks	Now, I am the man with the dogs people talk about. My dog right now, Egypt, he's a four-time winner and nobody wants nothing to do with us. Egypt is a low dog, will go for the legs and, well... Egypt is named for a country. I never been there, but I always liked the notion of the place, and Egypt will tear your leg down to the cords and water. *(Pause)* Always the legs, and even once we had to travel to Arkansas and even then we won, but I had my dog on an I.V., forget

about training and keep, I just wanted him to recover. It had been a long trip and Mr. Penix, he stayed up all night with me and that match lasted ninety minutes. The first half hour Egypt just held onto the nose, and used defense, and he just wanted to keep that big dog of Mr. Ellsworth's out a little. That dog was stronger than Egypt, and my dog knew that and so he never tried the back end but kept at the front legs and the nose, and finally he got a throat hold on the Ellsworth dog, and Mr. Ellsworth asked us to scratch 'cause that dog looked dead, not breathing, no sign of breathing, but when he scratched he came out on fire 'cause that was a dead game dog. But Egypt got him again in the same throat hold and this time we said no, no scratch, either you pick that dog up now or Egypt will just take his motherfuckin' life right there in the corner of the box. Well, Mr. Ellsworth picked him up and we both made good hard courtesy scratches, and you know it took me twenty-five minutes to calm Egypt down. He was screaming, screaming, and it took twenty-five minutes, and that was the greatest fight I've ever seen. *(Pause)* So I will match him maybe two more times, see, if the situation is right because I have nothing to prove, but I'm a sportsman and I won't avoid anything, but Egypt has nothing to prove, we have nothing to prove. *(Beats)* And Dog Mouth wanted to meet me, and I didn't ask why, but I seen him on TV, seen you both, and I knew his name from before anyway.

Nyah   Terry doesn't tell me his business, so I don't know why either.

Weeks nods. Pause.

Weeks	When's the baby due?
Nyah	Next week. But you never know, that's what I been told. But, yeah, next week.
Weeks	A little baby Dog Mouth. Now isn't that a concept.
Nyah	He has had other children, but this will be different.
Weeks	*(Beats)* When you get into Phoenix, into the city I want you to be careful. They have some serious police in Phoenix, just mean stupid men, about as mean and dumb as any police anywhere. It's a little like the south that way, Phoenix is. I live just outside these days, but still in Phoenix, and I am very careful. I wonder why I don't leave, but probably it's a sickness, a need to be feeling the bootheel of power stepping down on me. Must be, otherwise I would move. But since I crawled out of that eternal dream and out under the heat lamp of earth I have been feeling myself stepped on, so it's something I have trained myself to enjoy. You wouldn't have any idea what I am talking about, would you?
Nyah	No, I don't think so.
Weeks	You know in cafeterias, those heat lamps keep the food warm? That's us, all of us, mankind, just a giant lukewarm casserole waiting to be tossed into a trash bag.

WEEKS *laughs. Pause.*

Weeks	And now you are going to have a baby, and he'll be waking from his dream soon, and then he'll be mad and he'll be wonderin' how the fuck do I get back to the dream, to the night and the warm stuff, but there is no way, no way this side of death.

Nyah looks down at her large belly and then rubs it gently as Weeks laughs. Lights fade out quickly.

*

Scene 9

Lights up slowly. It's night now and the light is dim. Dog Mouth, Nyah, and Weeks.

Dog Mouth That was before Vietnam.

Weeks I remember.

Dog Mouth Was a lot more activity, and almost no states had anti-dog fight laws.

Weeks In Texas, shit, the governor I think, he played, he had his dogs.

Dog Mouth After Vietnam the laws started or started being enforced, and even old timers were being raided. I got out of it then. I had other things going on in my life and so I got out.

Weeks Well, I know who you are. Knowing that I'm wondering what you want to see me about?

Dog Mouth You know who I am?

Weeks I know who you used to be, too. You used to have dogs. You ain't got dogs anymore, that's not who you are now.

Pause.

Dog Mouth I only wanted to get a dog. You think maybe I have other business, and that's wrong. I wanted to see your dogs. Indian

	Sonny talked to me, and said you are the man. I want to have some dogs again, soon, and maybe start up a yard, go back to something I liked.
Weeks	Alright. My dogs are all good right now, and my yard is good and I got enough wins and a ROM bitch, and a four-time winner and isn't nothing half ass in my yard.
Dog Mouth	I guess you were mistaken about the other.
Weeks	Listen to me, when a man appears on TV and a reporter is asking him about murders and about a criminal organization that he runs, well, I think someone would have to be very stupid not to want to know up front what the reason for the visit is.
Dog Mouth	My reason for the visit is dogs, that is all, dogs: bulldogs, pit bull terriers *(Laughs)*—what people call 'em now, and I love dogs, and that's why I'm here.
Weeks	You gonna have a baby soon too. Man about to have a baby makes changes in his life.
Dog Mouth	*(Pause)* You think so? *(Pause)* Could be, could be, many would agree with that, many, and maybe it's so.

They look at each other. Lights fade out.

*

Scene 10

Lights come up slowly; it's night. WEEKS and DOG MOUTH both sit next to the tracks. It's late. The sound of the train whistle is in the distance. Silence.

Weeks	What will happen with that girl?
Dog Mouth	She'll have her baby.
Weeks	That's what I thought. *(Pause)* You ain't gonna buy no dog. You also ain't gonna get a house or some shit and become a father.
Dog Mouth	No, no I'm not.
Weeks	But you liked the dogs, didn't you? You know dogs, I'll give that to you. *(Beats)* But now I want to understand why you're here? I imagine it has to do with Muehler.
Dog Mouth	Muehler, yeah, it has to do with him.
Weeks	I expect Muehler will turn up, found at the side of railroad tracks somewhere, dead as my unemployment claim. Am I correct so far?
Dog Mouth	So far you're correct.
Weeks	I don't want nothing to do with Muehler or his business.
Dog Mouth	You already have something to do with Muehler.

Pause.

Weeks	That's true. But now I don't anymore. You can see that. *(Beats)* What I can see about you is that you're not feeling so good anymore, in your life, I mean I think you have medical problems of some sort, and here you are with this girl following you and getting knocked up and telling you she loves you and all the while you feel worse and worse, but nobody is supposed to know that because you are the big dog, right? Dog Mouth's the enforcer, that's how the reporter described you. The enforcer. *(Beats)* And one man went to prison for life in Mississippi because of you, of you killing someone, and he took the fall on that, and another

man went to the police somewhere, in Denver, somewhere, and he asked for protection from you. And now journalists are following you and the girl and want-ing interviews and offering money for interviews, and offering other things too. Is this right so far?

Dog Mouth How about I'll just stop you when you make a mistake.

Weeks OK. So I am a business associate of Mr. Muehler, I am not a friend, but I am a business associate, and it's true we did some business, several times, several different things, and Mr. Muehler is a man of German extraction, I think, and he does his business in a kind of way I guess they do in places like Germany, that's what I imagine. Sort of German business practices, and he is not a man many people are going to like, he's not a likeable man, not at all, he's a bad smelling man, and while he always had clean clothes he, in his body, he had odors, and his breath always, his breath was not pleasant and his manner of talking, he'd spit when he talked to you and he drank and so you could smell it on him, the odor of cheap wine, of Thunderbird, I know that one, and of Mad Dog, and cheap ports, and he had bad teeth, and he'd pick at his teeth see, he'd pick at them and you could see the holes in the goddamn tooth, black spots, black holes of decay, and he lied, and I never had wanted to do business with Muehler, but I did, because I can't afford to be choosey, see, I can't afford to pick my business associates, I can't and I have to look out for myself first and last, always had to look out for myself, always all times, and I've had a hard life, but I'm not complaining, I've seen worse off, seen people had worse lives, seen people had to do much worse than I have and in some ways I figure myself lucky. "Lucky

Weeks," I say to myself sometimes, I should be called Lucky Weeks. So that is all there is to the story. We did some business, sold a few pills, sold a little smoke, nothing very big, just some little piss ant shit, and didn't really rip nobody off, and I hardly was part of it truthfully, hardly a part of the damn business. So now I figure Mr. Muehler is dead, or about to be dead, and you are here to see me about some dogs you don't really want.

Silence.

Dog Mouth One problem is hemorrhoids.

He stands slowly, gingerly.

Dog Mouth I got hemorrhoids. I even, one time, after Vietnam, they built me a new asshole. That's how bad it was at one time.

DOG MOUTH paces.

Dog Mouth I am not sure what I thought would happen, I truly didn't know. My focus is about one hour, two hours in front of me, that's all, that's the truth. *(Beats)* And the organization, well, they may paint the name of it all over train yards across the western states, but hell, there isn't much of an organization, but when that reporter started talking about us then every-one started to make all kinds of claims about what we had done. And people I don't even know began to write the name of the organization on the sides of boxcars, on trestles, and the cement embankments of hobo jungles, anyplace they could find, and it started to seem that there were thousands of us, or hundreds, and there isn't that many, not nearly that many. Then other reporters took up the story and there were men who'd call up reporters to say they knew of some killing, they knew where someone had been killed, and they knew where the graves were or they knew something, anything. They'd say whatever they felt sounded good and might get them a few bucks. And they'd always mention Dog Mouth— he's the leader, he's the enforcer, he's a killer and you better watch yourself.

Weeks   Yeah, well, but I've heard you, and I've seen you on TV.

Dog Mouth   Sure you have, and I didn't deny a thing, did I? I didn't because, hell, some of it's true.

DOG MOUTH stops, rubbing his buttocks near his anus.

Dog Mouth   Now, it's worse than hemorrhoids, I still have those but I also have cancer of the asshole, cancer of the anus, somewhere down there I am being eaten alive, from the asshole up, in, and out.

Weeks   Who told you you got cancer? A doctor tell you that? What doctor? This was a doctor you trust?

Dog Mouth   At the VA in Los Angeles, a doctor out there, at the VA *(Beats)* The GI bill and medical benefits is what I got out of killing people for the government. I tried to get 'em to write me for some painkillers, but, you know how they are and they took a good look at me and said, no, that wouldn't be in my best interest. I said well, having cancer is not in my best interest either.

Weeks   That's the thing with these doctors. I expect they don't understand that death isn't an illness, see, they think maybe down the road there's a cure for the damn thing. But I don't want that cure, I don't want to cure death. I lived long enough already, you want to know, and maybe I'm scared as anyone else about it, but I know it's gonna be a relief nonetheless. I know that.

Dog Mouth I know I could have used codeine or whatever, I sure as hell could have used that.

Weeks *(Beats)* So I have to ask you, what is it you plan on doing? You want to kill me same as Muehler?

Dog Mouth Well, it's not something I can really give you an answer for, because anything I decide to do I would lie about anyway, right?

DOG MOUTH *finally finishes up pacing and sits. Silence.*

Weeks Little Nyah asked me why I was here, out here in Arizona. I been thinking how to answer that, how to answer it honestly. But I have no honest answer, because I've been pulled along all my life, moving from here to there and never having an answer for why. *(Beats)* There are not a lot of people here, that's the best reason, because the one thing I am certain of is that if there were a lot of people here then I would leave.

Dog Mouth I want to think about the dogs for a night or so, think about if I am really going to get back into the game or not. That OK with you?

Weeks You got a lot of things to think about, so you take all the time you want, all the time you need.

DOG MOUTH *nods. Pause. Lights fade out.*

*

Scene 11

Lights come up slowly. NYAH *is sitting and* DOG MOUTH
stands over her. It's night.

Nyah	I love you.
Dog Mouth	How do you feel?
Nyah	Like a girl about to have a baby. I guess I'm gonna have the baby soon now. *(Beats)* What's gonna happen, Terry?
Dog Mouth	Nothing to do with you. I don't have to talk to you at all if that's what you want.
Nyah	This is your baby, and I love you, and just because you pretend you don't care I know you do.
Dog Mouth	Then you're stupid and shouldn't be breeding. *(Beat)* I could do things would stop you from loving me.
Nyah	*(Pause)* No, I don't want you to do that.
Dog Mouth	You tell me when the baby is ready, you tell me and we'll get you to the hospital. I know where they'll take you and I talked to Weeks and he cut me into a couple people know the scene here and how to get welfare extras and food stamps and you'll be fine.

Silence. NYAH *looking at him. Lights fade out.*

*

Scene 12

Lights come up slowly. It's day, and it's hot. DOG MOUTH *and* BECKER. BECKER *is pacing and agitated.*

Becker No, no, no. I am telling you about this.

Dog Mouth OK, OK.

Becker This wasn't good, not good.

Dog Mouth Well wait, is Muehler...

Becker ... No, no, no Muehler isn't dead. Is Muehler dead? Is he dead? No, no, he's not dead. No, no, he's not.

Dog Mouth OK, OK.

Becker This is not good, how this happened. What happened is not good, is not fucking good. Do you want to hear or not?

Dog Mouth Yeah, yeah.

Becker Man, man, I was up there in Provo, in Utah, that's the motherfucker's home now, in Provo. In Utah, in Mormon Utah. Now, so now if I spend my life in prison it's going to be with a bunch of lapsed Mormons. Man, that's not right, that is fucked up.

Dog Mouth Tell me about it. Go ahead, slow down, tell me about it.

Becker I am there in Provo, and I ask around and everyone seems to know Muehler, knows his house and his old lady. Yes, yes, he has an old lady, and nobody told me that. Bitch is ugly too. So I'm there in the city, and I'm asking and I find out his house and I go there and, you know, I am hanging around waiting to see him. So later, after a couple hours, I see him and he goes inside his house. So I wait, and I am thinking I'll follow him when he leaves, next time he leaves. But he doesn't leave, and hours go by and it's about eleven now and some fucking Provo cops stop and ask me what who I am and what I'm doing and I tell them I'm just a bum and I'm on my way out of town, you know. So they tell me OK, and that I should get out of town quickly and all that good stuff and so I split. I split a little ways but then I come back and now I see the cocksucker. He's out walking the dog with his old lady and it's tough to tell which one is the dog, and I follow them, you know. And finally they come to a dark stretch of street with no houses and I just ran up on the motherfucker and I shanked him. I stuck him right there, and he started screaming like some bitch and I stick him again, and I stuck him once more.

Pause.

Dog Mouth   Go on.

Becker   His old lady is yelling and running down the street, yelling for help and Muehler is on the ground, and man, there is blood all over. Its all over the ground and he had on a light brown coat, and its red now, its, you could see how wet it was, red and wet and I looked down at him and I told him he was a punk and that he deserved this. Then I hear people coming, the fucking bitch had found people and so I ran. Man, I ran and ran, and I got to the tracks, and I jumped on the rear car of some commuter type... I don't know, I got on something for about a day. I jumped off and I was in New Mexico, and now I'm here.

Pause.

Dog Mouth	But he's not dead?
Becker	No, no he's not dead.
Dog Mouth	You know he's not dead?
Becker	I heard it on the radio and I read the newspaper, outside Zion I read a paper in a coffee shop, the paper had a report you know on the attack. Said a man was attacked allegedly by a member of...

DOG MOUTH holds up his hand and stops him. Pause.

Dog Mouth	This sucker didn't die, and he spoke to the police and accused us? Is that it?
Becker	On the radio, it said he was expected to make a full recovery. *(Beats)* I'm sorry man, I really am, but this, he, he's a tough old cocksucker all I can say.
Dog Mouth	All you can say.
Becker	I stuck him three times, maybe more, maybe four, maybe five, but for sure three, and all three man, I felt the blade go in there, felt it go in and I was gonna "run the gears" you know, let me die holding his fucking intestines, but it didn't happen like that.
Dog Mouth	Let me tell you something.
Becker	Yeah, yeah, go ahead.
Dog Mouth	You have to leave here and you have to go far away. Becker, let me tell you something else. You have to be smart and listen to me or you will find yourself on death row, and, man, they will shoot your ass in Utah.

BECKER starts pacing in circles again.

Becker	Alright, alright. Fuck, fuck, man, fuck that cocksucker.
Dog Mouth	He's going to recover, and he's gonna help the police any way he can, he's going to tell them everything about us. Everything he knows.
Becker	Yeah, but what's he know? I mean the fucker doesn't really know so much, if you think about it. He don't know anything.
Dog Mouth	I want you to go to Mexico. I can tell exactly how to do this, and exactly what to do, exactly. And you have to listen to me. *(Beat)* You want to be on death row?
Becker	No man, I don't, I don't.
Dog Mouth	Then you have to do what I am going to tell you to do. I have some friends in Mexico, and they'll help you.
Becker	How long I gotta be in Mexico, man? I mean I don't, you know, I don't like Mexicans, man.
Dog Mouth	Mexico is alright, Mexico is fine.
Becker	Shit. I hate fucking Mexican food. There, right there, I don't want to go and have to stay a long time.
Dog Mouth	There's good Mexican food too, there is bad Mexican food and there is good Mexican food.
Becker	Shit.
Dog Mouth	Enchiladas. *(Beat)* What, you gonna tell me enchiladas aren't good?
Becker	It's a matter of personal taste, man. I don't happen to fucking like Mexican food, I don't like enchiladas and I don't like tacos and I don't like Mexicans.
Dog Mouth	You like the food on death row? You like Utah penitentiary food, is that it, powdered eggs and chili mac, that what you like?

BECKER stops and squats down, head in his hands. He is moaning softly to himself. Long pause.

Dog Mouth   You can leave in the morning and head down to El Paso, and cross there, and you'll be in Matamoros.

BECKER remains moaning, not looking up.

Dog Mouth   I will call Arturo, Artie, he's got dogs, and I know him a long, long time. He will meet you somewhere and he'll drive you down, deep down into Mexico. Artie's family is part of the syndicate down there and he'll take you into someplace in central Mexico, someplace where the police work for the syndicate, and this is where you're gonna stay until I send word that you should leave.

Becker   Uh-huh, OK, alright, OK, fuck man, I don't like Mexico though, I'm telling you.

Dog Mouth   I reckon that's not really the issue, is it? I am trying to just take care of something you let get away from you. Now I know that can happen, but there is reason, if I wanted, to ask a couple questions. *(Beats)* Don't you think? Don't you think that?

Becker   No, I don't know, what questions? I guess you should ask any questions—if you got questions they should be answered.

Dog Mouth   I don't think you can answer them. It's those kind of questions.

They stare at each other.

Becker   You asked me to do this. You told me, you told me to go see Muehler.

Dog Mouth	That's right.
Becker	How long I known you? How many years is it? Eight? Ten? *(Beats)* Since the joint, right?
Dog Mouth	Ten years, I'd say.
Becker	You told me to go.
Dog Mouth	I knew you would say exactly this. I knew this is what you would say.
Becker	Ten motherfucking years.
Dog Mouth	Is there a point here? Do you have a point to make?
Becker	How come you sent me to see Muehler?
Dog Mouth	Because I was coming to see Weeks.
Becker	And what's been going on? I mean, it looks like all you're gonna do is buy a motherfucking dog.
Dog Mouth	I might buy a dog. *(Pause)* Man has good dogs. What are you trying to say?
Becker	I had, you sent me to kill a motherfucker while you came here to buy a dog, and see, that's alright, but now you're saying shit about it, or saying I didn't do something. It didn't go right, that's all. It just didn't go right.

DOG MOUTH nods and turns away. He walks away, pacing. Silence.

Dog Mouth	Maybe I should kill the nigger, what do you think?
Becker	*(Pause)* That's you. It don't, it isn't important, not anymore, not to me.

DOG MOUTH nods. Silence. Lights fade out.

*

Scene 13

Lights up slowly. It's twilight. NYAH and WEEKS both
stand looking upstage, their gaze following the tracks into
the distance. Silence. They turn away finally.

Weeks   There is a car I can use, nearby. When you're ready, you
say it, and I'll go get it.

Nyah   I can't tell. I am not certain what is supposed to happen to
let me know, and, and I guess I will just know.

Weeks   I believe you'll know, yeah.

Nyah   I had a boyfriend once who wouldn't let me out of his sight.
If I was away from him then he'd call, he'd call every five
minutes until we were back together.

Weeks   Yeah, uh-huh.

Nyah   He was never happy. It wouldn't matter what I did, or
how much I told him I loved him or anything. He couldn't
be happy, I think, I think that even the idea of being OK
about things, trusting me and all, just the idea made him...
made him shiver, and made him get afraid.

She looks at WEEKS. Pause.

Weeks   Some people need to be busy with something, anything,
even busy being jealous.

Nyah   That's how he was. And he drove me insane until I left him.
But I had to sneak out of the town because just to tell him
he would have beat the shit out of me. *(Beats)* I didn't want
to go, to leave that place, and I shouldn't have had to, that's
my point.

Weeks	You have to do a lot of things you don't want to do in this world. The world is real shitty that way.

NYAH gets up and walks around, looking around. WEEKS watches.

Nyah	I wonder what this is all about with you. Terry doesn't usually do anything with black people.
Weeks	We aren't really doing anything.
Nyah	He usually won't do nothing with black people. You follow me on this, he won't even do nothing if it involves a black guy.
Weeks	We're talking about dogs, maybe that's different.
Nyah	No, no, but something is different, I just can't see it.

She is walking in circle around WEEKS, looking at him. He turns his head to watch her.

Nyah	Aren't you a little worried about Terry, about Dog Mouth? Don't you know who he is?
Weeks	I know.
Nyah	Are you worried, a little?
Weeks	No, not worried.
Nyah	No, something is going on, why we came here, because if Terry wanted a dog he would buy a dog from a white guy, even if the black guy's dog was better.
Weeks	You think that?
Nyah	No *(Pause)*... something *(Pause)*... and I am a little nervous myself.
Weeks	Woman gonna have a baby shouldn't be nervous, it's not good for the baby.

Nyah	I'm not that kind of nervous. I'm not nervous about myself. I am fine. I am, however, getting a little nervous about you. About you, the black guy, you get it?!
Weeks	You thinking that the father of your baby, that he might have come here to hurt me, something like that?
Nyah	Well, something like that, yeah.
Weeks	Does that sort of make you feel all excited?
Nyah	No. *(Beats)* I'm not some sicko.

WEEKS *stands up. Pause.*

Weeks	What about black men? Does being close up to a black man make you feel something?
Nyah	You know what would happen if I told Terry you said that?
Weeks	I give a fuck what you tell Terry. Shit.

WEEKS *walks a few yards away. Pause.*

Weeks	I'm not trying to fuck you, I don't like white girls anyway, and I don't have much use for sex anymore anyway. *(Pause)* That's not something you can understand is it? A world without things of a sexual nature, a world without sexual charge everywhere.
Nyah	You think you're trying some head game with the dumb little white chick.
Weeks	*(Beats)* I think nothin' of the sort. *(Beats)* I think you're just a young girl in love and having a baby and wondering how that's gonna feel and what that's gonna be like.
Nyah	You have children?
Weeks	Nope.

Pause.

Nyah   I don't know why we're here and I didn't really want to
               come here and I'm going to ask you for something.

Weeks   Go ahead.

Nyah   I want to ask you to leave. I'm asking you to leave and go
               away for a few days so Terry will just take me and we'll
               go back to California and forget all about whatever the
               hell it is we came here for.

Weeks   *(Pause)* Someone came today for Dog Mouth. A friend of
               his. *(Beat)* You know who this is?

NYAH nods. Silence.

Weeks   Shit.

WEEKS walks away, looking up the tracks. Pause.

Nyah   Will you do that for me?

Weeks   Shut up, just shut the fuck up, 'cause I am getting very
               fucking tired of you.

Silence.

Weeks   *(Half to himself)* The fuck am I talking to this bitch for.

Pause. Lights fade out.

*

Scene 14

Lights up slowly. It's late at night. DOG MOUTH *is asleep in a sleeping bag next to track.* NYAH *is kneeling next to him.*

Nyah   Wake up, Terry.

DOG MOUTH *stirs, rolls over to face her, and then gets up on one elbow.*

Dog Mouth   What?

Nyah   I might be ready to have the baby.

Dog Mouth   You *might* be? *(Beat)* Are you?

Nyah   I don't know.

Dog Mouth   Then you aren't.

Nyah   One more thing.

Dog Mouth   Yeah.

Nyah   I saw Becker. *(Beat)* Saw him when I was in town around the truck stop there.

Dog Mouth   You saw him.

Nyah   Yeah, and I had a bad feeling about him all of a sudden. Just like that, all of a sudden.

Dog Mouth   Don't worry about Becker, Becker is leaving tomorrow. Should have left yesterday, but he's leaving tomorrow.

Nyah   No, no, I don't think he will.

Dog Mouth   Go back to sleep.

Nyah   I think at the moment I had that bad feeling come over me, I also, well, the bad feeling was part of how I could feel he wasn't going to do what you want him to do. He was going to try to do something to you.

DOG MOUTH sits all the way up. Pause.

Dog Mouth	Listen to me, Nyah. I have known many Beckers, and I understand what they are capable of doing and what they aren't.
Nyah	Christ.
Dog Mouth	He'll leave tomorrow. *(Beat)* We'll leave too, tomorrow, after Becker leaves.

NYAH stops, holds her stomach. It passes.

Dog Mouth	You going to have it?
Nyah	Now I don't think so.
Dog Mouth	You just...
Nyah	... Yeah, I did, but it was the wrong kind. Maybe tomorrow, maybe soon. *(Beats)* I want to ask you something again. *(Beats)* Tell me one time when you killed someone. I don't care about who, but I want to know about it. I want to know what you thought about, and what you did afterwards.
Dog Mouth	OK. *(Beats)* I'll tell you. I never killed anyone. Never. I never did, never, never killed anyone. I had a fight one time, and I hit this man, and he was hurt, fell down and I guess he fell on his head, and then I kicked him, kicked him in the head, kicked him in the face, in the crotch, everywhere I could. As I kicked him, I first thought, where can I kick him now, where haven't I kicked him yet, and after I ran out of places to kick him, I felt sick like I'd throw up. Not because I gave a shit about him or felt bad, I didn't feel bad at all, but I almost got sick and I went and sat down and sat there looking at this guy. I didn't have a single thought in my

head, except for thinking how I didn't have a thought in my head. That was all, just blank, and slowly this man got on all fours, face to the ground and blood dripped from his mouth and nose and somewhere else probably. Somehow I had torn the nail on my thumb, and it started hurting. I don't know how it happened unless it happened when I hit him. I got up then and went over to him, and I thought maybe I would kick him again because I was mad my nail was torn, but I didn't, I just walked off and I left, I think. Later on, I thought about it, but I didn't have any particular feeling about it. Then someone told me the guy had some real medical problems because of the beating I gave him, and I thought about asking, but then decided that would be stupid and that I shouldn't care. He got beat because he needed a beating, that's all, that's all the part I played in it. Fuck him, I thought, fuck him and his fucking real medical problems.

Nyah   Lots of people are scared of you, a lot of people think you're a killer and they're afraid of you. I've seen it in their faces when they meet you or even when somebody talks about you. They are afraid. How come they're afraid if you never killed anybody?

Dog Mouth They think I have.

Nyah   Well I know, but why do they think that?

Dog Mouth I don't know. I let them think that I suppose. I've just let them.

Nyah   Maybe you aren't telling me, and you really did kill some-one. Or many, many people. You're maybe a stone-cold killing machine.

Dog Mouth Why don't you go back to sleep?

Nyah	Maybe you were. Maybe before, you were a killer, and that's why people are so scared of you. But that was before, and I know you're not the same as you used to be.
Dog Mouth	You know nothing about it.
Nyah	Yes I do, yes I do, I know you're a changed man, I know that much.

NYAH gets up and walks in a circle, sort of skipping and hopping happily, in an exaggerated way meant to suggest happiness.

My baby will be like you, Terry. It will be a boy baby and I'm going to name him Terry, Terrance, and he will be like you. He is already like you because he's inside me, and I feel him. *(She stops)* I can feel him kick. Do you want to feel him? Come here... feel... feel here.

She kneels back down, extending her stomach for DOG MOUTH. He doesn't move.

| Nyah | Here... feel... it's your baby too... feel... here. |

He doesn't. Lights fade out.

*

Scene 15

Lights up slowly. WEEKS *and* NYAH. *It's day.* WEEKS *stands, straddling the tracks.*

Weeks I'll take you myself, if he isn't back soon. *(Beats)* Take a deep breath.

NYAH does. Pause.

Nyah I dreamed last night and in the dream was Lee Marvin, and when I was a little girl my father would talk about movies with Lee Marvin, who he loved, and Lee Marvin scared me, but he was there in my dream. *(Takes another deep breath)*

Weeks Well, if it's a boy, maybe you call him Marvin. *(Laughs)*

Nyah Fuck Lee Marvin and fuck my dumb ass dreams and fuck my father who loved Lee Marvin because he was a marine. *(She stops, taking a deep breath and then breathing deeply throughout what is obviously a contraction)*

Weeks See, maybe you should get to the hospital.

Nyah My father loved war movies best, best of all would have been a war movie with Lee Marvin. So he could talk to you about the army, or marines, whatever he'd been in, talk at you with a beer in his hand, and I'd always have to run off and get him another, another cold one he'd say. Bring me another cold one, honey. The only time he called me honey was when he was sending me for more beer. When I started to have friends, he'd buy us beer, or wine, the kind of wine he thought was fancy, but it wasn't really. I know that, and even then I kind of knew it, but nobody else did, not my friends, and so he felt like a big shot. Maybe he felt like a father then too, I don't know. So he'd order fancy wine or some shit, and he'd talk to my friends, and talk to them sometimes about being a marine, and he never hit on them or anything, I'll give him that, but he was just an asshole, and he'd give advice, sort of general advice on stuff, as though he could provide guidance, as though he were like a priest. A friend of mine said once, your dad talks like a priest, and really that is about as funny as shit gets in this life, my dad a priest. *(Stops to breath through another contraction)* Everything was just like that, half assed and full of shit. And then like my mother would just get backhanded for anything, for nothing, for something, something he thought was wrong, or if he started to feel bad, if he started to get into a depression he would smack her. This was to get him feeling better, I guess.

Pause.

Weeks   It's a long ways to the hospital. I want you to come with me, alright? You have everything you need? My memory isn't that good, so I need you to remember things for yourself. It's just something that's happened to me, that I will forget things, same as an old man. Do you have everything you need?

She looks at him. Silence.

Weeks   I'm taking you into the hospital where I am going to leave you. I know things you don't know. Man I wish I didn't, but then...

Stops. Pause.

Nyah	But then what?
Weeks	Then, by now, I'd be a dead nigger. *(Pause)* Do you have everything?

Silence. Lights fade out.

*

Scene 16

Lights up slowly. It's night and very dim. DOG MOUTH and BECKER crouch by the side of the tracks. From off-stage come flashlight beams, aimed by offstage VOICES. Two of them, possibly three, play all over the stage, but miss DOG MOUTH and BECKER.

Voice 4	*(Off)* There is nobody out here now. I can see nobody.
Voice 5	*(Off)* Man, shut up, why do you complain, I mean everything, every time, you complain.

Far upstage are the shadows of several men. The flashlight beams keep crisscrossing the stage. DOG MOUTH and BECKER crouch lower.

Voice 4	*(Off)* It's later than I usually work, that's all, and isn't nobody here anyway. Do you see somebody, because I don't see nothing.

Voice 5	*(Off)* Get Melvin to look up by the trestle, and we'll go down to the wash there...
Voice 6	*(Off)* Fuck, send Melvin yourself. Hell, I'll go, I'll go up to the bridge and back.
Voice 5	*(Off)* Somebody go, all I care.

Sound of a truck engine starting up, very close by and very loud. The voices continue but are muffled. The flashlight beams disappear. Sound of the truck idling continues...

Becker	Railroad, those are railroad cops.
Dog Mouth	They won't be back until tomorrow, when it gets light, then they'll come back.
Becker	Were they looking for me? You think even the railroad is looking for me?

DOG MOUTH straightens up a little, looking around carefully. Sound of the truck engaging and driving away.

Dog Mouth	I think the whole world is looking for you, Becker.
Becker	It feels that way. The fucking whole world is out looking to find me.
Dog Mouth	The entire planet is looking for you. Soon the police from other planets will be looking for you too. Don't you think?
Becker	*(Beats)* Well, that's how it feels, you can make fun of me, but that's how it fucking feels.
Dog Mouth	I'm not making fun of you. And I know just how you feel. Every stranger looks like a cop, and every time someone goes to a pay phone you think they're dropping a dime on you. You dream of being chased, like dogs dream, always

dreaming of chasing something. Same as you, except you dream of *being* chased. You didn't make a sound last night, though. A dog barks or whimpers in his sleep, but you didn't, you slept like a baby, silent and not even moving, far as I could tell. When a dog dreams you can see their little paws moving, running after that rabbit or whatever it is, and making little noises like little half barks, and chasing down their prey. I wonder though, how they know that's what dogs dream? Huh? Maybe dogs dream of empires and sacred books... or of hot girl dogs, dancing poodles or something. It could be, hell, they don't know. I like to think of dogs dreaming of unknown mathematical equations... of science and architecture. All things they forget when they wake up.

DOG MOUTH moves behind the kneeling BECKER. He takes out a piece of cord.

Dog Mouth I wonder do we dream after death? I'd like to know what those dreams are like.

He whips the cord around BECKER's throat and pulls. BECKER tries to fight...

Dog Mouth If you can, Becker, you come back and tell me, OK? Tell me what you dreamed... after...

BECKER slumps to the ground, dead, and DOG MOUTH releases him.

Dog Mouth Chump.

Lights fade out.

*

Scene 17

In the darkness, there is a sound of a baby crying. Light up on NYAH. *She stands in pool of light. She is no longer pregnant. She wears a hospital gown.*

Nyah In this hospital is a sort of day room where I spend a lot of my... of my day. I've been kept for observation because they say I had some irregularities. I believe it is because the police asked the hospital to keep me. *(Beats)* In this day room there is a television, but they keep the sound turned very low so as not to disturb us, the girls watching it. Some kind of thinking along those lines. *(Beat)* I find the television very upsetting, and so I don't watch very often. I never watch when the news comes on. I go and do something else like play with my baby. I named him after my father. I didn't name him after Terry. I named him after my father. *(Beat)* I guess it just works that way. No matter what. *(Beat)* Love, hate, like, dislike, none of it matters. Some things just work the way they work and you can do little to change it.

She turns away and walks out of the light as it fades out.

BLACKOUT.

The End

Times Like These
by John O'Keefe

Times Like These was produced at 2100 Square Feet by Padua
Playwrights in October 2002, under the playwright's direction, with
the following cast:

Oscar Weiss: Norbert Weisser
Meta Wolff: Laurie O'Brien

Characters

Oscar Weiss

Meta Wolff

Voice on the Radio

Scene

An apartment in Berlin, 1930.

Act One

Scene 1

OSCAR and META in silhouette facing each other. META is holding a bouquet of roses. OSCAR is kneeling before her. OSCAR is applauding.

Oscar   Did you hear them? They all cried out for you. You were wonderful "Meta! Meta! Bravo! Bravo!" And you, eating it up.

Meta   You were wonderful too.

Oscar   *(Mimicking her)* "You were wonderful too." I hate it when you're generous.

META clutches her flowers to her breast and peers down at OSCAR.

Meta   Oh, get up.

Oscar   I won't get up until you admit how brilliant you were.

Meta   Oh, stop it, Oscar.

She looks down at him. OSCAR remains in place on his knees. Then finally she shouts.

Meta	Yes! Yes! I was brilliant!

They laugh. Lights out.

⁕

Scene 2

OSCAR is pacing and working on his lines from "Woyzeck."

Oscar	"Yet, if a Wanderer, leaning on the stream of time..."
Meta	*(Off, correcting him)* "Wanderer," Oscar. What sound in the word gives it its meaning?
Oscar	"Wan."
Meta	*(Off)* Yes, "waaaaannn..."
Oscar	"Waaaaann..."
Meta	*(Off)* "Waaaaaaann..."
Oscar	"Waaaaaaann..."
Meta	*(Off)* It is his longing.
Oscar	"Waaaaaann..."
Meta	*(Off)* And then the sound of his feet, "... derer..."
Oscar	"... derer..."
Meta	*(Off)* Yes, but a light touch of the tongue,
Oscar	"... derer."
Meta	*(Off)* The word is so elegant.
Oscar	"Yet, if the Waanderer, leaning by the stream of time, in his godly..."
Meta	*(Off)* "... gawdly..."

Oscar	"... gawdly wisdom asketh and answereth himself..."
Meta	*(Off)* Snap those words.
Oscar	"... asketh and answereth himself: What is Man?"
Meta	"What is man?"
Oscar	"What is man? Verily I say unto you..."
Meta	*(Off)* Think the words through as you say them, they are not complete until the last line.
Oscar	"On what would the farmer, the barrel maker, the cobbler, the doctor live, if God had not created Man?"
Meta	*(Off)* Yes, Oscar, now dig in.
Oscar	"Yet, if a Wanderer, leaning by the stream of time, in his godly wisdom asketh and answereth himself: What is Man? What is Man? Verily I say unto you, On what would the farmer, the barrel maker, the cobbler, the doctor live, if God had not created Man? From what would the tailor live if Shame was not implanted in Man, from what would the Soldier live if Man did not come equipped with the need to slaughter himself? Therefore, doubt not, yes, yes, it is lovely and fine, yet everything on earth is evil, even money rots. In conclusion, my Beloved Ones, let us now piss on a cross so that a Jew will die."

META *enters, beautiful and radiant. She applauds him as the lights fade.*

*

Scene 3

META on the telephone. She is in her kimono. She is cradling the phone on her neck while filing her fingernails.

Meta   You know perfectly well that I'm too old to play Kate—You drive me crazy, Hans. You are such a charmer—

OSCAR enters, drying his hair. He is peeved.

Meta   Oh, do you? Well, if I play Kate, then I think Oscar should play Petruchio.

OSCAR waves for her to stop.

Meta   Why not? I think he's perfect for the part—*(She laughs)*—Yes, yes, he did tame me—I am tamed, I tell you, I am tamed—

OSCAR turns his back on her and leaves the room, only to return and glare at her.

Meta   No, you aren't the taming kind—What are you? Hmmm, do you really want me to say?

OSCAR begins angrily pacing.

Meta   You're a bureaucrat—How have I insulted you? A true German should take that as a compliment—

OSCAR stands over META.

Meta Listen, Oscar seems to be chomping at the bit, I've got to tend to his needs. It is my wifely duty—Don't worry about it—Yes, rehearsal in two weeks. Kate, my God, I hope there is enough makeup—Oh, stop, you're making me ill. Go to bed; drink a glass of hot milk. Tschüss.

Meta What's wrong with you?

Oscar I don't like that man.

Meta There's nothing to dislike about him, that is why there is nothing to like.

Oscar Yes, he's like a piece of paper, you can write on him anything you want to write and it will be there for everyone to see. Be careful what you say to that guy. In times like these Hans Johst can be a very dangerous man.

Meta You're exaggerating, Oscar. He's just a little man with a name in front of his desk. Hans says that things could go much better for theater artists, especially for actors. God knows the union is doing nothing for us. He said that there could be a special chamber for actors where untalented novices couldn't get in.

Oscar You mean the Jews?

Meta What do the Jews have to do with it?

Oscar Jews, intellectuals, foreigners. Who's going to pay for all this? What do we have to do in return? We would have to play folk art, folk art, Meta.

Meta What do you mean?

Oscar Polka Theater!

Meta That's not possible; this is Berlin.

Oscar Goethe, Schiller, Shakespeare, oh yes, but with changes.

Meta	What's wrong with Shakespeare? I could do with more Shakespeare, and Goethe and Schiller. There is a lot of self-indulgent crap out there.
Oscar	Yes, and Hans Johst.
Meta	Impossible, he's a terrible playwright.
Oscar	*(Pretending to tear his shirt open)* Yes, Expressionist sauerkraut!
Meta	Is it because he was my lover?
Oscar	No, it's because you could fuck somebody with so little talent!
Meta	My dear, dearest Oscar, it is you I love, only you. *(She puts her arms around his neck and sings)*

Du, du, liegst mir im Herzen
Du, du, liegst mir im Sinn
Du, du, machst mir viel Schmerzen
Weisst nicht wie gut ich dir bin.

The lights begin to fade as she sings the chorus.

Ja, Ja, Ja, Ja,
Weisst nicht wie gut ich dir bin.

They kiss as the lights fade out.

*

Scene 4

The lights rise just as META *is entering in a huff.* OSCAR *is behind her.*

Meta I don't understand why they had to postpone the rehearsal. It's unheard of. Casting problems? What does that mean? Well, say something, Oscar. What do you think? You must have some opinion.

Oscar I wouldn't worry about it, your job is secure.

Meta Of course, my job is secure, why wouldn't it be? And so is yours, but I think he should have cast you as Petruchio.

Oscar I'm perfectly fine with my role.

Meta That's your problem. You're afraid of success. You could have done that role; you could have stepped up into that role, yet you hung back. I swear you shrink every time you get up on that stage. You must focus. You must be sharp as a stiletto.

Oscar I hate that Johst; I don't want to work for him.

Meta Some of us don't have the luxury of picking and choosing our directors.

Oscar Who says he's a director?

Meta The Prussian State Theater! You are in the finest theater in all of Germany, Oscar. This is your chance.

Oscar I don't have your talent.

Meta You don't have my will.

Oscar I wish it were a matter of will. You and Marianne Hoppe and Grüdegens, I can't stand near you without being terrified, without shaking, without being fat. And him, that Johst, that smirk.

Meta	He just wants to see if you can stand on your own two feet.
Oscar	Are you picking on me?
Meta	There are always challenges, and they're not always pretty. In fact, most of the time they're ugly as sin, ugly as Hans Johst. And they're not always fair, most of the time they're not. There is always some little thing, some loathsome little thing that will get you in the end, that you stave off from moment to moment. From breath to breath you live, now, now, now you live just in the nick of time. That's acting. That's all it is. There is no mystery. *(She crosses to the downstage window and looks out)* You must find that thing, that loathsome little thing.

META *begins crying.* OSCAR *crosses to her.*

Oscar	My dear, what's the matter?
Meta	Will he become king?
Oscar	Who?
Meta	That little Austrian?
Oscar	*(Chuckles)* You mean, Hitler? No, he's chancellor.
Meta	*(Tasting the word)* "Chancellor…" If I remember my high school Latin, it's cancellerius. Isn't that right?
Oscar	I can't remember my high school Latin.
Meta	Oh, but you should. You must always remember the roots of your words, their primal meanings, the eggs in them that hatch on your tongue when you speak on stage. Cancellerius is the root of "chancellor." It means, "doorkeeper."
Oscar	Bellhop, you mean. Are you okay?
Meta	I'm a Jew.

The lights fade.

*

Scene 5

META is sitting on the couch. OSCAR enters. He is in a huff.

Oscar	Meta? Are you all right?
Meta	*(Quietly)* Shhhhh, relax. Sit down.
Oscar	Smarmy, bastard, practically licked my face.
Meta	*(Quietly)* Did you get Petruchio?
Oscar	Yes.
Meta	Marianne got Kate?
Oscar	Yes.
Meta	She's good.
Oscar	That smile, that sneaky smile, those snake eyes. God, I hate that man, that little smiling man. Did he call you?
Meta	No.
Oscar	Of course not. Meta, why didn't you tell me?
Meta	Is it important?
Oscar	Not to me.
Meta	My grandfather belonged to a Reform synagogue that was extremely liberal, so he didn't protest when my father became a Protestant and I was raised as a Protestant too. I've never thought of myself as a Jew. I've never known anything Jewish. I abhor religion. At best it's a kinky relationship to one's father. And Buddha, a rich boy who

gave up his ego because he couldn't take reality. I can't admire that. I'm not a humanist either. I'm not that nosey, nor that interested. I'm not even an atheist. It's a non-issue. I'm an actress. That's all I am. I like to be noticed. I like to be praised. I have a big ego. Anyway, people knowing I'm Jewish wouldn't do me any good.

Oscar	Didn't you register yourself as Jewish?
Meta	No, why should I? I'm German.
Oscar	He can't fire you. That smiling little unctuous man can't fire you. You're the best actress in that theater.
Meta	That seems to be debatable.
Oscar	What are we going to do?
Meta	You've got to take care of us for a while, Oscar, until we can get out of here.
Oscar	Get out of here?
Meta	Yes.
Oscar	Yes, of course.

Lights out.

*

Scene 6

There is a flickering light downstage. META appears and looks out. OSCAR appears behind her.

Meta	A fire. Where?
Oscar	The Parliament.

Meta   Oh, my God. Turn on the radio and see if there's anything about it.

OSCAR turns on the radio. The music to Wagner's "Tannhauser Overture" comes on. OSCAR returns to META and looks out. A song is heard on the street. It grows louder. "And they won't ever let go..."

Meta   Can you hear that? Turn off the radio.

OSCAR turns the radio off. The song is the "Horst Wessel Lied."

Meta   What is that song? I hear it every day.

Oscar   It's the "Horst Wessel Song." He was a Nazi hero who was shot in the face by a commie. He wrote it. A martyr for the Nazi cause.

Meta   It's big and dumb like a zombie. It feels no pain, has no reflection, cannot be stopped. *(Suddenly she can't stand up)* Oscar, hold me, I'm falling. I'm falling.

META sinks into his arms as the lights fade and the "Horst Wessel Song" grows louder.

*

Scene 7

META is sitting on a chair by the radio, expressionless. She is in her kimono. She is listening to the radio.

Voice on the radio A few days ago, Germany was astonished by the news of arson in the Parliament. The ringleader is a Jew Communist. A bloody uprising was supposed to begin throughout Germany. The burning of the Parliament was to be the signal for the attack.

OSCAR enters. He is wearing his winter coat. The VOICE ON THE RADIO continues through their dialogue.

Oscar How are you?

Meta Fine.

Voice The Jews did not succeed in carrying out their treacherous scheme. The National Socialist Minister Göring put a halt to their plans.

Oscar What are you listening to?

Meta The news.

Voice But the Jew will find new intrigues and crimes, will not rest until a new attack on Germany is ready. The Jew is guilty...

OSCAR turns the radio off.

Oscar Why do you listen to that crap? (*He takes off his coat*) Bernard has left. So has Sophie. Hector, Otto, Franz, Paula. There are a lot of new faces. Josht, he smiles all the time, says "the air is clear now. We will be a family." I think

	most of the new ones are embarrassed. Marianne says
	nothing. She smiles, she keeps to herself. She does her work.
	And Gustav, he just prances about as usual. He greets the
	new ones with big fat, hot handshakes. He came up to me,
	clapped me on the shoulder and said, "Congratulations.
	See, it's not so bad." He and Johst, they should be husband
	and wife. *(Notices a book on the table)* What's this?
	Goebbels on Horst Wessel. Why are you reading this crap?
Meta	*(Gazing out the window)* All these flags, I've never seen so
	many flags. It's like a big celebration. What are these flags?
	Are these the flags of my country? A flag should be like
	the Holy Host hidden in the Cross under glass that a priest
	holds above him when he is doing Mass. When there is
	war the flags will fly out of it, but these, what are they?
Oscar	What are you talking about? You've never been to a
	Catholic Mass.
Meta	Yes, I have. I liked it. It was very theatrical. It was like
	magic, they turned a piece of bread into God. Do you
	think they did it?
Oscar	What are you talking about?
Meta	Destroy the Parliament building?
Oscar	Who?
Meta	The Jews?
Oscar	No.
Meta	Who then?
Oscar	The Communists.
Meta	Perhaps.

OSCAR *looks at her.*

Oscar	The Nazis? Oh Meta, you can't be serious.
Meta	No one would believe they'd actually do it. Only a crazy person would believe such a thing.
Oscar	You haven't dressed.
Meta	There is a catastrophe. A building has been destroyed. People have been killed. Everyone is running around in terror. They don't know where to hide, what will happen next. This guy comes along, comes along who wasn't really liked that much before, but now, he's there in the ashes of disaster, in the still smoldering fires, naming the people who did it, promising to punish them. You'd rally around that man.
Oscar	Meta, you haven't left the apartment.
Meta	I never wanted to think about politics. I took it for granted that civilized people would act in good taste. Now everything I know has been turned around. Nothing is the same. I used to think there were crazy people and sane people, but now I know that we are all crazy. How else would one explain it? That little screaming man is our leader. I'll tell you something else, guys like him, once they're in office they never let go.
Oscar	I know you're frightened, but this foolishness, it won't last long, it can't.
Meta	Why not?
Oscar	Because this is Germany.
Meta	Oh, yes, of course, yes, I didn't think of that.

The lights crossfade.

*

Scene 8

META is still in her kimono. She is dialing the telephone.

Meta Hello? Hello, Marianne? This is Meta—Yes—Oh, I'm fine. How are you? I'm not interrupting anything am I? I just wanted to say "hello"—Yes, I'm sure it won't last—I'm glad it's you. I think you should have played Kate all along— Oh, please. That's one thing I'm not vain about, my age— *(Laughs)* Well, perhaps I am—Oh, don't, please, it's all right. I didn't call for sympathy. How is Oscar doing?— Oh, that's so good to hear. Take care of him, will you? What I mean is that he's not terribly confident around you. You understand—Yes. Yes, he should pipe up more. Perhaps some good will come out of this, a chance for him to stretch—Plans? Well, everything's happened so quickly, I haven't caught my breath. Yes, I think I will be planning something—Yes, I heard that and Franz too—Oh, to Paris—Hmm, he speaks French does he?—Oh, Paula, to Amsterdam. What is she going to do?—I'm sure she'll find something. Well, I guess I should think about that. Being married is a little complicated... It's probably not good for me to be speaking with you. I mean, has it gotten that bad? I'm sorry, what a stupid way to say it, but I'm very curious about it, like lifting a rock to see what kind of bugs are under it. *(Laughs)* I'm sorry, it's just so burlesque, isn't it all? I mean the flags. It's a miracle the birds can fly with all that cloth in the air—Oh, I'm sorry. Yes, you have to learn lines. I get absolutely incensed when someone interrupts me when I'm learning lines—Oh, yes, I'll call.

I'll tell you what's happening as soon as I find out. Make sure Gustav doesn't flail around him too much, Oscar gets nervous as a cat when people fling their arms about. And how is Johst?—Oh, yes, please, I won't hold you, but he is treating him well? Good, good, that's good to hear, oh, yes, of course, well, Tschüss.

MARIANNE has hung up. META still holds the receiver to her ear. She whispers into the receiver as the lights fade...

Meta   Go to hell, you blond bitch, go to hell, go to hell, go to hell...

*

Scene 9

Oscar is reciting lines from The Taming of the Shrew. *They are holding scripts. Meta is still in her kimono.*

Oscar   *(as PETRUCHIO)* Come on, I' God's name; once more toward our father's. Good Lord, how bright and goodly shines the moon!

META stops him.

Meta   Let me play him and you play her. Not Petruchio, Nazi Petruchio.

OSCAR kneels. META performs PETRUCHIO with a cold, homicidal intensity, strutting around OSCAR like a Nazi. META as PETRUCHIO shrieks at the imaginary servant.

Meta *(as PETRUCHIO)* Come on, I' God's name; once more toward our father's!! *(Steely)* Good Lord, how bright and goodly shines the moon.

Oscar *(as KATHARINA)* The moon! the sun: it is not moonlight now.

Meta *(as PETRUCHIO)* I say it is the moon that shines so bright.

Oscar *(as KATHARINA)* I know it is the sun that shines so bright.

She grabs OSCAR by the back of the hair. OSCAR is a bit surprised.

Meta *(as PETRUCHIO)*
Now, by my mother's son, and that's myself,
It shall be moon, or star, or what I list,
Or ere I journey to your father's house.
Go on, and fetch our horses back again.
Evermore cross'd and cross'd; nothing but cross'd!

Oscar *(as KATHARINA)*
Forward, I pray, since we have come so far,
And be it moon, or sun, or what you please:
An if you please to call it a rush-candle,
Henceforth I vow it shall be so for me.

Meta *(as PETRUCHIO)* I say it is the moon.

Oscar *(as KATHARINA)* I know it is the moon.

Meta *(as PETRUCHIO)* Nay, then you lie: it is the blessed sun.

Oscar	*(as* KATHARINA*)* Then, God be bless'd, it is the blessed sun: But sun it is not, when you say it is not.
Meta	*(As* HERSELF*)* The best place for the woman to serve her people is in the home, in the marriage, in motherhood. This is her highest mission. This is what Kate must understand. This is what Petruchio understands. He must set the example of German manhood, for the less German men are willing to act as men in public life, the more women succumb to the temptation to fill the role of the man. So he must tame her and once tamed, she will naturally understand what her task is as a woman.
Oscar	That's a pile of shit!
Meta	Oh, is it?

META *kneels before* OSCAR. *She mews with desire and adoration.*

Meta	*(as* KATHARINA*)* "Thy husband is thy lord, thy life, thy keeper, Thy head, thy sovereign; one that cares for thee, And for thy maintenance commits his body To painful labour both by sea and land."
Oscar	That's completely skewed.
Meta	You have to think like they think. An actor obeys the director.
Oscar	I can't stand that Johst.
Meta	You are an Aryan. The world embraces you and abhors me. Think of it. What is the logic, the sequence of particulars, the sense information of each subsequent step in the chain of experiences that lead you to believe that you are superior

to me? Where is that ugly maggot in the dark of your brain? You must find the fault to find the power. Only then can you believe it and let it speak through you beyond morality. When the maggot in the dark has walked out of your head and stands naked on stage for all to see then they will cry, "He is magic!" If you keep thinking you're a "good boy" then you are not worthy of being an actor. Think of it, all you have to do is get rid of me. Oh, what a relief it would be. It's only going to get harder. I'm the unwanted dog in your house, the one that shits on the rug, that howls in the night and keeps the neighbors awake. Think of it. Doesn't it tempt you to throw me out on the street for the dog catcher?

Oscar   No, Meta, no!

Meta   Then start thinking of it. You must be that ruthless to be that Aryan Petruchio Goebbels wants you to be.

Oscar   I don't know what Johst wants. He's the director, not Goebbels.

Meta   *(Laughs)* Johst wants what Goebbels wants, he just doesn't have the balls nor the talent to know what it is. Your job is to show it to him so he can take credit for it. That's what every director does. Now, my dear, let's begin again, but with magic.

Lights out.

*

Scene 10

META is on the telephone. She is still wearing her kimono.

Meta   Edgar, I must get out of here. Can you help me?—No, Oscar doesn't know. I don't want to tell him. It would destroy his focus and he needs his focus. He needs a lot of work, but I think he can do it if he applies himself. I'm going to be his crutch until opening night, but then after that I must go. Oh, please, can you help me? I'm so terrified—Palestine? I don't think I'd like the weather—Constantinople?—South Africa?—America? Yes, that would be nice, but it's awfully far from Oscar—Of course, of course, I can't be picky. But couldn't you find some place closer, like Paris?—Yes, once I'm out of here I can go other places. At least, I used to be able... until I became a... *(She breaks down in tears)* I don't want to leave my city. I'm from Berlin. I was born in Berlin—I'm sorry, please, please forgive me. *(She recovers)* Switzerland? Do you really think there might be a possibility?—Yes, I know several theater directors there. God, I can't believe I'm even considering this. Things have happened so quickly, without transition, they keep hitting you and before you can recover, they hit you again. I can't go to the theater any more, I can't even attend my own husband's performances. Can't they make an exception in my case? I won't tell anybody I'm a Jew—I'm sorry, I'm sorry, Edgar. Please don't hang up. I know what a risk you're taking by helping me—Yes, I have talked too long on the phone— Yes, I'll watch my phone use—

The lights begin to fade.

Meta   I won't call you, but you'll call me soon, won't you? Yes, yes, I will, yes, anywhere, yes, anywhere, I'll go there—

The lights have faded to black. META continues in darkness.

Meta   I'll go there, I will, I'll go...

*

Scene 11

OSCAR is pacing. META is in the bathroom.

Meta   *(Off)* How long will it take to get this identity card?
Oscar   It might take a little while. I'll be with you, but we really must get going.

META enters. She is in an elegant hat and scarf.

Meta   Do I look all right?
Oscar   You look beautiful. But take the scarf off and change your hat.
Meta   Why?
Oscar   You're a little overdressed.
Meta   Do I look like a Jew?
Oscar   No, you look like a diva. Everyone is dressing down right now. Everyone is trying to be invisible.

META exits into the bedroom.

Meta *(Off)* I'll have a pedigree. I'm a complete Jew.

Oscar Hurry, Meta, please.

META enters. She has a simpler hat and the scarf is gone.

Meta Do I look like a Jew?

Oscar I don't know what a Jew looks like.

Meta Of course, you do. Big nose, big ears, big lips, shifty eyes.

Oscar Well, maybe the ears.

Meta Really, do you think so?

Oscar Don't be silly. Come on, let's get this over with.

META starts for the door, then staggers and holds herself up.

Meta I can't, I can't go. *(She goes to the floor)* I haven't gone out on the streets for days and now I have to go to the police. What will they do to me?

Oscar They won't do anything. I'll be with you.

Meta Because you'll stop them? Because you're an Aryan? Hell, you can't even act!

OSCAR turns away from her.

Meta I'm sorry, I didn't mean that. I'm just terrified. Will they hurt me? Will they scream at me? Will they spit at me? Please forgive me, I need you.

She falls to her knees.

Oscar   *(Shouting)* No, I'm not a good actor! I know it! What do you think it's like? You've never needed me. You're always the boss. You can't stand it that I can help you. Don't start believing that shit. I'll kill anyone who touches you. You are with me. For once I'm useful. Let me be useful, Meta. Stand on your feet. You can't show any weakness. They're animals. If they sense a weakness they'll attack. Stand up for Christ's sake. Think about it, you've stood on the stage for thousands to see, the most sophisticated people in all of Europe. These are beerhall idiots. They are dogs. They will cower if you stand straight and tall. You are magic, Meta. You can make yourself invisible with a thought. You're always yelling at me to concentrate, well, it's your turn now. Concentrate. Stand up, goddamn it.

He kneels too and takes her in his arms and kisses her.

Oscar   You've got to last this out. It can't last forever, it's too insane. Things have to change, my darling. They will. You'll see, it won't be so bad. Breathe. Breathe. Breathe. *(He pulls her to her feet)* Yes, that's it. Now, let's go.

The lights fade.

*

Scene 12

META is wearing a plain bathrobe. She is tying OSCAR'S tie.

Meta Many actors clown around in the dressing room—they poke and mimic each other. They quack like ducks and bark like dogs. On the surface it all looks quite harmless, as if they're simply doing it to relieve tension and oil the joints, but don't let it fool you. When actors pretend that out of humility they should make light of their work, they are really saying, "Don't excel; be one of the gang, be like us." Don't do it. Be respectful; treat them with dignity. Watch out for Gustav. He'll test you every moment. No one will notice it but you. He'll delay his lines, pounce on yours, smile at you unexpectedly. He'll try to wear you down—stand your ground. Watch him. See him. Soul to soul—meet him without decoration and he will come to you like a cat chasing a string; he won't be able to stop himself. He is too curious and he's just too good. You look very nice, my love.

Oscar I'm terrified.

Meta Good. Your terror is your stallion. Ride it well.

Oscar Oh, Meta, I wish you would come with me, at least to the theater.

Meta I'm sure you do. *(She makes the German expression of "good luck," a rapid spitting gesture)* "Teu, teu, teu." *(She directs him to the door)* I'll be here, waiting for you.

Oscar Meta...

Meta Shhh, go; do.

She pushes him out of the door. When OSCAR *is gone, she takes her bathrobe off. She is fully dressed beneath it. She brushes her hair, straightens her clothes, then exits into the bedroom and reenters with a suitcase. She puts it by the easy chair next to the telephone and sits. The phone rings.* META *grabs the phone.*

Meta   Hello?—Yes—Yes. Oh, my God, yes, thank you—Midnight? I've got to wait for Oscar. I'll be there—Yes, I understand.

She hangs up. She begins pacing. The lights shift. The door opens and OSCAR *enters.* META *turns to him.* OSCAR *stands there, crestfallen.*

Meta   What?

OSCAR *looks at her, then breaks into a laugh. He can barely contain himself.*

Meta   They loved you?

She flings her arms around him.

Oscar   A standing ovation! It wasn't just for Marianne, it was for me. They called out for me but they didn't know my name, I swear it.

Meta   I knew it, I knew it would happen. You've worked so hard, you deserve it.

Oscar   I've never known such a feeling. I know I shouldn't indulge in it.

Meta	Yes, indulge it, indulge it. If the audience wants to give you love, let them give it.
Oscar	Oh, my Meta, I couldn't have done it without you. You should have seen Johst, he was drooling. I wanted to slug him, that grinning little gargoyle. I wanted to pummel him! Do you know what he said just before I went on? "We're counting on you. Goebbels is in the audience." And the great Gustav Gründgens. He knelt to me and kissed my hand.
Meta	Yes, next he'll be trying to get you in his bed.
Oscar	And then, backstage *(He enacts GOEBBELS with his small stature and his limp)* that hideous little man, Goebbels shook my hand and clapped me on the back and said, "Congratulations, I'll be keeping an eye on you." Can you believe that? I didn't know whether to be glad or shit my pants. *(He sees META'S suitcase)* What's going on?
Meta	I've found passage to Switzerland. Isn't it incredible, Switzerland? I won't be far from you.
Oscar	Why didn't you tell me?
Meta	Does it matter? You're on your feet. It will be just for a little while. Like you said, it won't last forever.
Oscar	Yes, of course, when do you have to go?
Meta	Immediately. I only have a few minutes. Now kiss me, Oscar, and let me go.

META *kisses him.*

Oscar	Where do I write you?
Meta	Basel, at the Theater Suiss in care of the director, Kurt Jörger. Now I must go.

Oscar	What am I going to do without you? You should have told me. You should have warned me.
Meta	I couldn't have done it if I had told you.
Oscar	Please!
Meta	Oscar, I must go. This is my last chance!
Oscar	Yes, yes, I understand.
Meta	Do you? Oh, please understand!
Oscar	You could have told me. My God, what am I going to do? I'm sorry, I understand, I do. Go, Meta, go, hurry!

She pauses and looks at him. He pushes her toward the door.

Oscar	*(Screaming)* Get out! Get out of here!

He shoves her out of the room and closes the door and breaks down in tears. There is a moment when Oscar *is by himself; then,* Meta *flings open the door and flies into his arms.*

Meta	I can't. I can't.

The lights crossfade.

*

Scene 13

There is a flickering light downstage. META is standing there looking at it. The radio is on and a VOICE is speaking over it. The action and lines continue while the announcer speaks.

Voice   The Jew Herschel Grynszpan brutally murdered Third Secretary Ernst Von Rath in Paris. Throughout Germany there has been a spontaneous outburst of indignation.

OSCAR bursts into the room.

Oscar   Oh, my god, you're safe. They stopped the rehearsal.

META shushes him. OSCAR crosses to META and stands behind her. The lights dim as the VOICE ON THE RADIO continues.

Voice   Seventy-six synagogues demolished. And seventy-five hundred stores ruined in the Reich. According to reports, one hundred and fifty Jews were arrested by yesterday afternoon. So much glass fills the streets that the German people have named this night Crystal Night. All together there are one hundred and one synagogues destroyed by fire.

While the names of the German cities are spoken the "Horst Wessel Song" is heard.

Voice   Synagogues were destroyed in Berlin, Leipzig, Dresden, Linz, Munich, Baden, Nuremberg, Hanover, Bremen,

Hamburg, *(The lights fade to darkness)* Munster, Essen, Düsseldorf, Brunswick, Bonn, Mannheim, Saarbrucken...

*

Scene 14

In the darkness there is the sound of the room being torn up.

*

Scene 15

The lights rise. The living room is in shambles. OSCAR *enters.* META *is not in the living room.*

Oscar   Meta?

He goes into the bedroom.

Oscar   *(Off)* Meta?

He comes out of the bedroom. He is frantic.

Oscar   Meta?

He sees a card on the table. He grabs the phone and dials the number.

Oscar	*(On the telephone)* Security police, please. Security police? Yes, this is Oscar Weiss.

Lights out.

*

Scene 16

The lights rise on OSCAR *picking up things.* META *is standing in the middle of the room. She is in a kind of brittle, vigilant shock. She doesn't move from the center of the room and only shifts her eyes and head to enact each character as she relives her experience.*

Meta	"Do you have any weapons?" They made me look for weapons. "Do you have any weapons?"
Oscar	No.
Meta	Yes, you do. You have a stage sword.
Oscar	My épée? It's ancient. It has bandage on the tip.
Meta	He said, "What's this?" I said it was a stage sword. "A what sword?" I said, a stage sword. "What's a stage sword?" I told him that it was to practice fighting scenes, but it wasn't dangerous. Every actor has one. "Is this yours?" "No, it's my husband's." How stupid, I should have said it was mine. "So your husband is an actor? You have scripts. You're an actor. So where is yours?" "My what?" "Your sword!" I told him that I didn't know. I didn't do swordplay anymore. I must have just, what the hell did I do with it anyway? "I

lost it," I told him. They searched the house for hours. I asked the big one to be careful, please. He started throwing things around. "Cheap Jew garbage!" The animal had mustard on his chest. They tore everything up. They took my scripts, all of the plays that I have done with all the notes in them. I asked them what possible importance do they have? There was this littler one, but not small because he was too muscular; he was the more dangerous of the two, and they were dangerous. My god, I had never imagined any two people so dangerous, so violent, so free to do anything. This littler one said, "Up until now you looked okay, but this hostile attitude. It makes you wonder what does she have to hide?" I said that they weren't important; they were just personal. Then the big one screamed at me, "You ugly Jew sow, do you think I'd want anything personal from you?" And then he said, "Take her to the station. They've got guillotines there, electrical ones that chop off heads electrically." They took me there. They walked on either side of me so that all the neighbors could see. When we got to the police station I had to sit... for hours, Oscar. Then an old man with a party badge came and got me. He said, and he said it almost in a whisper, "Don't worry, honey, they do this to everybody." He led me down a hallway and to an office with a tidy little man, and this man was actually little, but perfectly proportioned. He said, "Hello, I'm Dietrick Dieter. Meta Wolff, God, I know you! You are fantastic! How could you be a Jew? Well, this is very unfortunate. Don't worry about it." He looked at my file. It was very big. How can they know so much about me? Why would they even be interested? He said, "Ah, your husband is an Aryan. Oscar Weiss? I don't know him. It says here he's an actor." "*The Taming of the Shrew*," I said. "Ah," he said, "I didn't see that one." He stamped my papers. He said, "This inconvenience should never happen again. My God, Miss Wolff, it is an honor to have met you." I loved it, Oscar, now that I am through it. I am through it, aren't I? *(She notices that the radio is gone. She suddenly screams)* They took my radio!

Oscar   I'll get it back.

She attacks him. He restrains her.

Meta   Because you're superior! You look just like them!

Oscar   I don't look like anybody. Meta, it's Oscar. It's just me.

Lights out.

*

Scene 17

There is music on the radio. It is a kind of jumpy tune sung by Zarah Leander. META is in a housecoat. She's doing a strange dance to the music. At the close of the song OSCAR enters with a bag of groceries. He puts them on the table.

Oscar   *(Softly)* Meta?

META doesn't answer.

Oscar   Meta?

She ignores him.

Meta   I have new teeth.

Oscar   New teeth?

Meta   Yes, you remember that Aryan dentist you couldn't get for me and my teeth were so sore they were falling out. I had maggots in my mouth. I went to a Jewish dentist. He was able to put in a new set. He got them from the cemetery. See, look a fine set.

META shows her teeth. OSCAR looks at her teeth.

Oscar   Meta, these are your teeth. He didn't put any teeth into your mouth.

OSCAR grabs META and holds her in his arms.

Oscar   My darling. My darling.

The lights fade. There is the sound of rain.

*

Scene 18

The rain continues. A melancholy vocal of the period is on the radio, Zarah Leander's "Ice steh'im Regen." META is alone, sitting by the window, careful not to be seen. She is wearing a house coat.

Meta   People are missing from the streets. They've gone away or have disappeared. And it's so strange. No one says anything about it, but I know they notice it too. *(She crosses behind the couch)* And in the Jewish cemetery there are so many fresh plots. I can't walk in the park, only in the Jewish cemetery. *(She smoothes the pillows, then lays her head on them)* I look at the grass there, at those fresh graves and I have this longing to rest, to get it over with. But then I see these Jews strolling among the gravestones and I begin to hate them for their resignation to it all. *(She rises)* I've never really known hate until now. And I can understand how civilized people would be resigned to death rather than be filled with so much hate. It is crushing, this hate. One has to constantly be reminded to hate, but it keeps me alive.

The lights shift.

*

Scene 19

Music on the radio. OSCAR *lights a match and touches it to a candle on the dining table.* META *is sitting at the table, subdued, observant.* OSCAR *pours wine into her glass. He is trying desperately to make contact with her.*

Oscar   Things are changing, my darling. Come on, drink. Gustav has taken over the theater. He knows about you and the problems we have had. He said he would do everything to help us. He is a horrible man in some ways but you must admit he is talented. He admires you. He had me into his office. He asked me about you. He said, (*Oscar does an impersonation of Gründgens*) "My dear, poor Meta, I'll do anything for her. She's a genius. She must be protected." He's gotten us food. Look, French wine. He said, "She must not lose hope. I am disgusted, revolted by what is happening, but what can we do, what can any of us do but survive this madness? It can't last forever. All we can do is take care of our own." (*He kneels beside her*) Meta, please snap out of this. You're killing me. (*He pushes her hair from her face*) Listen, my darling, I'm going to play Hamlet!

META *slowly raises her eyes to his. She looks at him for awhile, then...*

Meta   You're what?

Oscar   I'm going to play Hamlet.

She gazes at him. Slowly a laugh issues from her.

Oscar Yes, isn't it hilarious?

META begins to laugh in earnest. She laughs and laughs. OSCAR joins her in her laughter.

Oscar Isn't it funny?

META laughs.

Oscar Well, it's not that funny. Don't you see, I need help. You've got to help me. *(He shouts)* Help! Help! Help! Oh, my darling. My darling, don't you see, we've got work to do.

META continues laughing.

Meta Who's playing Ophelia?

Oscar Marianne.

Meta She's perfect; high cheekbones, blond hair, a little on the severe side, good hips for birthing and totally harmless. She will simply "go mad."

Oscar And I suppose that you feel that way about me?

Meta What way?

Oscar Like I'm some Hessian ox?

META looks at him and laughs.

Meta Yes. Yes, you are, aren't you?

OSCAR laughs.

Oscar	Yes, I am. Didn't you know? I'm a member of the Master Race, the Hessian ox race.

He picks up META'S glass of wine and brings it to her lips.

Oscar	Meta please, drink. It's good. Gustav can get us more. Gustav wants you to help me.
Meta	You? You're beyond help.
Oscar	I know, I know.

META rises.

Meta	Is Pamela Wedekind still in the company?
Oscar	Yes.
Meta	Marianne is a superb actress, but a better choice, a more delineated one, would be Pamela Wedekind: that black hair, that pale white skin, those ice-blue eyes. And she's mad. She has that shrill upper register like some terrible addendum, something she can simply unpack and throw on a bed. And she is relentless as a tick. She's a stalker. Once Hamlet gets her attention he's a goner. She'll lurk and skulk about, appear out of nowhere.
Oscar	And what about me?

She looks at him mysteriously.

Meta	If I could run that company and make that play for this place, in these times, for these people, I would make a Hamlet that would pull the devil right out of its bottle, expose the maggot on a dark stage under a bright white

light and make the Germans eat it whole. "Elsinore," with its race of old aristocrats, a castle full of zombies, venom pumped by their rotting hearts; utterly beautiful dead Ophelia floating through dark halls. God, it makes you want to vomit blood. Oh, Oscar, think about it. Wouldn't it be fun? Right from this room we could give them a show and it might just be possible.

Oscar   What do you mean?

Meta   If I know Gustav, he'll try to get away with anything he can. He's a different kind of sneak from "The Smiler," Mr. Johst. The Smiler cheats everybody but his masters. Gustav is a ubiquitous cheat and he's creative. His only problem is which devil to serve.

Oscar   What do you mean?

Meta   Goebbels or Göring? Goebbels never liked me very much. He didn't like my edge, but Göring loved me as he loves Gustav. Goebbels is a sneaky little puritan; Göring is Bacchus. Haven't you seen them snap at each other's ankles? Goebbels is the Minister of Culture—by rights he should be in charge of the Prussian State Theater—but it is Göring's plaything and Hitler doesn't want to get involved. Gustav has to decide whether he will serve Goebbels or Göring. When he cast Marianne as Ophelia he was thinking Goebbels, but if he recasts her with Pamela Wedekind he will be thinking Göring. And Göring is ever so much more fun. Listen, my darling, with a little ingenuity, like Goya we can paint the Nazi family royal.

Oscar   This is a very dangerous game.

Meta   Dangerous? Have you looked outside lately? Listen, darling, it's a German thing. *(She puts her forehead against his* *forehead)* Nobody takes us seriously unless we have a war.

Lights out.

End of Act One

Act Two

Scene 20

The lights rise on OSCAR *asleep in the easy chair. There is a rose in a vase on the table.* META *enters silently. She has disguised herself as a man. She has one of* OSCAR'S *overcoats and is wearing one of his fedoras. She bends over* OSCAR *and looks at him.* OSCAR *snaps awake with a start.*

Oscar   Meta, where have you been? It's past the curfew.

She takes off her coat and hangs it up as she speaks.

Meta   I went to my first "Jewish thing." It was a reading by Hans Heinz Ewers, a banned writer. It's funny, he's banned for Germans but he isn't banned for Jews. He's an old man now living with a half Jew architect. He's a homosexual. He has a face like a skull. He wrote a book about Horst Wessel.

Oscar   My darling, darling Meta, I never want you to do this again. I waited up for three hours. You could have been shot.

Meta   I've got the model for Hamlet. Horst Wessel.

Oscar   Who? The Nazi hero?

Meta	Hero? Do you know what he really was? Hans Ewers told me the real story of Horst Wessel. *(Playing with a German accent)* "I thought he might have been a Bavarian boy making a song to Germany when they bring the cows down from the mountains, wreathed with flowers: lung soup and beer, girls in dirndls with edelweiss in their hair, fathers in leather shorts bringing down the cheese for the May Fest." Do you know who Horst Wessel really was? He was a pimp and his wife was a prostitute and he was killed in a jealous rage by a gangster named "Ali." Isn't it perfect? For our play, that is, for that castle in Elsinore?
Oscar	What are you talking about?
Meta	Hamlet is Horst Wessel. Ophelia is Erna Jaenicke.
Oscar	Who?
Meta	Erna Jaenicke. Horst Wessel's "woman," the prostitute. Pamela Wedekind has to play Ophelia.

OSCAR crosses to the rose and plucks it from the vase.

Oscar	I have a little flower.
Meta	Yes?
Oscar	Her name is Pamela Wedekind.
Meta	Gustav went for it! How did Marianne take it?
Oscar	As well as can be expected, she's a trouper.
Meta	*(Smiles ironically)* Yes, she is. Did you begin working with Pamela?
Oscar	Immediately. Gustav did it with such speed that it seemed Pamela had always been in the role.
Meta	What did you think of her?
Oscar	Of Pamela? She was terrifying! Honestly, you were

	absolutely right. I could tell some of the cast was a little taken aback but they didn't say anything.
Meta	Of course, they're good Germans. What did Gustav think?
Oscar	Gustav ran to the lobby where there were roses, picked one out and gave it to me. He said, "It's for your dear wife." Then he winked at me, Meta. He winked. "I think your suggestion was a stroke of genius. Let me know if you have any more suggestions. Keep them between you and me, alright? I'm really interested to see what you and Hamlet come up with."

META kisses the rose. Lights out.

*

Scene 21

OSCAR is standing in his underwear. They are the 30's kind, and he looks a bit ridiculous in them. He is irritated.

Oscar	I don't like this.

META enters with an SA uniform. She lays it on the couch and begins circling OSCAR, watching him with a certain sexual curiosity.

Meta	I do. You've got to dress for the role.
Oscar	Can't I put my costume on at the theatre?
Meta	Put on the shirt. *(She hands it to him)*

Oscar	You're impossible.
Meta	Perhaps. Oscar, you must stop feeling like the good guy.
Oscar	I don't feel like a good guy, God damn it.
Meta	Yes you do!
Oscar	No, I don't.
Meta	Yes you do. I can see it in your eyes. They're full of apologies, like some sneaky little puppy. *(META reacts to OSCAR'S look)* That's better.
Oscar	What? Is the sneaky little puppy gone?
Meta	A bit. Now the pants. *(She hands them to him and then kneels in front of him, watching him closely)* This is good.
Oscar	*(Buttoning his pants)* Are you sure you want me to button these?
Meta	I want you to look this part. I want you to feel this part. I want you to feel what it is like to wear this uniform on the streets of the Third Reich.

OSCAR *continues to put on his SA uniform.*

Meta	Now the boots.
Oscar	Is this a game?
Meta	This is no game. *(She hands him the hat)* I want to see him.
Oscar	Who?
Meta	Horst Wessel.
Oscar	Horst Wessel is dead.
Meta	No, he's not. He's not dead.

META, *finished dressing him, slips the swastika armband on him.* OSCAR *looks embarrassed. She points at him and begins laughing. She then starts crying, crosses away, and as* OSCAR *reaches for her the lights fade to black.*

*

Scene 22

OSCAR *is pacing in his SA uniform.* META *is on the couch, watching him.*

Oscar   I can't seem to concentrate. I'm watching myself doing the role like a puppet. It's as if I were separated from my body, that my body is working independently of me. I'm not saying my lines, "It's" saying them. I look at the actors. I can see them mouthing their words. The saliva on their tongues. It seems so silly that I'm standing there. I realize that I could ruin everything in a single moment. I could just walk offstage and leave them standing there, or worse, I could do something crazy, like licking Ophelia's face; or I could slap her, or strangle her. Perhaps a murderer feels that way, not out of control but being "taken over." Then I come to my senses; I'm suddenly in my body again and I don't know where I am, don't know my lines. Oh God, Meta it happened tonight in rehearsal. I was just looking at them and I didn't know what I was doing. I felt so small, like a stupid drooling child.

Meta   You're afraid of your potential.

Oscar   What potential?

Meta   He's sitting in the back of your head watching me, Horst Wessel, can you see him? Can you feel him?

Oscar	Horst Wessel?
Meta	Is he looking at me? Is he looking at me?

OSCAR'S face begins to change. As he gazes at META his face hardens and at the same time becomes aroused.

Oscar	Yes.
Meta	What is he seeing?
Oscar	He doesn't know, you're just an object.
Meta	What does he want to do?
Oscar	I don't know.
Meta	Come on, what does he really want to do?
Oscar	He wants to break your neck.

META approaches OSCAR seductively. She exposes her throat.

Meta   Come on, do it, break my neck. Say your lines and break my neck.

OSCAR is Horst Wessel, tender in his hunger to kill, sweet in his ruthless need, efficient in brutal act, cunning in his seduction. As OSCAR speaks, he first places his hands on her head, as if to simply snap her neck, then he slides his fingers over the soft warm skin of her throat and begins strangling her. META begins to sink to the floor. As she chokes, OSCAR flicks his tongue against hers. She goes to the floor.

Oscar   *(as HAMLET)* Get thee to a nunnery: why wouldst thou be a breeder of sinners? I am myself indifferent honest; but yet I could accuse me of such things that it were better my mother had not borne me: I am very proud, revengeful, ambitious, with more offences at my beck than I have thoughts to put them in, imagination to give them shape, or time to act them in. What should such fellows as I do crawling between earth and heaven? We are arrant knaves, all; believe none of us. Go thy ways to a nunnery.

META throws her legs around him and kisses him passionately.

Lights out.

*

Scene 23

META is in shadow. OSCAR is by the window. He is dressed in his SA uniform. He is on one knee in a heroic pose sur-veying the scene below his window. There is a flickering of torches and the sound of marching feet.

Meta   Tell me what you know.
Oscar   *(With growing intensity)*
              First the election without a mandate:
              then the catastrophe:
              the enemy, then the scapegoat.
              Indignation follows emergency.
              Fear turns to anger, anger to revenge.
              The objective is to create a state of continuous emergency.

When the state of emergency is over we can afford to
question. It is never over.
In the terror of confusion we must seek solidarity, find our
basic values.
We clean up our streets,
enlist our neighbors as informers.
"This shall not happen again. We will strike back."
Fortinbras has taken Poland and now he's taking
Denmark.
He clears the castle in Elsinore of vermin.
The charlatan is vanquished.
His slut mother drinks poison like honey.
The hothead is easily slain.
The dottering counselor is run through.
The virgin whore goes mad with heat and cools her lust by
drowning.
The would-be king meets his justice at his nephew's blade.
The good and loyal friend remains,
but Fortinbras will have none of it:
at his signal, he too is killed.
All are slaughtered.
The blood is washed from the walls and floors;
the Danish court disinfected:
Hitler is marching on Czechoslovakia. It has begun.

OSCAR *makes the Hitler salute.* META *steps downstage.*

Meta   Are you ready?

OSCAR *rises.*

| Oscar | Yes. |
| Meta | Let's open our play. |

*

Scenes 24/25

META is pacing.

| Voice | The goddess of history looked down to earth. German troops entered Bohemia and Moravia, and with breathless excitement the German people and the whole world saw the Führer take up residence in the castle of Prague... |

OSCAR is heard unlocking the door. META runs and turns the radio off. OSCAR enters. He is still in the SA uniform. He gazes at her, she at him. He crosses to her. He takes her into his arms and kisses her. Lights crossfade to another look. META, sitting. OSCAR is in the process of performing for her as the lights rise. He quotes from Fortinbras *in Hitler's voice.*

| Oscar | *(as FORTINBRAS)*
"Speak loudly for him.
Take up the bodies: such a sight as this
Becomes the field, but here shows much amiss.
Go, bid the soldiers shoot." |

OSCAR breaks character and enthusiastically relates the events.

Oscar   And then the soldiers shoot Horatio and all the court. It's
a blood-bath. Everyone is writhing on the ground. The
cannons blast and the curtain falls and then... silence. *(He
pauses and waits, then...)* The curtain rises for the curtain
call and... *(He pauses and waits)* silence. Meta, you've
never heard such a silence. I looked out at them; their faces
were all agog. They were in shock. It was as if they had
ingested some huge seeping pig that had fairly rifled through
them. I tell you, I've never seen so many satisfied Germans
in my life. Then, miracle of miracles: spontaneously, in
unison, they began to sing the "Horst Wessel Song," tears
streaming from their eyes.

*He begins singing the "Horst Wessel Song." The phone rings.
META and OSCAR start. They watch the phone in dread as
it continues to ring. OSCAR looks at META, then crosses
and answers it.*

Oscar   Hello? *(He looks at Meta)* Yes, Gustav?—Oh, yes—Oh,
thank you so much—Is that so?—You think so?—He is?
And that is good?—Good. When?—You'll let me know,
won't you?—Thank you. Goodbye.

*OSCAR hangs the phone up. He looks at META in
apprehension.*

Meta   Yes?

Oscar   Gustav congratulated me. He wanted to extend his compli-
ments to my *(Indicating META)* "Hamlet." He said Doctor
Limp was not so happy. He said that Mr. Diamond was

not in attendance but he was sure to come when the word got out. That he would let me know when he came.

Meta	Doctor Limp?
Oscar	Goebbels.
Meta	Goebbels was not happy.
Oscar	Mr. Diamond...
Meta	Göring? Wasn't there?

He takes her in his arms.

Oscar   He's coming. You wanted war, my darling. We have one.

*

Scene 26

META *is asleep on the easy chair. She snaps awake, disoriented. She crosses to the side of the window and cautiously looks out. She looks at her watch. She paces. The phone rings. She watches it in apprehension. She waits for it to stop ringing but it does not. Slowly she crosses to it, waiting for it to stop ringing. Then, impulsively, she snatches up the receiver.*

Meta   Hello? *(No answer)* Hello? *(She waits)* Is someone there? *(No answer. She hangs up)* My God, what have I done?

She looks at the receiver in dread as if something was hiding in it, then slowly places it in its cradle. She sits then falls asleep.

The door opens. OSCAR *enters. His clothes are in disarray. His face is bruised.*

Oscar   Meta?

Meta   My god, Oscar, where have you been?

Oscar   Are you okay? I'm sorry, I've got to hurry. It's almost curtain time.

OSCAR *exits into the bathroom.*

Meta   What's happened to you?

Oscar   *(Off)* The bruises look good! It was even better, Meta. It was incredible. You should have seen it. They had to close the curtain on the applause. They just wouldn't stop. I thought the theater would explode.

Meta   Never mind that, you were gone all night and day.

Oscar   *(Off)* I no sooner left the stage than two men grabbed me by the arms and pulled me out of the theater to Gestapo headquarters. Oh my god, I had the scariest night of my life. The Gestapo boys roughed me up; called me faggot, Jew-fucker, bolshevist, traitor; they ran out of names. They were really pissed. I thought they were gonna kill me. Then some bigwig in a leather suit came in, I swear, Meta, it was leather. He took one of them aside and whispered frantically at him. They untied me, but before they did one of them slugged me in the face. The guy said, "This is from Herr Goebbels so that you'll look good for Prime Minister Göring." *(*OSCAR *enters from the bathroom)* I'm so inspired. Goebbels was trying to stop the show but Göring intervened. It is a miracle, it is magic. They're fighting each other, Meta. And we little actors—no you, Meta, you're doing it. I've got to go. Prime Minister Göring is coming tonight. Wish me well.

OSCAR starts for the door.

Meta	Oscar.
Oscar	*(Impatient, looking at his watch)* Yes?
Meta	I answered the phone.

OSCAR takes on that Horst Wessel look again. He becomes cold, pins her with an icy glarae.

Oscar	You what?
Meta	I answered the phone.
Oscar	How could you be so stupid!
Meta	I didn't know where you were. You were out all night.
Oscar	Did anyone answer?
Meta	No.
Oscar	Of course not. If the phone rings again, don't answer it no matter what happens. Do you understand me? Now wait here. I'm going to kill tonight. I'm going to burn the house down with my performance!

He exits. META gazes at the door in amazement.

*

Scene 27

Offstage in the dark, OSCAR *is heard loudly singing the "Horst Wessel Song." He is drunk. The lights rise as* META *approaches the door cautiously. He knocks on the door.* META *steps back. He knocks again. Silence.* OSCAR *unlocks the door and springs in.* META *gives a startled shout. He's wearing his SA uniform. He has a rose and an open bottle of wine from which he's been drinking.*

Oscar   My darling! *(He drops to one knee and thrusts the rose to her with his head bowed)* From the Prime Minister of Prussia, Founder of the German Airforce, Creator of the Gestapo, Reichmarshal, President of the Reichstag, Chairman of the Council for Defense of the Reich.

She stands back and looks at him, irritated by his carelessness.

Meta   You're drunk.

OSCAR *remains kneeling with the rose extended.*

Oscar   Is that what I am? Yes, that's what I am, a victorious drunk! *(Realizing that she's not going to take the rose, he stands and throws the rose on the table)*

Oscar   Aren't you happy to see me? Don't you want to know how it went?

Meta   You met Göring?

Oscar   None other.

Meta   You told him about me?

Oscar	I didn't have to, he knew who you were.
Meta	He knew I was your wife?
Oscar	He knew from Dietrich Dieter.
Meta	Dietrich Dieter?
Oscar	The little man at Gestapo headquarters. He was there too. He wanted to get close to Göring. He clicked his heels and introduced himself. "Herr Prime Minister, your Hamlet is none other than the husband of the famous Meta Wolff. She was in my office only a few months ago."
Meta	Oh, god, then Göring knows I'm a Jew.
Oscar	Don't worry, my darling. Everything is going to be all right. Göring is going to take care of us. He loves us. He loved my Hamlet. He loved everything about it. He grabbed me by the hand and almost broke it with enthusiasm. He's huge, Meta, enormous.

OSCAR laughs. META laughs mockingly.

Meta	Yes, fat with Jewish corpses.
Oscar	Don't be a spoilsport. We are victorious! *(He drinks from the wine bottle)* Czech wine. From the Front.
Meta	"The Front." What are you doing, Oscar?
Oscar	I'm celebrating, if you let me. Come on, drink with me, drink with me, my love. Gustav took us into his office, Göring and me. Can you believe it? He had a sky blue uniform with huge lapels and ten pounds of medals. He had this French aftershave. There were four SS men with him everywhere he went. He loves Gustav. He put his arm around him. Every time he looked at me he laughed. He sat and looked at me and laughed and slapped his

knee. He wasn't a bad guy, you know, for a killer. Gustav told me he has four castles. He has a pet lion that he takes with him everywhere and he calms himself by immersing his hands in a fish bowl full of diamonds. Can you believe that?

Meta   Diamonds stolen from Jews.

Oscar   *(Laughing)* Where else would he get them? Listen, my darling. I don't approve of the guy, but if you're going to have somebody on your side he's the next best thing to Hitler.

META laughs incredulously.

Meta   I can't believe you're saying these things!

Oscar   *(Roaring)* Why not, you're the one who did it!

Meta   Quiet down.

OSCAR approaches her. She avoids him. He laughs and feigns surprise. He goes one way, she goes another. This goes on for a bit, then he grabs her and tries to sit her on his lap.

Oscar   Come on, my darling, come and sit with me. Drink to our success.

She resists. He throws her on to the couch.

Oscar   Fucking Jew bitch! I do everything for you. I go out on stage and I do everything you say. I go to Gustav and risk telling him how to direct the play.

He drops to his knees next to her. She covers her face with her hands.

Oscar   I'm sorry. I'm so sorry. I'm acting like them, aren't I? *(He puts his face in his hands and cries)* It's been so hard, so frightening. I'm sorry I called you a Jew.

OSCAR cries. META watches him. Finally, OSCAR'S tears subside. He sits there in silence.

Oscar   I never mentioned you, Meta, I swear it. I wouldn't be that careless. Göring knew you. He loves you.

He goes to the rose and then crawls to META on his hands and knees.

Oscar   When Göring left he plucked a rose from a vase in Gustav's office and gave it to me. *(He holds the rose out to her)* He told me that you were the finest actress in all of Germany, in all of Germany, Meta. Göring said that.

META takes the rose.

Meta   *(With a certain surrender)* And that is my death sentence.
Oscar   No, no, it's not. When he left, he drew Gustav aside and spoke with him. Gustav was excited. He told me that Göring told Goebbels to keep his hands off of the production or else he would tell the Führer about a certain mistress Goebbels is keeping. Gustav said that while the stand off lasts we must get you to Switzerland, Switzerland, my darling.

Meta	*(Quietly)* While the "stand off lasts." Yes, my dear, while it lasts. I'm going to the performance tomorrow night.
Oscar	You can't do that.
Meta	I must do that.
Oscar	But if people see you. Goebbels has spies everywhere.
Meta	It doesn't matter anymore, Oscar.
Oscar	Don't think that way. It's just the beginning. We'll get you to Switzerland.
Meta	Yes, of course.

The lights fade.

*

Scene 28

OSCAR is in his SA uniform. He is nervously pacing.

Meta	*(Off)* I want to go by myself. I want to take a taxi. I'm going to get out a few blocks from the theater and look at the shops.
Oscar	I don't want you to do this. It is against the law.
Meta	*(Off)* Whose law?
Oscar	You know very well whose law it is.
Meta	*(Off)* Don't nag. I know what I'm doing. You're going to be late. That's not only careless, but it's discourteous to the stage manager. Who is the stage manager?
Oscar	Georg.
Meta	*(Off)* Georg, he's held on? Well, he's a bear when he's crossed. Get along.

Oscar	I can't stand this, Meta, really, I don't think you should do this.
Meta	*(Off)* Where is the ticket?
Oscar	On the dresser. So is the money. You shouldn't be going alone.
Meta	*(Off)* I want to taste things. I want to feel the street as a human being. I want to climb out of my hole and see the lights of the city at night. I might get some pastry at Koppels. Then I'm going to sit at a sidewalk café and drink a glass of Riesling. I want to see the fashions. I only look at them from my window. I want to see the women parading down the street on a spring night. I want to hear their shoes clacking on the sidewalk. I want to smell the trees blooming. I want to see gentlemen open doors for ladies. Perhaps one will open a door for me. I haven't been out past nine for ever so long. I want to be a part of Germany's new prosperity. I'm going to watch my husband's triumph. I'm going to meet everyone backstage. Now get along, you'll be late.
Oscar	Meta...
Meta	Go, go. I'll be fine. I'll meet you backstage.

OSCAR exits. META sings "Du, Du Liegst Mir Im Herzen" as the lights fade.

*

Scene 29

OSCAR enters and opens the door for META. META sweeps into the room in all her diva glory. She is wearing a blond wig with braids encircling her head. She is ecstatic.

Meta   I can't believe it! It was even more than I expected. Those jowly servants of the Reich, weeping and grinning, winking at each other and the stage winking back at them like one great eye, the curtain slamming down and then up again midst tears of rage—the Horst Wessel Song and you standing there with your "Hitler Salute." Franz Weber covered with blood, taking a bow. I almost choked. I thought he would break into laughter right there in the curtain call: all of them, they were practically airborne. *(She runs to OSCAR and embraces him)* Oh, Oscar even if I never see another night I will have this one fixed in my eyes for all eternity. Thank you, my dear! At first they didn't recognize me. They thought some grand duchess was paying them tribute. Kitty Stengel came up to me and she gazed at me as if I were a mummy under glass and then she recognized me. I never heard anyone shout in a whisper before and all of them, they suddenly recognized me. And they crowded around me. "Oh Meta, Meta," and then, "shhh, shhh." They kissed me in all of their powder and makeup and stage blood.

She begins crying. OSCAR goes to her and strokes her hair.

Oscar   It was good, wasn't it?

Meta   They were so happy to see me. Marianne slipped her hand

	in mine and she whispered in my ear, "Oh, my brave darling, be careful, please." Only Pamela Wedekind stood apart. She watched me. Her eyes were endless. It made my hair stand on end. She said, "Heil Hitler, honey." *(Meta laughs. She turns to* OSCAR*)* And you, you, my love, I'm so proud of you. You were practically howling on that stage.
Oscar	You will be on the stage again in Switzerland.
Meta	I can't even dream of it. God, do you think…? Oscar, I want to be onstage again. It's been so long. I know so much more. Wait. *(She runs into the other room) (Off)* I kept them. *(She enters with a bouquet of dried roses)* Remember? It was the last time I was onstage.

The phone rings. OSCAR *picks up the receiver.* META *begins murmuring.*

| Meta | No. No. No… |

OSCAR *turns and smiles at* META.

| Oscar | Yes, Gustav? *(As he listens the smile slowly vanishes from his face)* Are you serious?—*(*OSCAR *listens for a long while, then cries out)* Why did you do that? *(*OSCAR *turns from* META*)* I can't understand you—That's absurd. I won't do that—Go to hell, you bastard! Don't hang up. |

OSCAR *stands with the dead receiver to his ear, then slowly he hangs it up.*

| Oscar | *(Quietly)* The play is cancelled. |

META sinks to the chair, her roses still in her arms.

Meta	Goebbels and Göring... they've made up?
Oscar	Gustav said that Göring thought the show was too exciting.
Meta	What else? What else?
Oscar	Göring practically fired him, then and there.
Meta	He turned me in.
Oscar	Gustav told him that it wasn't his idea.
Meta	That it was mine.
Oscar	He said he was "sorry." He said we should leave immediately. He began sobbing and hung up.
Meta	Where can we go?
Oscar	I don't know. We'll just go.

He starts for the bedroom.

Meta	Stop, Oscar. What else did he say?
Oscar	It doesn't matter.
Meta	Yes, it does. Tell me.
Oscar	I can still stay in the company.
Meta	If you let me go.

OSCAR takes META in his arms. META holds the dried roses as she embraces him.

Oscar	I won't let you go. Wherever you go, I go. We're in this together. The Gestapo could come at any moment. We've got to hurry.

OSCAR exits into the bedroom.

Meta	There's nowhere to run. Fortinbras is on the move and the nation is moving with him. The play was in the audience long before it was on the stage. Oh, Germany, my Germany, you go to meet your destiny.
Oscar	*(Off)* We'll take one suitcase. We'll take the tram west to the final stop. We'll go on foot...
Meta	There's nowhere to go, my darling.
Oscar	*(Off)* I won't let them take you to a concentration camp.
Meta	I won't let them either.
Oscar	*(Off)* What are we going to do?
Meta	I...
Oscar	*(Off)* No, "we."
Meta	I don't want to be here anymore.

OSCAR enters.

Oscar	What do you want to do?
Meta	I want to be in this moment forever with you.
Oscar	That's what I want too. Do you think I want to go on without you; in this place; in these times? I watched them, Meta, these important actors of the Prussian State Theater. They looked at you with such sympathy and hunger. They envied you, poor slaves. They live in silent immigration. I don't have poison. I don't have a gun. But we have gas.

They gaze at each other.

Oscar	Yes, Meta, yes.

META *gives the dried roses to* OSCAR, *then removes the blonde wig. The lights fade.*

*

Scene 30

In the darkness, there is the sound of hissing gas. The lights rise on OSCAR *and* META *lining the door and the window with sheets.*

Oscar   Get me another sheet. Hurry.

META *exits into the bedroom and then enters with a sheet and a pillow. She throws the sheet over* OSCAR *and then begins hitting him with the pillow.* OSCAR, *looking like a ghost, grabs her and pulls her to the floor. He kisses her through the sheet. She struggles free and runs.*

Meta   I'm out of breath.

OSCAR *stands in his sheet, then pulls it off.*

Oscar   We can stop this, Meta.

Meta   No, we can't, not unless you want the Gestapo to chop our heads off with electric guillotines. *(She laughs)* That's German efficiency for you. I feel faint. Do you?

OSCAR *checks himself.*

Oscar	I don't know.

They look at each other and laugh. META *sinks to the floor.* OSCAR *goes to her and sits.*

Oscar	Are you all right?
Meta	*(Laughs)* No, am I supposed to be? Oh, God, I'm frightened. *(She grabs him)* I don't want you to die.

He kisses her.

Oscar	By God, I am faint.
Meta	Oh, Oscar...

OSCAR *wraps the sheet around her and cradles her in his arms.*

Meta	Are we who we are? Who are we? Are we our actions? Do we have a choice, or are we driven to do what we do? What I do each moment is undetermined and yet when I do it it is there forever. The world is full of magic. It is so much around us, so much in us; the light that falls through the window, the moisture on your lips, my hunger for you. It is so close that we cannot see it. We are making our marriage bed.
Oscar	I love you, my darling. In all the evil, the ugliness, I don't know where that love came from. I feel so lucky to have met you. Now we will know no separation. They can do nothing more to us. Now they have only themselves.

META *is still.* OSCAR *cries out.*

Oscar   Oh, Meta, my Meta! My Meta, my Meta...

He lays his head on her breast and murmurs her name into silence. Then suddenly there is a loud pounding on the door: bam-bam-bam! bam-bam-bam! bam-bam-bam! The lights bump to darkness. bam-bam-bam! bam-bam-bam! Then silence.

The End

Wilfredo

by Wesley Walker

Wilfredo *was produced at* 2100 *Square Feet by Padua Playwrights in* *May* 2002, *under the plawright's direction. The set was designed by* *Jeffrey Atherton, with original music and sound design by Robert* *Oriol, and costumes by Bridget Phillips.*

With the following cast:

Wilfred: John Horn
Tanner: George Gerdes
Esther: O-Lan Jones
Nestor: Barry Del Sherman
Roberta: Christine Marie Burke
Rutledge: Jack Kehler

Characters

Wilfred *Mexican gentleman, 50s.*

Tanner *American man, 40s.*

Esther *Mexican woman, 50s.*

Nestor *Esther's husband, Mexican man, 50s.*

Roberta *Mexican woman, 20s.*

Rutledge *American man, 40s.*

Scene

Old barroom in downtown Tijuana.

Act One

Throbbing music. Behind the bar, WILFRED *appears. He wears a slightly worn suit and speaks with formality.*

Wilfred My name is not Chingado. Do not call me that. Do not call me Chingado. My name is Wilfred: the boss and keeper of this Tijuana bar. You have heard, no doubt, of my famous exploit. You have heard of my crowning. Did they torture me? They did. Did they scar poor Wilfred with fire and defecate on his person? But I hardened. Hardened, and now I am before you. Happy. The hero: famous Wilfred. I laugh. But what a man learns is not always of benefit. The lessons pull at his flesh. I do not want to learn another thing ever. Unless. Unless I will learn of treasure. Because treasure is that thing which causes the heart of a man to thump. I have such a thing, a tiny special, special. I call it my bueno. To hold onto my bueno I use every muscle. They used the wire and the caliper and the hammer. They broke my toes with a bucket of paint. But I… digress. This is the story of how I lost my bueno, how with its loss came freedom from all suffering. But it is also the story of how I got my bueno back. For now I will be quiet. Because an American customer enters the bar.

Music. An American man, TANNER, enters bar from outside. He wears a business suit, no tie. The men stare at each other.

Wilfred   My name is not Chingado. Do not call me that. Wilfred is my name, I am your barkeep. Please. Let the customer instruct us. How best to serve his needs.

Pause. TANNER says nothing. An awkward moment follows. Suddenly, WILFRED produces a bottle, pours a glass, offers it to the American.

Wilfred   This is the very best tequila and I pour it in the traditional way. It is made here in town. By two famous brothers across the street. One of the brothers is Ralpheo, the other is Juan: they have a dangerous streak and between them they share a daughter. She is cut diamond. She is loveliest, loveliest stone. I sometimes imagine…

Tanner   I would, uh…
(Pause) I would love to drink this tequila, Wilfred, if it didn't smell like sperm.

Wilfred   What?

Tanner   This tequila, it smells like semen. I can't…

Wilfred   I see.
(Pause) Do not call me Chingado. Do not call me whore.

Pause.

Tanner   I won't call you Chingado.

Wilfred   You have heard, then, of my splendid exploit.

Tanner   May I try a different tequila?

Wilfred	With pride I will tell you now the story.
Tanner	Stories bring me down.
Wilfred	What is your name?
Tanner	Tanner.
Wilfred	I will change the ending of this story for you, Mister Tanner, to make it appeal.
Tanner	I'd see through it. I'd know the real ending.
Wilfred	With the apology from my very deepest part, Mister Tanner, I differ. You would not see the ending.
Tanner	*(With inappropriate vehemence)* I could tell you the fucking ending right fucking now.

Pause.

Wilfred	We admire our friend's forcefulness and we imagine it carries him far. How far, pray tell us, does the force carry our friend with the woman?
Tanner	Pardon?
Wilfred	Does it make the woman succumb? *(Pause)* I have in my recollection a technique for the woman. I will show this to you now.

With a flourish, WILFRED begins a clearly rehearsed performance. He shifts his voice, radiating gravitas and tragic romance. He speaks to TANNER as if he were the woman.

Wilfred	"There is within my hand a bird, a bird who's come from an intimate location: he's come from out of your heart.

Music swells. Soon, it drowns out WILFRED's words.

Wilfred	His feathers! Still wet! Still wet with blood from your heart...

WILFRED continues under the music, clearly swept up in his speech. TANNER seems to be too. After long moments of this, WILFRED is again audible. His speech has hit its passionate peak.

Wilfred	I love you. If I cannot have you, I will sing of you. I will sing of you till I die."
Tanner	*(A little embarrassed by his own enthrallment)* Wow.
Wilfred	Right away or in a moment or in a series of days, the woman will succumb.
Tanner	I don't like women.
Wilfred	Do you like men?
Tanner	I like to be alone.
Wilfred	I like this too. We are alone here together, very much. Listen... *(Silence)* The night: how small we are against it. Men so small, how could they do the harm? Do you do the harm, Mister Tanner?

Pause. TANNER is uncomfortable with the question.

Wilfred	Do you visit for the purpose of business?
Tanner	I do.
Wilfred	I have poured my tradition and feeling into your cup. Please, Mister Tanner.

WILFRED pushes the glass toward TANNER.

Wilfred   Please.

TANNER refuses to drink. They stare at each other.

Wilfred   Why? Why must the other man always hurt me? *(Pause)* When I was a boy, my best friend hurt me: he tied a bottle to a part I wish he didn't. Now every man I meet: enemy!

Tanner   Are you Mexican, Wilfred? *(Pause)* You don't look Mexican.

Wilfred   Night! Night is my only friend!

Suddenly, ESTHER, a woman slightly younger than WILFRED and wearing the clothes of a shopkeeper, enters from outside.

Wilfred   And Esther. Esther is my friend also.

Esther   I was in the store sweeping. Two men went by dragging a third. In his palms, Wilfred: two gold coins! He stole these, I think, from you.

Wilfred   My two gold coins?

Esther   Yes. That you sometimes polish when it's late at night or cold.

Wilfred   These are my bueno! My favorite thing!

Esther   Up Revolución, past Tilley's, they dragged him.

Wilfred   Were the coins in his palms, were they old? Like mine?

Esther   The coins were old but still shiny. We saw them flash.

Wilfred   I cried when I first saw them. I discovered them under Nestor's bed. *(To TANNER)* Nestor is an idiot we hope you never meet.

Esther	But Nestor is my husband.
Wilfred	I remember.
Esther	And your name he says with respect.
Wilfred	He hid his two favorite coins under his bed. The first place I looked!
Esther	And you took them.
Wilfred	Sometimes I set them out here on the counter just so I can take them again. I keep them in their secret place so no one ever could find them.
Esther	Why don't you look there now?

WILFRED *looks for and, with surprise, finds his two coins.*

Wilfred	My bueno! My joy!
Esther	Let us see.
Wilfred	No one ever could steal them!
Esther	Show them to the American.
Wilfred	One is from Spain, one Portugal. They were dug as ore from the earth near this coast. On galleons, they were shipped back, minted, and returned to this land as currency against tender. I look at them late at night when I am hopeless. Or when it is cold. When you hold these coins I want you to think of your truest wish, my friend. What is your truest wish?

Pause.

| Tanner | I wish all suffering would cease. |

Pause.

Tanner	I wish all suffering would cease.
Wilfred	Please. Hold my bueno for the evening's remainder. This privilege you've earned with your wish.
Esther	That was a good wish.
Wilfred	Esther is the daughter of Ralpheo and Juan—the brothers who own the distillery. Also, they own this bar. Esther has in her mind a wonder-trove of knowledge . She knows especially tequila, the process of manufacture. It is her family's tequila you will now enjoy.

TANNER doesn't drink. ESTHER and WILFRED stare at him.

Wilfred	To avoid the grievous insult. (*Pause*) Please. (*Pause*) And the shame.

TANNER waits, then finally relents, tentatively sips the tequila. He stifles a grimace. WILFRED is pleased.

Wilfred	They keep her in the gift shop polishing glasses with her stupid husband Nestor, but she'd find better suit in the distillery. Her intelligence is a rebuke to men. She's due some money, isn't she? When the brothers die. We're very curious about her, all of us. But also we are afraid. No one is sure which is her father. Is it Ralpheo? Is it Juan? It can't be both!
Tanner	It's a... It's a fine tequila.
Wilfred	It's from a certain agave, which is speckled.
Tanner	It's a fine tequila, but it reminds me too much of pain.
Wilfred	The speckled agave is the sick agave. We call it: manchado densamente con los dolores, or: speckled thick with sores.

Tanner	Ah.
Wilfred	We drink the sick cactus to restore what once we had.
Tanner	Pardon?
Wilfred	We drink the sick cactus, friend, to restore what once we had.
Tanner	It's a sharp pain. Right here.
Wilfred	Yes.
Tanner	I... I wish I could sit up straight.
Wilfred	The spine, yes. And we miss the upright posture. But the night rolls forward, does it not? and through the discomfort we bear up like men.
Tanner	Oh!
Wilfred	Yes.
Tanner	My groin! God!
Wilfred	Well but the oaths and the deprecation... even the gift of speech—we release them. Because now you'll want to excuse yourself. After looking at your palm.
Tanner	*(TANNER looks at his palm; he's frightened by what he sees)* What is it?
Wilfred	It's the "unfortunate hello." Esther will, if she likes, guide you to the restroom now for men.

TANNER attempts to gather himself. He's disoriented, hurting. ESTHER and WILFRED stare at him expectantly. He stumbles toward ESTHER. She recoils slightly then points him offstage. She exits behind him, then returns.

Esther	Is he very sick? Will he die?
Wilfred	We hope not. He's a good man.
Esther	Is there not some comfort we could offer? It is a horrid life.

Wilfred	It's a pinching, pinching life.
Esther	And it's in Mexico you feel it.

Enter ROBERTA. *She's a young and pretty bar waitress.*

Esther	Here is Roberta who is always late.
Wilfred	You are late again, Roberta. Perhaps there is some reason.

No response from ROBERTA.

Wilfred	Perhaps there is some reason.

No response from ROBERTA.

Wilfred	So the punishment won't come.
Roberta	I'm sorry I was... distracted.
Wilfred	Yes?
Roberta	By a man. With a fur coat. Who was kissing me, just kissing me. To distract me from the fight.
Esther	The fight?
Roberta	His name was Romel, he kept shouting: "I am Romel." Into my mouth. And kissing. I thought he was a badger. Because of the eagerness. And the fur coat.
Esther	I saw a fight earlier. Or, two men dragging a third up the street.
Roberta	"There are three places in my heart," he said. "Now one belongs to you." I don't think he'll remember me. I'm not very good in bed.
Esther	In the fight I saw, the one man had two coins. And the other two dragged him like a sack of fruit.

Roberta	Whatever it was, it was terrible. I heard the crowd applaud. I wanted to see the fisticuffs. They sounded so wet and real! But Romel was very clear about it and he got me under the tree and put his knife on my neck to steal my favorite thing.
Esther	What is your favorite thing, Roberta?
Roberta	It's... why, it's my girls, Esther. Is that a thing you have to ask?
Wilfred	Did you see into the eyes of the badger?
Roberta	*(Baffled by his question)* It was... I don't...
Wilfred	Did you grasp the angry spirit?
Roberta	I'm sorry I'm late, Wilfred. I won't be late again.
Wilfred	You will be late again tomorrow. Did you grasp the angry spirit? Did you? With your comprehension?
Roberta	He... He seemed... injured.
Wilfred	All men, Roberta, all of them are injured. And they do it to themselves! We have a sick American in the restroom now.
Roberta	I'm sure he will be fine.
Wilfred	We are thinking he will not be fine.
Roberta	Feed him a radish; tell him a story. *(Pause)* A good story. And a radish. That's what I do with my girls.
Wilfred	Put on your apron. Cut the limes.
Roberta	I'll go back there; I'll visit.
Wilfred	No. Limes. Then do the ice.
Roberta	When my girls are scared I tell them the story of the pine box. It's frightening. In the end the boy loses his eye. But after the story the girls sleep like rocks. I'll go back. Because I need to wash. Mix a little water drink with a pepper in it and a radish. *(She exits toward bathroom)*
Esther	Maybe she will know what to do. Because she is younger than me and strange. And our friend will come out again.

NESTOR enters from outside.

Wilfred Here is your stupid husband, Nestor.

Nestor There are high crimes and there are high crimes! I'm going to leave forever! If you love me send me a letter. I'm going north. To El Centro.

Esther What's in El Centro?

Nestor It is not what's in El Centro, it's what is not. Your father, Esther, your father and his brother are not in El Centro.

Esther Poor Nestor.

Nestor He says I spilled. I was moving the bottles. He says, "You spilled tequila on the floor." I did not spill tequila. I do not think I did.

Esther Oh, Nestor. Was it a big spill or a small spill?

NESTOR starts to cry with remorse. No one moves.

Esther Poor Nestor!

Wilfred Poor Nestor!

Nestor I try.

Esther You do try.

Nestor Why is everything made of glass?

Esther What did my father say?

Nestor He said, "In heaven or in hell, Nestor, I will find you and I will tear your skin out and I will eat you and I will shit you out and I will take that stool in my mouth and eat you again until you are brown water..." *(Stumbles slightly, recovers)* "... I will go on 'til the sun cracks open, I will eat you; when you no longer come out as refuse I will chew out my stomach to make sure you are nothing and nothing. Until my own welcomed death prevents me from killing you." Hello, Wilfred.

Wilfred   Hello, Nestor.

Nestor   May I see my two coins?

No response.

Nestor   Because, because... I'm... sad.

Esther   They're in the bathroom.

Nestor   Oh.

Esther   With an American. A good man.

ROBERTA enters from bathroom.

Nestor   Hello, Roberta.

Roberta   It's dark in there. Is there a candle? We don't want to inconvenience the customer.

Esther   Is he ill?

Roberta   We need a candle. Or maybe just a... I can't find him. I can't find the customer.

Esther   He's left? He's gone?

Roberta   It's dark. Or someone took him. I need a light or a match or... Please? I shouldn't have opened the window.

Esther   You opened the window?

Roberta   Wait!

She exits to bathroom. Returns.

Roberta   I'm embarrassed. He's there. Am I blushing? He's got nice teeth. But I hope he meant what he said.

Esther	What did he say?
Roberta	He said I was perfection. And he made a promise. I doubt it was the truth. He has a house. In Malibu, he says. And a speed boat. And some good art from France. I would be his girl and we'd drive to Starbucks in his tank.
Esther	His tank?
Roberta	He owns a tank, he says. And a drawbridge and a moat. I know it's... I know it's not love I'm feeling. And a ring of guards with halberds. And a ferocious yellow dog. Am I blushing?
Esther	Is he ill?
Roberta	Well... But. I could salve his sores and drain his pocks. And wipe the spittle. If there is snot I can take care of the snot and his ears and the blood. And his distended abdomen and the skin flakes and his punishing smell. His smell, Esther: it makes me want to confess. I should maybe play aloof. I could suck the crud and fluid from the dirt-producing wound. And spit it in the garden in order to fertilize plants. And lick his dirtiest problems and be kind with my lips and mouth. And powder him with sweet talcs. And sit with him by his feet while he trembles his slow trembles and looks dumbly at the sky. I could read to him. The lesser, less demanding works. Of the poets, Fuentes, Paz, whoever. Or some English writer he might prefer. Or the bible, the holy bible: "Fear, and the pit, and the snare, are upon thee, O inhabitant of the earth." But then the sun will go down and the dark will find us in our pose. And I'll stand over you to guard against things bad. And you can sleep the sleep of the dead, darling, for as long as you like. Forever, darling, because I will never leave you: I will guard you till the end of time.

	(To WILFRED*)* What should I do? I don't want to love him.
Wilfred	There are limes to do and glasses. There is ice. If you want to be happy, do these things, Roberta, because these things are your job.
Nestor	Hello, Roberta.
Roberta	Hello, Nestor.
Nestor	That man in the bathroom, does he have my coins?
Roberta	I didn't see coins, Nestor.
Nestor	That may be because he swallowed them. Men do that sometimes. They steal. Why don't we go back there, you and I? For a visit. For the threat we'll use a knife. And some towels. And water.
Roberta	I don't... This is not something I'd like to participate in, Nestor.
Nestor	Wilfred. May I have a towel and a basin. And a large cooking knife.
Wilfred	No.
Nestor	The coins, Wilfred, he swallowed them. The cooking knife will be used to dislodge. I feel strongly...

No one budges.

Nestor	Or something sharp and metal... I'll use my keys!

NESTOR *exits toward bathroom.*

Esther	Nestor believes God protects him, but God does not protect him: I do. Even from literature books, I protect him. "Stop crying, Nestor. Put the book down."
Roberta	You must love him very much.

Esther	I set out his clothes in the morning. When he's asleep I put up the little fence. Sometimes I doubt my motive.
Roberta	Your motive?
Esther	For marrying him.
Roberta	It must have been affection.
Esther	He was beautiful the way a child is beautiful. He made everything in this world new. It was like marrying the morning. Affection was one reason. But there was one other reason also.

Pause. ROBERTA waits to hear it.

| Esther | Wilfred knows it. He can tell you if he likes. |

They look at WILFRED, waiting for response. Nothing.

| Roberta | You are happy, though, Esther. You are happy. |
| Esther | As happy as the human being who is a woman in this time will be. |

Pause.

Wilfred	*(Gravely)* The limes are what I would like you to do, Roberta. Also glasses. But if you will not do these things maybe you will do something else.
Roberta	I hope I do, Wilfred.
Wilfred	Go get a bucket of peanuts from Escobar down the street. Get the best looking peanuts with the shells all intact. Take your time in selecting. It's these little things, Roberta, that in the end pay off. But if you are late coming back or

the nuts you choose are shabby, something bad may occur and the punishment will approach.

Roberta   I will do my best this time, Wilfred.

Wilfred   Thank you, Roberta.

ROBERTA exits outside.

Esther   *(To WILFRED)* When I heard the American make that wish I was reminded of someone else. A young man I met in a bar. In Comala.

Wilfred   Comala!

Esther   He cornered me in his stable, the young man, and spoke to me, spoke to my chest, in which, it turned out, a bird resided.

Wilfred   A bird!

Esther   He beckoned it. I felt it come out.

Wilfred   Astonishing!

Esther   Yes, and he cried. He would rather yearn for me, he said, than have another girl.

Wilfred   A brave romantic!

Esther   Full of promises.

Wilfred   Full of lies.

Esther   My father is from Comala. So is his brother.

Wilfred   Yes.

Esther   You three have that in common.

Wilfred   We do, yes. But that is the only thing. There is nothing else on earth that we have in common. *(Pause. Suddenly paranoid)* If they... If they told you something, Esther, about me... I have always been a Christian.

Pause. ROBERTA enters from outside empty handed.

Wilfred	Do I see no peanuts? Can she have failed again?
Roberta	There's a crowd of men. Outside, Wilfred. With picks and shovels. A crowd.
Wilfred	Are they angry with me?
Roberta	Should they be angry with you?
Wilfred	No. I am a hero in this town. I won't tell again the story.
Roberta	Thank you, Wilfred.
Wilfred	But the fame of my exploits has reached as far as the wind will blow it.
Roberta	They probably come from the desert, looking for work.
Wilfred	Did the men out there say my name? Did they say Wilfred?
Roberta	No. They stare at your door here and wait.
Wilfred	Sometimes one does things one is not ashamed of yet others find it repugnant. And there are those with overly strict ideals and mores who can envy... I won't be judged. I won't be judged by you.
Roberta	They may just be looking for work.
Wilfred	I won't be called Chingado. Or Dupe. I won't be judged by a barmaid! Or a mindless, bloody mob! *Roberta!* Find something to do!

NESTOR enters from bathroom.

Nestor	O God, why do I doubt you? Why do I everyday ask, is there a Father? Is there a God? This American in your bathroom, Wilfred, he is genius. But he doesn't have the coins.
Wilfred	My bueno!
Nestor	He is good news and sweet triumph. The sweat on his skin

	shines like steel. I asked him for the coins; he was quiet on the subject. I think, Wilfred, our coins are gone.
Wilfred	Oh no!
Nestor	His skin is blighted with sores but sores not unlovely. They remind one of pink tomatoes or beef. His face is hard. His tongue clicks. His eyes loll and flip like fish. And what hands!
Roberta	Is he naked?
Nestor	He has hands like these, but bigger, and he raises them like this. He speaks with the voice of heroes. Underneath you hear the pain. I fell to my knees. "Please," I said. "Heal me."
Esther	Oh, Nestor.
Nestor	I... I think he will heal me, but first I have to do some things. I have to say a little... a little speech he gave me. To the crowd. Which has gathered outside.
Roberta	What? What are you supposed to say to them?
Nestor	I cannot tell you. I can only tell the crowd. I am no longer afraid. *(Reflects)* I am still afraid. But less so.
Roberta	What will you be telling the crowd?
Nestor	I cannot say but I can say I will be telling them naked— this was his recommendation. *(He stops at door)*
Esther	Nestor...!?

NESTOR disrobes, exits outside. ESTHER, distraught, exits after him.

| **Wilfred** | It started sad, now it's sadder: this happy hour. |

An American, RUTLEDGE, enters from outside quietly, sits at bar.

Wilfred	Do not call me Chingado. Do not call me Fool. My name is Wilfred. I am from Comala, Mexico: home of the yellow cypress, home of the sour wind.
Rutledge	Rutledge, Hills of Hollywood, Los Angeles. Home of the Lakers, Clippers, Dodgers and Kings.
Wilfred	Pardon my demeanor, Mister Rutledge, but my bueno, I've lost it—my one favorite thing. Do you have a bueno?
Rutledge	I do. This... my lucky tie.
Wilfred	Close your eyes. Your tie! It's gone! See the problem?
Rutledge	I picked it up in Vegas, this black guy bet me his tie I couldn't jump the hood of his car. Check it out.

WILFRED touches RUTLEDGE'S tie.

Wilfred	I can feel the luck.
Rutledge	Put it on.

WILFRED dons the tie.

Rutledge	What's the biggest thing, Wilfred, now you're wearing it, what's the biggest thing you could hope to win? In a bet?
Wilfred	I would bet and beat hoary Satan to prevent the torture of men for their crimes.
Rutledge	Wow.
Wilfred	Because I don't want to suffer. I don't want to suffer.
Rutledge	I don't want to suffer either, Wilfred. Perhaps you could help me with a drink.
Wilfred	*(Produces bottle)* Manchado densamente con los dolores.
Rutledge	We'll assume that's Spanish.

WILFRED pours some tequila.

Rutledge   You don't look Mexican, Wilfred. Are you Mexican?

Wilfred   Would you like your tie back, Mister Rutledge?

Rutledge   Keep it awhile. You earned it with that bet. The hoary
devil, wow. That's what I like about Mexico. You guys
come up with that weird-assed shit. This is nasty tequila,
Wilfred. But that is one attractive youngster.

Wilfred   Roberta.

Rutledge   Roberta. Reminds me of my wife. My wife always reminded
me of my mom, so... And I loved my mom. Wait. Am I
sick from this tequila already? No. Yeah Mom could bend
all the way over. Hatha Yoga. Bend over touch her butt
with her tongue. She'd do that in front of the TV. I loved
her so much it was a problem. Drew pictures of her, bragged
at school. Made a statue of her out of wood. Part wood,
part plaster of Paris. She had the world's most terrific grin.
Then she got Alzheimer's, forgot who she was. Forgot me, my
little brother. Ate old meat from the trashcan. Embarrassed
my father. Load up his phone-mail with messages. We've
got her out now on some ranch for older women, some
ranch out near Saugus. They give her structure. She let her
looks go. But I carried my statue—it was three feet tall—
around New York when I lived there, around DC and
Decatur. I do news, TV news. One day a guy offered me
ten bucks for the statue. I took it, and with the money
bought a bra. Went home, put it on. Now I'm going to
throw up. Nope, still good! Yeah, a sports bra, real simple.
And I walked down the sluiceways and trash-drops of old
Decatur, past the rot, stench and ruin, ducked into The

Lawrence, an old bar off Lincoln, and quietly became new to myself there, mother to myself there: a more generous, more complete vessel. Over some nice vodka they were pouring and lemon. This tequila by the way is making me DIE! Where's the bathroom? But you're a terrific looking woman, Roberta, no, you have a salable face; you might entertain the idea of a trip north. Sell soap, or something. No, we'd love you up there. I'm heading back up tonight. Buy you a dress; give you some dollars. I'll get you on the news. You like soccer? We've got soccer up there now, sure, the Galaxy. I'm a trained boxer, kick boxer. I'll fucking pepper you with diamonds. Oh, God! *(Blood issues from his nose)* No, and we'll attend the Lakers' games. At night people, crowds will come by, they'll gather outside our place; you might deign to, on occasion, wave a hand. The sick, the stunted: they'll congregate, they'll sing. Streams of laser blue light will shoot from your eyes, illuminate the hillside. And people will picnic up there. Like it was day. I can't think of a better life for you than the one you'd lead in Los Angeles, little girl. Struggle though I might. God this death I'm drinking! Agghg! Guess I'll, uh, excuse myself to your uh… headquarters now, uh… *(Blood)* Seem to be running up against some sort of hemorrhage. Should be fine. Oh! I wonder who I am! I wonder who I am!

Roberta   You're the American.

Rutledge   I don't want to cry in front of you folks, is there some-where…? My tie! Who has my tie?

Wilfred   I'm wearing your tie.

Rutledge   That's my tie? Wait! Who just entered the bar? Who just entered the bar?

ESTHER enters the bar from outside.

Rutledge   Is she talking to me? Is she talking to me?

Esther   He's saying things to the people, Nestor is, but because he's dancing you can't understand it. He flicks his head like a fire hose. I'm reluctant to intervene. They call him shit monkey and throw trash. I wonder, am I the best wife for him? Another woman might be more patient. Should I just put him on a bus to El Centro? It would please my father, my father and his brother.

Wilfred   Which of the brothers, Esther, Ralpheo or Juan, which is your father? It can't be both! That would be an aberration.

Esther   How did our friend find his way from the bathroom?

Wilfred   This is not our old friend, this is a new friend.

Esther   Hello, friend.

Rutledge   *(Exaggerated diction)* I have trouble understanding you.

Esther   Hello.

Rutledge   Not your fault.

Esther   You've had a nosebleed and you're far from home. I'm unhappy too. Is that a comfort?

Rutledge   Is she talking to me?

Esther   It's my fault I'm unhappy, I know it is. But why? I picked the simplest life I could, I picked the simplest man.

Rutledge   What's she saying? Is she being friendly?

Esther   Did I choose wrong?

Rutledge   What's her name?

Wilfred   Esther.

Rutledge   Is she being friendly? Is she saying, "Yeah, I know, you've got your problems; but I like you and would be into helping you. With them. With your problems. Even if they're sexual in nature," right? Even if they involve sex and lots of pain for the woman, lots of bite marks and trouble for the woman. And my penis, with its veins, like a white thumb strangled by worms. And she'd willingly become my goat, whose every hole is pried to breaking. And the venom from my tendrils leaks into her veins and organs. The very fiber of their walls it unweaves. She cries, pisses blood; each visit to the toilet brings worse news. She watches her guts tumble out in bundles of red. Still I fuck her just to cause more harm. I kill you, saint! And I laugh at the God who made you! Ha! Now. We understand each other. *(Pain, tears)* I feel good. Just about good to go. Need a minute or two, but...

Wilfred	Maybe señor would appreciate a visit to our restroom.
Rutledge	No, thank you.
Wilfred	The customer suffers. It is not our policy.
Rutledge	Wilfred? I don't want to be a gargoyle! Look at my back! Please! Don't make me change!
Wilfred	We can empathize. We can appreciate your pain from a distance.
Rutledge	I was so good, so natural looking!
Wilfred	We can watch and feel pity.
Rutledge	Infection! Traitorous flesh!
Wilfred	Poor son of man.
Rutledge	Foul Nature! And the fools who worship your evil cunt! I kill you all in one last scream:
	(He draws breath as if to scream. He doesn't. He contorts, freezes in grimace)
Wilfred	Where is the pity for such men? Why does God make us play a part in such things?

Esther	He won't stay like that. Will he stay like that?
Wilfred	We wonder. And we grow cloudy.

NESTOR *enters from outside, naked.*

Nestor	Please do not heckle. Please do not throw trash. I do what I am told to do. The men out there! How like donkeys! They ignore the shining word. I spoke in the language he taught me, the language of pain and fear. Why do they not listen? Am I boring?
Roberta	What did you say to the people?
Nestor	I said what I was told to say. I won't repeat it here. Apparently, it's not appropriate. They threw cucumbers and trash. I am worthy. I am good. I did as I was instructed in exactly the right way. *(Starts to cry, stifles it)*
Esther	Poor Nestor!
Nestor	His words were clear and should have had a good effect.
Roberta	What were his words, Nestor?
Nestor	They were these: *(Nothing)* They were: *(Nothing)*
Wilfred	You are stupid, Nestor, it's not your fault. Please put on your clothes.
Esther	We have another American friend, Nestor. Look. This one is silent.
Nestor	Can there be two? There can be only one.
Esther	He won't speak. He's suffered. Do you think he's a genius too?
Nestor	I don't think so. I'll go ask. *(He exits to bathroom, returns)* No. I was right. There's just one.

He crosses to RUTLEDGE. *Furtively kicks* RUTLEDGE. *He hesitates, then bites him.*

Nestor   (*Addresses the women*) Help me.

The women, not comprehending what it is he is asking them to do, don't move. They look at each other. ROBERTA begins to smile. ESTHER, after a hesitation, returns the smile. WILFRED realizes what might come next.

Wilfred   This is not the thing to do.

The women ignore WILFRED and turn, with deliberate wickedness, to face RUTLEDGE. They grin like beasts. Music swells. They set upon him, biting, molesting his body. They work his skin with knives, press their feet into him. They cut relics from his face and hands, lifting to the light fingers, nose scraps and tissue. They open his chest, display organs. The women rub their crotches against his legs and shoes. The wickedness has left the proceedings and all is carried out with curiosity and deliberation, the way children would explore a new game. No frenzy. Finally it ends, they're sated.

Nestor   I think this was his lesson. Let's reveal to the public what it is they have done.

NESTOR drags him outside. Women collect body scraps and follow NESTOR. WILFRED is left alone, rattled. He begins the following conspiratorially, as if to one man.

Wilfred   In my youth there was a lady, a mother to a friend of mine. Nervous, asthmatic. Marina was her name. In all things we'd do, my friend and I, Marina would prefer me to her son. She'd praise my manners, praise my appetite for her cooking. One night she said, "Watch the way Wilfred eats his chorizo. He flatters me with his enjoyment!" My friend then showed me that part of his eye where vengeance hid. Later, I played chess with him. There were pornographic books—we looked through these. When his mother was asleep, I suggested we go to the kitchen to steal some tequila. We each filled a jar, snuck out the window and looked at the sheep. The drink hit us hard. Soon I was crying. He threw up in the trough and passed out. Then I went to him. "Amigo. Amigo. Do not harbor anger. Do not hurt me. Do not hurt yourself. Your mother, your mother is very agitated. She favors me. It's not my fault." Then he fell asleep and I removed his pants. I remember repeating to myself a single word: victim. The word produced in my mouth a flavor. Then I removed my pants. It is as clear to me now as this bar is in front of me. Because I was naked like a ghost. And I found a beer bottle to play a trick so he would remember in the morning. And the anus on a boy is a tiny thing, a gentle thing. Luckily I avoided this. Then with twine I bound his testicles to the bottle. Later it was clear I bound them too tight. Then I tied his wrists to the fence and we slept. In the morning, I went home. I learned later my friend was beaten and scolded by his parents, found as he was, tied to the fence. He was blamed for corrupting me, poor Wilfred! and his mother baked me a tray of pana dulce in apology. My friend was quiet about that night, and when that year I ran for President of Students he worked on my campaign. Later I won his girlfriend, Rosa, in a bet. Neither did this he protest. His name was

Nestor, this friend; his crazy mother, Marina. But hardly do I tell anyone this story. In fact I only tell you.

Tanner enters upstage of Wilfred. His shirt is wet. He glares at Wilfred with groggy menace. Lights down.

End of Act One

Act Two

WILFRED behind bar, TANNER seated.

Wilfred   But hardly do I tell anyone this story. In fact I only tell you.

Pause.

Tanner   I'm not accustomed to the Mexican ways.

Wilfred   It may just take some time.

Tanner   I'm not accustomed to the vomit. I say this in apology. In my distraction, I missed the gist of your story.

Wilfred   My story is not important. What is important is the customer. And his impression. What is the customer's impression?

Pause.

Tanner   You were cruel to poor Nestor, in turn he loved you for it. That was the gist.

Wilfred   I was cruel.

Tanner   And the crime of it fell on the two boys evenly.

Wilfred   In one way, sir, it was he who did this thing to me.

Tanner	The crime spills down, Wilfred, like so much wine or mud. We can say this man wears more of the stain. Or this man, or that. But...
Wilfred	The businessman is very suave with us. And also cunning. The bueno, which he was vouchsafed, when does he foresee its return?

ROBERTA enters from outside, shaken from the goings on.

Wilfred	Here is Roberta. She is always late. This man here is Tanner. He will not... *(Suddenly very upset at the notion)* Evidently, return to me my coins. They're in his greedy pocket. Or his bowel. Why won't he confess it? *(Pause)* Perhaps... perhaps it's for my sake he hides my bueno. No? For a lesson. Perhaps I clutched them too tight. Or maybe he protects me from what I'll see. My coins... have they... *(Stifled sob)* changed?
Tanner	*(To ROBERTA)* I have a trampoline. In my house. And marvelous track lighting. I have a hill of my own, blue with ice-plant. In Malibu, Roberta, the sky is orange, and they love Mehicanas there, they'd love you. I have a ceramic puma, encrusted head to foot with stone. And a rack-mount stereo and a hutch. In the kitchen, you could cook dinner. It's white, white with off-white trim. The afternoon light sets it afire. You could read to me in the library. And I could fall asleep. You could put me in diapers, boss me around. I could forget how to use the potty. You could whip me and call me selfish. Selfish baby. Or... We could go the other way, I could whip you. Keep you in a cage. I have one, an actual cage. You could read, sit and read, and smoke ciga-

rettes, like the French. Write miserable letters about your captivity. Or we could just share it. The responsibility. And drive around. Like a normal couple. I have a tank and a jeep, so safety isn't a worry. Normal couple smiling, Zuma wind in our hair. And we could buy clothes. Matching shirts. I don't know. I've never been in love.

Roberta   I have two children, two girls. They were fathered by my cousin Hector.

Tanner   *(Retreating)* Oh.

Roberta   One is developmentally tardy. The other one is fine.

Tanner   Oh.

Pause.

Roberta   *(Stung)* There is love and succor out there, I can feel it, but it's not out there for me. It's under the ocean, perhaps. It's not for me, not for anyone I know, but it is there—a bountiful love.

Pause.

Wilfred   Tanner, you're looking well enough to handle another drink.

Pours. TANNER, *reflexively, drinks.*

Wilfred   Yes.

ROBERTA *bolts from the stage.*

Tanner	*(Regarding his glass)* I'm, uh... lost.
Wilfred	I understand your ploy, and I thank you. You protect me from myself. To see my coins now might... A man's terror, it's said, is revealed to him in things most familiar. In his possessions a man's death is revealed. Even... even gold. You are kind. I will not hurt you. Though your innards clutch my coins.

ROBERTA enters from outside. She's alone.

Roberta	Here they are, my two girls! *(Music)* My two girls. Here they are. Wait! *(She exits)*
Wilfred	*(Continuing to TANNER on earlier thought)* A man's possessions, it's said, are the skeleton of his brain.

ROBERTA returns alone.

Roberta	Look at them! They're intelligent. Well the one is. And they really won't make much sound. You could buy them dresses and cut their hair and do the lice. I would do the rest. I'll go get them. Here they are! I don't really... love them. I don't really love them. *(She cries)* It's too much. I'm young. It's too much. *(Long silent sob. Men watch)* Who will help me? My two girls will grow and one has a terrible flaw. It would take one thousand dollars. Or two thousand dollars. Nothing. Nothing to a man such as you. *(Pause)* Of all the cruel jokes that are played in this world, the cruelest are played on the woman.

TANNER suddenly reacts to the tequila and convulses in

*pain. Blood trickles from his nose. W*ILFRED *is not surprised.* R*OBERTA is enraged.*

Roberta	Oh, yes! How sick! How sick he is with his contortions! All of us feel very sorry! So pleasant to be the male in this world—it must be—the center of everything!
Tanner	Excuse...
Wilfred	Yes.
Tanner	Excuse me I...
Wilfred	Yes.

T*ANNER recovers slightly, starts to walk, thinks better of it, stops.*

Wilfred	The customer is ashamed.
Tanner	No.
Wilfred	Because he is a thief.
Tanner	I got rich from my good idea. I remember the night it came to me, I was sampling a scotch at the hotel bar—this was in Phoenix on the tail end of one of my junkets. I was rounding up some capital for my next big foray—and, bang! Sure as night, the intuition hit me. "Gold," I thought, "gold! And silver and your other precious ores. What we need is a more powerful method for the detection of such things." So with a pencil the barman lent me I limned the first hints of a sketch. In that first sketch were the things I would later put to patent—marriage of magnet to processor, lightweight shell design. Now, of course, I'm famous. They put me on the cover of *Business Week* with my robe and Turkish knife. Just as streams come to the river and the river

then comes to the sea, the events that led to that moment, my epiphany at the Marriott, are clearer to me now and make the whole thing look inevitable, but in the moment it came as a flash and I explained this to my partner, who at the time was dying of thrush, just a disgusting, disgusting disease. White patches in the mouth. I think it must have been due to some systemic weakness on his part. Nobody ever dies of thrush. Anyway, "Don't fuck me," he said. "Don't fuck me on this design." He thought the idea was his, you see. "I would never fuck you," I said. But of course I did. And I had to work to get through it, I meditated and saw a shrink. Signed up for some Learning Annex classes on breathing. I took his idea and fucked him. Fucked his wife out of the profits. No, it was terrible. I had to learn how to breathe through my flaws. But... and accept the Buddha nature of things. The face behind the face. The press, they build me up, I let them. It doesn't matter, the Buddha says it doesn't matter. All of it, all of this: *(Encompassing gesture)* Illusion. We announce our quarterlies next week. They call me the Turk. The Genius. And, you know...? You know, they're right. The thief is always genius. Providing his theft is great.

Wilfred

No. The thief is never genius.

Tanner

The thief is genius, Wilfred, when he steals what's beyond his grasp. *(Pause)* The great thief steals from great men, the greater thief steals from God. And when God is asleep and lying down the genius thief steals His dream.

Pause.

234

Wilfred	*(Frightened)* To say such things! To even think them!
	NESTOR *enters.*
Wilfred	Here, again, is Nestor to compound our deep displeasure.
Nestor	We set the corpse on the bus bench, put newspaper on his head, called the people over to see. I waved my hands, did a dance. The people got bored and left. I try every single thing but everything I try is spoiled. I disappointed Esther.
Wilfred	The crowd has left?
Nestor	No. They just gnash their teeth and wait. I have to go to the bathroom. I need some good advice.
Wilfred	But the American is here. No one is in the bathroom.
Nestor	Who is this man?
Wilfred	His name is Tanner. He's pregnant with my coins.
Nestor	I'm going now in back. *(He exits)*
Wilfred	*(Silently pouring and offering another drink to* TANNER. *He's afraid; his hands shake)* This... dream you speak of, God's dream: have you seen it?
Tanner	No. I haven't.
Wilfred	Is there a man in the dream? Does he look like me?
Tanner	He does.
Wilfred	Oh, terrible!
Tanner	Let's talk about something else.
Wilfred	Yes. *(Pause)* Does he have my features? Does he have my voice?
Tanner	The man in the dream marries a worm.
Wilfred	No.
Tanner	He couples, couples with a worm.
Wilfred	No.

Tanner	He tells it his romantic feelings.
Wilfred	Repulsive.
Tanner	I wish it weren't true.

Pause.

Wilfred	Does he... does he have my proud bearing?
Tanner	He drags it around town like a garden hose. And controversy follows, because it's wet, the worm is, and it resembles very closely his mom.
Wilfred	No.
Tanner	Yes and you see them kissing the way teenagers do when they're drunk.
Wilfred	I can't listen.
Tanner	Yes, let's stop.
Wilfred	The man in the dream, he's... he's confused.
Tanner	He's kissing his mom like a sex toy, right there in the center of town. You see them in the garden or behind the produce shop. Then he goes too far, gets her pregnant. Which, of course, produces kids.
Wilfred	No.
Tanner	Two, a pair of angry boys. Hungry. With fangs.
Wilfred	Frightening!
Tanner	Their fingers, long and clicking; they squeak like bats when they eat.
Wilfred	If I saw them, I would never sit still. I'd run as far as I could.
Tanner	They'd chase you down, Wilfred. In the desert. They have the legs of cougars.
Wilfred	No.
Tanner	The legs of wildcats. You don't run, you wait for them.

	They call you out; you don't respond. Then they enter, and the world hisses like a thousand snakes. They grab you, Wilfred, and drag you into the street.
Wilfred	What an awful dream!
Tanner	Up Revolución, past Tilley's. You try to resist but...
Wilfred	I would never have married the woman if I knew it would come to this!
Tanner	And Wilfred, you're pitiful. You're pitiful clutching your coins. Out of view, up the street, they drag you. Do they set at you with pliers then, Wilfred? Do they break your toes?
Wilfred	*(Slightly unhinged)* I don't appreciate God for dreaming me into this dream! I don't appreciate you for telling it.
Tanner	I don't appreciate you, Wilfred. Or your tequila. Thumbtacks perforate my gut and anus. It feels that way.
Wilfred	We all have our complaints. I, for example... I, for one... I... *(Pause. Whispers for TANNER's benefit)* I was unsuitable. With Nestor's mother. Marina. I tell you this now. We kissed. Nothing more. I'm not sure Nestor knew. *(Pause. Standard voice, so ROBERTA can hear)* Perhaps we should enjoy now our jukebox so full of the Mexican hits. *(Pause. Whispers)* I kissed her with my mouth and made some promises. No crime. You are familiar with my technique. In the spirit of fun.
Tanner	*(TANNER is suddenly struck with pain; more blood issues from his nose)* I don't want to make a mess. *(Goes to his knees)* Uh... discomfort! And...!
Wilfred	We don't like to hear it!
Tanner	I'm... afraid I....
Wilfred	Why does God make us see this thing?
Tanner	*(In agony)* Oh!

Music. NESTOR *enters from bathroom.*

Nestor Three times have I visited, three times have I been saved! The genius is the man on the toilet!

Wilfred But your genius is here.

Nestor He has given me the next plan, which I shall carry out.

Wilfred You are stupid, Nestor.

Nestor It's the best thing for our city. It involves digging underground. It requires picks and hammers. The benefits will make us rich.

Roberta Rich?

Nestor In the center of the ground is a pocket, a pocket of water and light, he promises it's under Tijuana, the people will find it there.

Roberta How will they find it?

Nestor They will utilize the steam shovel. With picks they'll tunnel down. If the hole is as he says it is the benefit will spread. Deposits of rich mineral and metal such as gold. We will sluice and blast free with water the good flecks from the chaff. The jobs are for the workers outside. Ungrateful dogs! It will be fun to watch them dig!

Wilfred Is this the business you spoke of, Tanner? Is this the reason you came?

TANNER doesn't answer. He appears horribly stricken, crumpled on the floor.

Wilfred Your metal detector, so fancy in your story. Did it lead you to our bar? *(Pause)* Would you like another drink?

Tanner I shouldn't.

238

A couple of beats pass. Suddenly, TANNER *lurches to his feet, hurries to the bar, takes up the tequila glass, and, as if by reflex, finishes the drink. He groans terribly...*

Tanner   Oh! *(And again roughly meets the floor)*

Nestor   I'm happy I understand so little of life! What I do understand makes me sad.

Roberta   Mister Tanner is sick but we don't know the name of his disease.

Wilfred   We have seen the old figurines—men twisted, with pustules.

Roberta   We have heard the stories.

Wilfred   The Olmec, the Toltec: those olden peoples. The Aztec shoved their first god into the oven because he was sick with this same thing, but none of us knows the name of the disease.

Roberta   Maybe it's pretty, the name. Maybe if we're quiet we'll hear someone blurt it out.

Silence. TANNER *lets out a harrowing moan.*

Nestor   I am happy I understand so little. I wish I understood less.

RUTLEDGE *enters from outside.*

Rutledge   What I don't like about women is the perfume! What I don't like about rebirth is the mess! What I don't like about Mexico is Mexico: too much goddamned dirt. The people here lack manners. And college kids come down to throw up. I'm a little turned around; you'll excuse me. I just had sex out there. Ugly sex. Can't recall her name.

Nestor	Was it Esther?
Rutledge	Might have been Esther, yeah.

ESTHER walks in. All in the bar, save RUTLEDGE, regard her.

Rutledge	She was talking the whole time, couldn't understand a word.
Nestor	What did she say?
Rutledge	I, for a second, got confused, thought I was the woman, because it felt so good.
Nestor	What did she tell you?
Rutledge	Tough to say: I was on my back like a woman, you know, receiving.
Nestor	Esther is a generous lover.
Rutledge	There's the word: generous. But some might accuse her of rape. She works her love up in there with her digits. And mine was the erection of a corpse.
Nestor	The what?
Rutledge	The erection of a corpse.
Nestor	I myself do not have the erection. Wilfred can, if he likes, tell you why.

All in the bar turn to WILFRED for an explanation.
WILFRED turns away.

Nestor	Esther has always been patient.
Rutledge	Well she is patient. Reminds me of my wife. Who reminds me of my mom. But my wife always brought a razor blade to bed; just different, different type of person.
Nestor	Esther is a mother to me. *(Pause)* She's taken over the thankless duty—from Marina, the slut! The Black Genital!

She's taken over the duty of mothering weak Nestor, the cause of all that smells!

Esther   Nestor... *(Pause)*

Nestor   Was there... pleasure... in this act for you?

Esther   *(After hesitation)* There was... yes there was pleasure.

Nestor   And this should not cut my heart?

Pause. He cries. Recovers. Pause.

Esther   I wasn't aware he was living. I thought I was using a corpse. *(Pause)* The things I said to him I shouldn't have. So there's guilt.

Nestor   What did you say?

ESTHER *hesitates.*

Nestor   Please, Esther.

Esther   I said: "Never have I loved anyone, it's always been a lie. Nor have I loved Nestor, nor have I loved Wilfred, because men, men all of them: vacío. In each one you see his copy, the counterfeit posing as fact. But the fact itself is counterfeited. I wish it were not this way. Never was there just one man; always were there two. From out the stony head they leapt: the twins, to create this world. Call one Adam. Call one God. Each wanted what the other had, be it dominion, be it a girl. The quarrel has lasted till now; I doubt it will end tonight. Even men not brothers now were brothers once—Wilfred and Nestor sprang from the same sack— and they vie, they vie like vermin, sometimes over a girl. I still bear scars. Each man is a copy, each of his acts are false. Show me one true act of man and I will love him again." And that is when our friend here revived.

Wilfred *(To RUTLEDGE)* Would you like another drink?

Rutledge No, thank you.

Esther I... encountered with especial longing the smooth coldness of his penis: it was hard not with desire, false desire, but with death.

Wilfred *(To RUTLEDGE)* Would you like another drink?

RUTLEDGE accepts the drink. He drinks.

Rutledge I don't want to be a gargoyle. I don't want to be a saint.

Tanner I don't either.

Rutledge I don't want to fall prey to what's dark in man. Again.

Wilfred We are all of us sorry for our roles in this.

Rutledge I mean... I'm... working, you know, to understand your... custom. I don't want to overreact. I don't want to get the cameras down here, please, don't make me get the cameras down here. I don't want to see this go away, this unique, uh, cultural, uh, whatever you've got here. I don't want to see it replaced with a Starbucks. I don't want the forces of global capital to win out, to crush you and win out, stomp on your children, shit in your hair. Because that's what they'll do. But I feel bad, 'cause I've already made the call. The crew is on its way. I called them, told them to get down here, expose this weird-assed shit. Expose this... *(Pained)* I thought I was special! I was led to believe...! My mother... I was promoted from Weather to Headline four different times. Miss Hickey asked me to read my paper in third grade assembly. In the boys room they would always call me Cheese. All the things I hoped for, will they fall away? Will I be forced to witness them? Falling away?

RUTLEDGE is now totally convinced he's dying. TANNER looks on, self-pity posing as pity.

Rutledge   Will I be alone? On the scaffolding?

Wilfred   No.

Rutledge   Will I be... alone?

ESTHER crosses to him, touches his face. RUTLEDGE resists the kindness, then breaks down and embraces her, resting his head upon her breast.

Rutledge   I don't...

He cries. ESTHER comforts him. His eyes settle on TANNER.

Rutledge   Who's this guy?

Wilfred   This is Tanner.

Rutledge   Why's he staring at me?

Wilfred   He's ill.

Rutledge   Tell him to stop staring at me!

Wilfred   He stole my favorite coins.

Rutledge   I can forgive him that. *(To TANNER)* I forgive you.

Esther   That's kind.

Rutledge   What have you done, Esther? What have you done you're ashamed of?

Esther   I. Well. I.

Rutledge   I forgive you. Wilfred? I forgive you. I forgive you all.

Young girl. You obviously have something... But you're free now; I forgive you.

ROBERTA begins to cry, exits.

Rutledge OK, now I'm ready. Am I ready? Why does it hurt so much? *(He falls to his knees, similar to TANNER)*

Wilfred In my mind there are several virtues. There is the virtue of patience. There is the virtue of keeping still. There is the virtue of decorum and properly modulated speech. But there is one virtue I lack. And that is the virtue of new thinking. I follow, I follow what has been laid before me. By my ancestors. Someone is to blame for these things, but it is not clear to us now who this is. I hesitate to blame God or my employers. I hesitate to blame your American state. But the hatchet will fall. Blood will breathe. Suffering will rule the day. And while some of you think it best placed at my feet, I think the blame falls on you. Nestor. Go outside. Tell your workers to leave. Esther go with him. Don't let them begin this bad tunnel.

They exit outside.

Wilfred In the meantime I produce my little axe. *(He does)* See it glitter. We are none of us too good. We are none of us too lasting. Gentlemen. Crawl toward me. With your necks.

The Americans sleepily inch toward WILFRED.

Wilfred Oh gracious! Oh beneficial! And the singing will ring in your ears.

ROBERTA hurries on from outside, alone.

Roberta   Wilfred! Wait! I brought my two girls. *(Indicating imaginary girls with a flourish)* We'll ask them to sit on the bar. Sit on the bar, girls. Now we'll ask them to sleep. Should I tell them the nighttime story? There once was a boy who had a pine box. And in the pine box lived a fairy. She was a good fairy and would do whatever the boy would ask. She did have, though, one stipulation: "I will do what you say," she said, "but never peek in." The boy would ask for gold and he would get it. He would ask for a bicycle or a knife. But soon his curiosity nagged. She gives these things too easily, he thought, no creature is so generous. She must be hiding something. So one night... he peeked in... and the eye was ripped from his head. The top flew from the pine box and the fairy ran for the door. With his one good eye the boy saw the fairy's attire. Belting her waist: a string of children's eyes. *(End of story)* There. There. Now everything is easy. OK, Wilfred, do it.

WILFRED raises his hatchet.

Roberta   Stop! Are their necks waiting on the bar? I could not... love them until right now.

WILFRED chops and chops at the empty bar with extreme, punishing violence. It's as if he were killing two repulsive insects. Finally, he relents. The two Americans watch, struck with awe and confusion. They look to WILFRED *for a clue as to how they should react. Suddenly,* ROBERTA *begins to cry.*

Roberta   Oh! *(It's as if she's shocked by what* WILFRED *has done, as if she hadn't volunteered her kids—imaginary or not—for the sacrifice)* Oh, Wilfred!

WILFRED *is shaken. He looks at the bar. He looks at* ROBERTA. *He begins to stammer an apology.*

Wilfred   I... I...

ROBERTA *runs for the door and exits.* WILFRED'S *violent aspect is gone. He looks defensively at the Americans. With sudden, wounded vehemence, he launches into the following.*

Wilfred   I don't care if the world knows it! I loved a woman very hard. She was my woman and we ambled through town. Nothing is so passionate as the first kiss. But the second one ruins your life. I was in love then and we would watch movies. Her favorite actor was Charo. This is the truth, and she would cradle me. All other woman I would shoo away. They brought flowers and pretty letters, Esther did, all of them. These gifts I threw in the trash. I was famous because people thought I was loving my mother in the sexual way men do. "There goes Wilfred!" But I was not capable of this. I made do with the kiss and the flirtation. If nothing came of this I am happy but unfortunately I think something did. I think there was a baby. Or some bad result. They came out looking like tumors. No one was more appalled than I. I tried to leave them behind. But you can never leave your mom. Because her love will follow. Like a shark does. Or the moon. If I could favor her with my love, I would have. Because she was so pretty even without her canine teeth. Marina, Marina just the sound of it. And I was large in her eyes.

Roberta enters empty-handed.

Roberta	Look what we found, Wilfred. Only they're not so pretty. Your two gold coins.
Wilfred	My bueno! Where are they?
Roberta	Wait! Hang on. *(Her hands are still empty)* Here they are! And ruined! In the bowel of the earth.
Wilfred	Oh, they were beautiful! I found them under Nestor's bed.
Roberta	They're stained now with filth from the earth.
Wilfred	Nestor says they're his. They're mine. They always were. Where are they?
Roberta	Take them from my hands.
Wilfred	I can't see them!
Roberta	Take them, old man!
Wilfred	I can't...
Roberta	Here.

She finally produces from her pockets two coins, huge, resplendent, sparkling in the light. Stricken, Wilfred and Roberta avert their eyes.

Roberta	And where was your debt before it was in the earth? Where did you hide your lies? Before they shined. I despise you, Wilfred, and your every act.
Wilfred	Take them out of my sight!
Roberta	I leave them at your feet as a curse.
Wilfred	Little witch! Bruja!

After hesitation, ROBERTA relents. She is struck with a better idea. She leaves with the coins.

Wilfred	Don't let me see them again.
Tanner	I... I'm sorry about the coins, I...
Rutledge	Gold coins. Wow.
Tanner	Yeah he, uh, leant them to me at one point and I, uh, in my, uh, stupor I... I...
Wilfred	*(Launching again into his confession, as if there had been no break)* I slept with my head between her legs. That's how we had the pillows. Perhaps my thoughts, or, uh, spittle, uh... trickled... We can hope our dreams have no consequence, but my story, I fear, proves the reverse case. In that they crawled out of my mind into her uterus. And came out looking like boys. Oh, the pride! The pride I felt! One of them is good with a pistol. His name is Ralpheo, the other one is Juan. Juan is by far the more engaging. The stories he tells, just funny, very lively. But he tends to embellish. Which I hate. And he pretends he's from Seattle. They were harsh as youngsters. They'd bite and do the tantrum. And Marina was no help. All she would do is eat. But they softened, my two boys did. Bought this bar to keep me local. It's good. And I was proud. In sports, they were good in

sports. They've made it clear they'd prefer I stay local. They had me sign a document. But we don't much see each other anymore. Two, three phone calls. I know when they're angry. It's a... It's a taste.

Enter ROBERTA.

Roberta   I buried them. Again. They won't come back. If my girls ever came back I don't know what I'd do. I don't think you can run from these things. These are the things that hound you.

RUTLEDGE sees an opening and, meekly at first, begins the following very long speech. By the end of it he is able to stand again.

Rutledge   Perhaps the sandy beaches and the turning surf and the young men and the telephones and the Lamborghini Countach, perhaps this is a chance for you, this city north, named for angels. Perhaps this is the chance for you, Roberta. There are lots of young people there. Just like you. With hopes. Oh you see them on TV. They really are so young. With hair. It's an occasion.

Tanner   Also there is Malibu. And the places up the coast. Or the nicer suburbs. Where things tend to go smoother.

Rutledge   Who is this talking?

Tanner   In Malibu we eat at Geoffrey's. We ride bikes and look at the sun. We leave the windows open for the smell. And you can catch up on sleep.

Rutledge   You can sleep in the city, where I live.

Tanner	You could sleep in Malibu to the sound of the sea.
Rutledge	You can buy one of those ambient cassette tapes in L.A. Run it on the stereo, sleep to that.
Tanner	You would sleep deeper and for longer periods by the ocean, you'd have ample time to dream.
Rutledge	Is that what you want, Roberta? To dream?
Tanner	You could for all intents and purposes live in bed and, like a sand speck in the oyster's mouth, rest and dream and change.
Roberta	I could lie down right here.
Tanner	You could.
Roberta	I could go off to sleep. For a considerable amount of time. I might in that way change.
Tanner	You might.
Roberta	I might forget the bad things.
Tanner	And remember the good.
Roberta	I think... *(She finds a spot on the floor, curls up like a cat)* I think... *(Deepest sleep)*
Rutledge	*(Turning slowly to* TANNER *in absolute, quiet violence)* What have you done?
Tanner	Let's not quarrel.
Rutledge	Let's not quarrel?
Tanner	We have too much in common.
Rutledge	We have nothing in common.
Tanner	We want the same thing.
Rutledge	We don't want the same thing.
Tanner	I want the girl.
Rutledge	I want the girl.
Tanner	She's asleep now. We'll just... watch. Over. Her.
Rutledge	We will?

Tanner	We'll, uh…
Wilfred	Gentlemen, now, gentlemen, it is at, again, this juncture we would do well to remember the sickness in our gut.

TANNER and RUTLEDGE double in pain.

Wilfred	And the horrid new curvature.

Their spines contort.

Wilfred	And the frightening display.

They shrink into hideous gargoyles, poised over ROBERTA. Enter NESTOR, ESTHER. Noise of picks and jackhammers offstage. ESTHER carries the two gold coins, places them in WILFRED'S hands. He is afraid of the coins, doesn't look at them.

Nestor	Well the ground is broken and we've made some good headway. Esther's dad and uncle are pleased with all I've done. The workers are glad for the work and the promise of good cash. The smells are as follows: sweat, dirt, oleander, tar. There is good cheer and respectful speech. We have all of us our debts to pay but in time we will meet these debts. I have been surprised at the snap in my voice, the ease with which I convey my orders. The men run and hurry. If there is a prouder sight than excavation, you should tell me what it is. It's a very clean evening; everything is in its place.
Esther	My father and his brother are happy. They have never

seen such dirt. They have donated to the cause a case of tequila. They feel good about the hole. Some say it will bring wealth, others contentment. Some say there's a garden down there with geysers of unusual milk. The notion that we were all once pilgrims holds special attraction for me. We were all once pilgrims barred from our goal, but now we have found our Mecca. It was always underneath.

Nestor   I wouldn't predict wealth right away. Or even satisfaction. But I would predict over the long-term a steady flow of new energy, new ideas that will slowly make us better.

Esther   Nestor thinks we'll move, all of us. And live down there. In tents.

Nestor   The day of the city is over. That's my idea. Let's join hands, and go. Start something new underground.

Esther   My fathers convey their love to you, Wilfred. They have not forgotten. But they want you to retire.

Wilfred   Retire?

Esther   They asked us to ask you step down. They asked you cross the street and talk to them. About severance and pay. You can now travel. You can find your expression.

Wilfred   I cannot. I cannot cross the street. I've grown accustomed...

Esther   I love you. Nestor loves you. Step out and away from the bar.

Wilfred   I've grown... quite... If they have bad plans for me. Tell them to come here. I have...

Esther   Wilfred. I love you. Nestor loves you. Step out. Step here. We will lead you.

Thunder, tympanies.

Wilfred	I find I cannot.
Esther	Then I will ask them to come here.

Music. NESTOR and ESTHER exit. WILFRED begins to sob. His tears flow, anguish lashes his face. Great trembling, great pain. The gargoyles do not move. ROBERTA continues to sleep. It is clear she will sleep forever.

The End

G-Nome
A Play by Murray Mednick

G-Nome *was produced at The Powerhouse Theater by Padua Playwrights in June 2003, under the direction of Guy Zimmerman. The set was designed by Jeffrey Atherton, with original music and sound design by Robert Oriol.*

With the following cast:

Jacko: Christopher Allport
Cleo: Lynnda Ferguson
Emile: Murray Mednick

G-Nome *continues Mednick's reimagining of the relationship between performers and dramatic texts. Here, the actors shift back and forth between portraying naturalisitic characters and addressing the audience directly as choral figures. Mednick purposely omits attributing speech to particular characters in many places — challenging the actor and director (and reader) to interpret the text in his or her own way. In addition to energizing the performances, this dynamic shifting raises intriguing questions about how theater relates to human identity in general — the explicit subject matter of this play.*

Characters
Emile
Chorus I
Chorus II

Characters portrayed:
Joe
Betty
Emile's First Wife
Louis
Celia
Primo Levi
Paul Celan
Martin Heidegger
Gisèle *Celan's wife.*
Saul Schwartz

Scene
A stage. EMILE *sits with a photo album.*

So so so so so so

I'm looking at a picture of my grandfather
—he's holding my cousin Winnie
wearing a bowler hat.

Winnie is?

No no no no no no.

Louis, Lazer, my grandfather
in California
of all places
He's visiting my Uncle Phil

Also a Gnome

In California, San Diego
San Diego, California.

Correct, right.

So so so so so so

He's holding her and he's got a little smile
He's about five-feet-two

On his face

On his face.

It's not a smile, it's not a grin
It is a gnomic expression of

Benign.

It is not exactly benign
It is malevolent indifference.

No no no no no no

It is beneficence bestowed
With not exactly a grin

"I'm here but I'm not here
I'm not really here."

Just like my father, Joe

It's kind of a sly grin
By a little sexual man
Wearing a bowler hat

With his arm around my cousin
Who is maybe three or four.

The picture must have been taken
In 1951 or '52
By my Uncle Phil

(Also a Gnome, like me.)

Like was said
I must have been in the fifth grade

At the time
And here I am now

Again.

So so so so so so
The story is:
He comes to America
From the steppes of Ukraine

From the Ukrainian steppes.

And my grandma
Celia
Came from Pinsk
The legendary Pinsk.

They got on a boat in Odessa.
They all got on a boat

(The whole town got on a boat—
It was a town on the Ukrainian steppes
Tamashbele
Called Tamashbele
Pronounced Tah-mash-bah-leh.)

The whole Jewish town of Tahmashbele
Got on the boat
And sailed for America
A wild and verdant land.

Whoa whoa whoa

Where there was gold
(Gold gold gold)
For a young guy like Louis
to pick up
off the streets.

(And that's where they met,
on the boat
Louis and Celia.)

And here I am again
I was born in 1939
The year the War began

The War against the Jews.
A whole section of the planet
rose up like a blister

(Or like a bloody red rose.)

And I was not safe.

No no no no no no

Not safe in America
Where Louis and Celia were headed
On the boat in 1905
Married to two different people.

No, not to each other.

No.

No, because they died.

Not true
Because one died and one abandoned.

One abandoned ship?

No no no

My Grandma Celia's husband
Abandoned her in Brooklyn

And meanwhile Louis was in Canada
Where his first wife died.

So so so so so

Nobody knows what happened.
She died.
And he took the kid out
Of the wilderness of Canada

In the dead of winter

And the kid survived
And his name was Harry
And Louis brought him to Brooklyn
And he looked up my grandmother
And he courted my grandmother

(This is Louis we're talking about
Here.)

Whom he had met on the boat
Already
He met her already on the boat.

It was a marriage of convenience
As my Uncle Phil calls it.

He had a kid named Harry
And Celia had a kid

Named Saul

Who was a Schwartz.

So these two got together and had eight more kids.
No, nine.

Pause.

(Yeah, eight, eight.
And one of them was my father, Joe,
One of them was my Uncle, Phil.)

But who is Schwartz
What happened to Schwartz?
If Schwartz doesn't take a hike
There's no you am I right?
There's no Emile.

So so so
What happened to Schwartz?
Where did he go, Schwartz?

He's buried in the ground
There's no doubt about that
No doubt about that.

But my half uncle, Saul,
Remains alive in Las Vegas
Saul Schwartz

Alive in Las Vegas.

Maybe I'll go and see him.
Maybe not.

I'll ask him questions about his father
And where he went
Schwartz
And why he left my Grandmother
And anything else he knows

(But I'm not sure if I'll go.)

About the family.
And all the terrifying reproduction
All the terrifying biology

Which led to me,
Now,
Emile.
Pause.

So.

And now.

Pause.

I

I imagine him in Vegas—
He looks like an aging movie star or a gambler
(with a mustache
and a walker, he's ninety-two)

A certain type
Like his father
A ne'er-do-well and a ladies-man
A Schwartz.

(But not an illiterate peasant like my grandfather, Louis
Who was also a ladies-man married five times
Famous in his day for sexual prowess.)

The world is a slaughterhouse
For no reason that has anything to do with us
Except to provide food and fodder

And everything else is an illusion.
Everything you think
And everything you want
Is an illusion.

So. Okay.

So these photographs are calling to me from the other side—
From the Dead
From the other side of the veil of illusion.

Oh oh oh oh oh *(Weeps)*

I blow you a kiss
Winnie and Uncle Phil—
I blow you a kiss.

Oh oh oh oh oh *(Weeps)*

Emile?

What?

Emile?

What?

Stop crying, Emile.

Stops. Pause.

Celia
I blow you a kiss.

I have her picture right here in front of me
Right here.

She's a teenager, a *maidel*, in the hues of the old country
On the steppes of the Ukraine.

(Now I cough and spit
I cough and spit like an old man
Who doesn't give a shit

Who doesn't give a shit.)

And it's true.
And she's got this amazing hairdo
Must have been the fashion of the day
I've never seen anything like it in my life.

And nothing bad has happened to her yet
On the Polish/Ukrainian steppes
(Except for the seasonal pogrom)

And she's not looking into the camera
She's looking at something else
A little sly, a little hysterical
Look in her eyes.

(I don't know what she's looking at
I don't know what she's thinking.)

And she's holding a flower to her breast
With her right hand.
And she's holding some lace
In her left hand.
And her right elbow rests on a book.

It must be the Talmud or the Bible
(At least she could read
The book is there to tell us that
And I can tell you she spoke four languages.)

Her family were horse traders on the Ukrainian steppes.
She is buxom and well-built, wearing a nice blue dress
In the fashion of the day
And the table is a good one and it's polished.

She has a big wide face with oriental eyes
And she's not smiling
And she's not about to smile.

Thick black hair.

And I'm asking myself
Did she love me?
Did she really love me,
Or did I make it all up in my head?

She loved you, Emile,
She loved you very much.

So so so so so so

And don't you forget it.

Who was this guy, Schwartz?

She saved your life and the lives of your brothers and sisters
She is the positive through-line here.

You're right.

Who was Schwartz
Who abandoned Celia
In the East New York section of Brooklyn?

Eh?

If you want to know, go to Vegas.

Say, what?

I say, if you want to know, go to Vegas.

Okay!

Talk to your Uncle Saul, your half uncle, Saul.

I had a fight there.

Where?

In the parking lot. I had a fight in the parking lot in Vegas
(There's *one* parking lot?)
In front of a casino in Las Vegas, Nevada.
I spent two nights in jail there.

(What does this have to do with Schwartz?)

In nineteen and sixty nine, A.D.
(Saul Schwartz.)
I had a lot of fights, like my father, Joe.
(Emile?)
I had some shit in the car. I had some shit in the car.

Say again?

In the glove compartment of the car. I had some smack
and I had some grass.

Jeez, Emile.

I had some smack and I had some grass in the glove compartment of the car.
And they had me cold in the county jail.

But they let me go.
They let me go on a Monday.

It was a fucking miracle because I drove right out of there
Even though
Even though I was holding
Because the minister of St. Mark's Church
On Second Avenue of New York City
And the Rockefeller Foundation,

And the Rockefeller Foundation,
They vouched for me and they bailed me out.

And so I drove to the City of San Diego,
Where it rained for three and a half months
And the police kept an eye on me.

But I was able to cop some Mexican brown.
And I had a very nice time with Janice Lebaud
(God bless you Janice,
I hope you're alive somewhere.)

And there was that fucked up kid
Whoever his name
Whatever his name
He hung himself from the lighting grid,

I can't remember his name.

(Where are we now?
Now we're in a theater here.)
I mean, this photograph was taken in Poland,
On the Polish/Ukrainian steppes.

(But where is he,
Emile?)

And my father, Joe, wasn't born, wasn't thought.
They say he fell out of a tree.

Actually, he fell out of trees and off of buildings.
He was autistic or a retard
Probably.

He never even finished grade school.
He was a wild and reckless boy
He lost half his teeth by the time he was twelve,

But if you look at this photo you can see he was a

handsome guy.
Not a Gnome.

No, he was of average height for an American.
But he was dumb or autistic or retarded
Or brain damaged.

So his brothers and sisters had a little smile
When they said, Joey, they had a little smile,
When they thought, Joey, they smiled.
Knowingly.

The first fight I had was with a black kid on DeKalb
Avenue.

That was my first fight.
And I put the other kid in a garbage can.

(Poor blacks and Jews, we all lived together in Brooklyn.)

And then the kid's father comes over and then my father,
Joe, came down and they have a big fight right there on
Dekalb Avenue in Brooklyn, they're slugging it out.

They must have been startled. Your grandparents, they
must have been startled to see black people.

I never thought of that.

African-Americans and immigrant Jews who can't even

speak the English language and they're living together in the Brooklyn slums.

I'm thinkiing that was maybe the only time my father went into battle, so to speak, on my behalf.

And Italians and Irish. And then the Puerto Ricans.

What was he, twenty-seven years old? Still a street kid, you know? I think it was hard for him. I think he had a hard time in that fight. But he stood there and slugged it out. Then his nose was bleeding and it was a big deal. It must have been a Saturday or Sunday on a late afternoon. I remember the look of the sky over Brooklyn, bright grey, with the street car cable and the black telephone wires and the roofs.

Joe	So there's a colored kid in the garbage can, and Emile is banging on the can, and he's crying his head off.
Betty	Yeah?
Joe	Yeah.
Betty	Yeah, so?
Joe	He never cries. The kid never cries. What's wrong with him?
Betty	Nothing's wrong with him, it's only his father.
Joe	His father what?
Betty	Just his father.
Joe	Just his father, what?
Betty	Come on Joe, then what happened?
Joe	I went down there, and he's crying his head off, and there's a colored kid in the garbage can.
Betty	Come on, Joe.

Joe	What?
Betty	COME ON, JOE.
Joe	I don't know what to tell ya, Betty.
Betty	I KNOW YOU DON'T.
Joe	My nose is bleeding, okay?
Betty	Put your head back.
Joe	Okay.
Betty	Put your head back.
Joe	Okay.
Betty	Put your head back more.
Joe	I AM. *(Noise from EMILE)*
Betty	Emile, shut up!
Joe	Leave him alone.
Betty	Once in your life, you defend him, once in your life you come to his defense.
Joe	Shut up, Betty.
Betty	It's about time.
Joe	Do you have any cotton, at least? Do you have a rag or something?
Betty	Do I look like a nurse to you?
Joe	Use the toilet paper.
Betty	What?
Joe	Use the toilet paper why don't you?
Betty	I don't want to waste it.
Joe	Are you kidding me?
Betty	There's a war on, Joe.
Joe	I know that.
Betty	There's a war on!
Joe	Oh, what do you care?
Betty	It's beyond you.

Joe	Get a piece of newspaper or something.
Betty	You can't even stay in a CC camp for five minutes.
Joe	What are you talking about?
Betty	In the middle of war, even, you can't stay still!
Joe	Oh, shut up.
Betty	Stay still now, why don't you?
Joe	Pay attention, Betty.
Betty	You'll live, Joe.
Joe	I know that.
Betty	You have a little nosebleed, that's all.
Joe	He's got a black eye, that one.
Betty	You'll live.
Joe	Toe-to-toe we're standing there, belting each other in the head.
Betty	Don't cry, Joe.
Joe	Who's crying? Not me!
Betty	No, because you're such a tough guy, Joe.
Joe	Not me!
Betty	Poor Joey...

One little moment from a Brooklyn slum in 1945.

So so so so so

Everybody thought they would have a good time in
America
And instead they went nuts
They went bananas
Trading wives
and bigamy was rampant.

Guys would marry one woman in Philadelphia and another one in Boston.

It's amazing the stuff that happened.

"Where are you going?

I'm not going.

You're going to Philadelphia?

I'm not going to Philadelphia.

Where are you going?

New York City is where I'm going.

When are you coming back, sweetheart?

I'll be back next week.

Next week?

Don't bother me, Missus,
Business is business.

Business!"

So now I hear Louis talking to Celia:

"So, I'm here.

You're here?

I'm here.

What happened to whatshername?

She died.

She died?

Dead. I buried her in the ground.
(In the cold, cold ground.)

Why? She was such a youngster, she, such a youth.

She gave birth to him, my Harry, in the middle of a blizzard.

Oy.

And Schwartz?

He's not here, Schwartz.

So goodbye to Schwartz?

Goodbye and good riddance.

And him? Saul?

He's a Schwartz, Saul.

I'll make you a deal.

What?

We'll bring together the Schwartzes and the Brasmans.

Oy.

We'll make one family.

So so so

(Who knows if they even got married?)

Listen

He said

Here we don't need a rabbi.

We have to have a rabbi.

Schwartz, you don't know where he is. My wife, may she rest in peace, I can never find her grave again.

So?

So we'll register, we'll be married."

(My grandfather, the Gnome, believed in registering with
the synagogue. He had no observance, he had no practice,
but he believed in registering.)

He had a gleam in his eye.
He had that smile.
Neither here nor there
He had a gnomic dick-like smile

Did Louis "Lazer" Brasman
Father of my father.

They're all buried up there in the Jewish Cemetery of Glen
Wild, New York.
My father and grandfather and brother and grandmother,
Who has her picture on her gravestone,
An expression of woe.

OY, VAYZ MIR

She used to say

Woe woe woe woe.

I hate to tell ya what I'm thinking.

(Is he talking to us?)

I hate to tell ya what I'm thinking.

Which is?

There isn't a tradition of happiness.

Say what?

There isn't a tradition of happiness.

Say again?

In the family.

In the family?

There is only the tradition of woe.

So what did they do for a good time?

I hate to tell ya what I'm thinking.

Which is?

I think they thought it was sex.

Oy, vayz mir.

Up in the Catskills: murder, mayhem, and fooling around.

Is that why you're depressed? Emile?

I'm not depressed.

Murder, mayhem, and fooling around?

Emile?

Yes. Wouldn't you?

What?

Be depressed.

Yes!

I was depressed.

(Can you hear me, Joe?)

No!

It could be chemical!

It was chemical!

There you go.

You should take something for it.

I did.

There you go.

What did you take?

I'm not telling you.

Fine.

I will not reveal the names of the chemical or chemicals.

You don't have to.

I'm not.

So then what happened?

I have revealed enough already.

You have.

Typically.

It's true. Reveal, reveal.

I was a heroin addict for goodness sake.

We know.

I'm talking about chemicals!

We know that.

There's no end to the chemicals!

We know all that.

Rivers of chemicals, oceans of chemicals!

It's true.

How could that fucking happen?

Chemicals up the wazoo! *(Laughter)*

So then what happened?

Louis and Celia?

No, George and Harriet.

So so so

So on they proceeded through life.

Say?

On they proceeded through life. *(Chokes)*

Are you all right?

No.

I'll get you some water. *(EMILE stares at audience)*

(I have no idea why I'm choking. Excuse me. I'm sorry.)

(With water) Here you go.

Thank you. *(Drinks)* That's good.

Water,

Good.

Water.

I am an ignorant, stupid man.

Oh?

I don't know anything about how you talk to a woman.

Really.

How you're supposed to behave.

No.

And what the proper approach to sex is.

No.

And also, I don't know what money is. I don't know what attitude you're supposed to take, for example, to money. Everyone else seems to know but me. Even though I've read a lot of books and had half a dozen or twenty-four nervous breakdowns.

Say again?

I've said a lot of stupid nasty things in my life and I deeply regret them.

Who are you talking to now?

I'm talking to you and I'm talking to them.

Fine and good.

I said them out of anger and defensiveness and hostility.

So so.

I was hostile to anyone above me and everyone was above me.

So?

Go on.

That's all. *(Pause)* You talk now.

Well.

It's okay to say things because if you say them you're not there anymore.

Sure.

You've advanced. So it's okay to keep talking. It's fine.

Okay.

I pray to G-d that I can make up for all that shit. I really do.

The truth will make you free.

I hope you're right.

I think I am. Right.

For example with my first wife, who was a sexy beauty. I can't remember what it was, but there was some nasty, hostile comment I made.

"I'm sick to my stomach," she said.

I remember the light, in the apartment on Avenue D.

"That was a terrible thing to say, Emile."

Some nasty comment about the middle class. I regretted it immediately and I regret it to this day. Wherever you are, I hope you're happy and I hope you're well. I hope you're happy and I hope you're well.

"You sit there reading all the time and you're stoned. You sit there looking at the book, and looking out the window, and looking at the book—stoned. How can you read? How can you follow what you're reading? You understand what you're reading?"

"I think I do, yes."

"You want to be a waiter and sell dope for the rest of your life?"

"No."

"Emile?"

"No."

"You need to do something, and fast, because you're ruining your life and I'm not going to participate."

"I will."

"Go back to school, Emile, or your days around here are numbered."

"I can't do that. I can't go back to school. Go back to school?"

"Why not?"

"I'm a radical hipster who is alienated from society."

"I see."

"I'm a poet."

"Great. Pack your bags and hit the street."

Passive and terrified. I met her at a party on the Lower East Side. She was wearing a tight green dress. It was 1963. I was a good-looking young poetry writing gnome with latent hostility towards those above me which was just about everybody and she was a couple inches taller, needless to say. And I say now in the most biblical way, I get down my knees, I could not believe or accept my good fortune to this day.

So.

Passive and terrified.
And then nasty
And then paralyzed.
That's your story, Emile.

Don't blame Joe and Betty.

Don't blame Grandma and Grandpa.

Don't blame your wife,
Who loves you and helps you.

(There is no blame!)

So let's go on.

Low class Jews in America:
"Make money or die!"
"And what did you do, big shot?"

"I never made a dime."

"So what brings you to the table?"

"I have a wish to be clean,
And purified."

"Then go on a diet, stupid,
Clean the shit out of you,
Your breath stinks."

Ah ah ah ah ah ah!

What's that, amigo?

That is pain, my friend, that is anguish.

You think they want to hear that?

No, I don't think so.

No, definitely not.

I just want to say one more thing.

Isn't clean the same as purified?

I did it all on purpose, which is absolutely amazing—that all could be so artfully arranged for failure! In the fucking Catskills—the grey cold fucking Catskills! Cold! Cold! Cold! Cold!

Okay, calm down.

AND PRIMO LEVI STANDS FACING THE ABYSS.

AND PAUL CELAN.

Calm down.

Okay.

You inherited that hysteria.

I did.

You inherited it on both sides of the family. Hysteria and

insecurity which comes from grief and persecution, okay?

Okay.

Who am I now?

You're asking us?

You're good.

Good.

Thank G-d.

God?

G dash D.

I see.

I spell it like a Jew, because I am.

Good.

I am a Jew.

Good.

I'm glad I'm a Jew.

(Pride. It's the sin of pride.)

And who's the other guy?

Bad.

Nasty little paralyzed motherfucking gnome.

Why? Because he likes sex?

And what is that, but a bit of reproduction?

A bit of reproduction here,

A bit of reproduction there.

So what if he says nasty things to women?

So what is that?

So what?

Because he is dependent on them and afraid of them at the same time—

Vavoom—

He is dependent on them and afraid of them, and he loves them and he hates them.

Amen!

And he loves them and he hates them especially when they yell at him or reject him or yell at him and reject him— then he is out of his mind with fear and loathing, fear of Her and loathing for himself.

Does this remind you of someone?

Eh, what?

I say
Does this sound familiar?
Do you know anyone like this?
Does this remind you of someone?

Yes!
(Aging and resentment
The failing of the body
The putrescence of the corpse.)

AND G-D BLESS PRIMO LEVI AND PAUL CELAN!

Did you hear what I said?

Eh, what?

I said, G-d bless Primo Levi and Paul Celan.

Good. Fine and good.

Finally, at last.

Does this remind you of Joe and Betty?

That's G-d with a dash.

I say, does this remind you of Joe and Betty?

G dash *D*.

Yes or no?

Oh, yes it does, Oh, yes it does.

That's how we learn, my friend, that's how we learn
Everything we know.
We learn from them
Our parents.

Joe and Betty.

And there they are right there grimacing into the Camera.
There they are.

I want to scream
I want to break their fucking heads.
They act like no crimes are being committed
The fucking idiots.

(Pause) Calm down.

While they're taking that fucking picture

She's grimacing like a madwoman,
And he—

Is hiding his resentment,

And he—

Is pretending he's not himself,

And he—

Is acting like nothing ever happened—

Anywhere—
To anybody,
Least of all to him.

So.

Fuck him!

And I'm not sorry!
Even though I wept uncontrollably for five minutes
At the mention of his
Name
Joe
I'm not sorry.

And there you are, too,
Emile.

I am the same exact person
I was then
And I know exactly what I was feeling
Which was shame.

SHAME SHAME SHAME

And there I am
I'm playing with Gilbert's hair
And he is annoyed
Now dead in the ground the poor fucking bastard.

Shame on you,
And on us all,
The gnomic idiots,
Coming down from the faithless Louis,

Dead in the ground from the colon cancer
Which was also the killer of
Matinee Joe, my dad.

Dead in the ground together in Glen Wild, New York,
In the cold cold Catskills ground,
Eaten by worms and bugs,
Along with Louis and Celia,

All in the same ground.

C'est la.

It's fucking cold up there
And dead in the winter.

"Dead in the winter"
They used to say.
"And it gets dark early."
Cold and dark.
You wanna get fuckin' warm
Anyway you can
You wanna get warm.

That sounds like you, Emile.

Yeah. Warmth. Warmth.

And Celia's not looking at the camera.

She's looking at the guy behind the camera.

Whoever the fuck that was
On the Polish/Ukrainian steppes,

Some short little Ukriainian Yid
Gnome she's looking at.

He made a living tearing up people's plumbing and roofs,
Louis did,

(He didn't make a living, pal.)

And he couldn't read a word in any language.
And his kids hated to work with him.
(Because of his temper with the tools
because nobody could tell him anything.)

DON'T TELL ME ANYTHING.
I DON'T WANT TO HEAR IT.

This with a strong Yiddish accent.

LEAVE IT ON THE GROUND AND GO HOME.

He had no patience with his kids.

"Pop had strong hands, the strongest hands
I ever saw," my father said,
And that was all he said.

So Louis avoided them,

Get away from me.

And he married five times.

(Gittel. Gittel Kanterman.)

Yeah, Gittel, on Belmont Avenue
East New York
With the pushcarts and the Yiddish
Where I rented a room.

Louis took you.

So Louis took you to Brooklyn?

Louis took me on the subway.
He never said a word.
We're on the subway to Rockaway Avenue.
The IRT,
Two gnomes.

He was leaning forward, his hands clasped in front of
him like somebody who knows how to ride the subway.

Emile?

Emile   Yeah?

WE GOT OFF AT ROCKAWAY AVENUE IN EAST NEW YORK AND
WALKED UP TO BELMONT AVENUE, OF WHICH I REMEMBER
NOTHING.

Emile?

OF THE WALK. I WAS FRIGHTENED.

Louis   Emile?

I HAD NO IDEA WHAT WAS GOING TO HAPPEN TO ME, AND
THERE WAS NO ONE TO HELP ME.

Louis   Emile?
Emile   Yeah?
Louis   You'll stay with this woman, Gittel, Gussie Kanterman.
She's a nice woman who I know very well. You'll have a
room in her apartment.
Emile   Sure.
Louis   It's okay?

Emile   Sure.

Louis   You'll have a place to sleep, a place to lie down.

Emile   Thank you.

Louis	A place to sleep, a place to lie down.

SAY SOMETHING ABOUT GITTEL.

Emile	Oh, it was cold and dark. Cold and dark in the winter.

NO, ABOUT GITTEL.

Emile	She never talked to me and I never saw her and the apartment had a smell. She stayed in her room and she sewed. Her husband, when he was alive, owned the store downstairs. Now she lived alone in her room and I lived alone in mine. My room was dark. It had a bed and a bureau and that's it. Downstairs were the pushcarts. A few blocks west was Rockaway Avenue. To the North was Pitkin. Loew's Pitkin was down the street. Amboy street was in the neighborhood, home of the Amboy Dukes.

Pause.

Emile	And that's the last memory I have of him, Louis.

Wait.

Emile	So I'll tell you the symptoms of depression, okay.

Okay. What are the symptoms of depression?

Emile	I hate cars and people and sound. And if you want to go to hell, go to a discount drugstore in America.

Wait.

Emile   TRY THAT SOMETIME, GO INTO A DISCOUNT DRUGSTORE IN AMERICA AND TELL ME YOU'RE NOT IN HELL.

Go.

Emile   *(Stepping downstage)* It's a very short distance
Between here and the grave.
There's almost no distance at all.

It's like a very fine veil.

We'll put that on your stone
Along with the double triangle.

Emile   Just don't put me in Glen Wild.

It's almost nothing at all.

PRIMO LEVI STEPS OUT OF HIS APARTMENT.

Emile   He comes out of his apartment and onto the stairs.

PRIMO LEVI COMES OUT OF HIS APARTMENT AND APPROACHES THE STAIRWAY.

Primo   No distance at all.

HE SEES: A LONG FALL.

HE HEARS: I CAN'T BEAR THIS ONE MOMENT LONGER. IF I
MOVE MY LEGS JUST A BIT, IF I LEAN OVER JUST A BIT, IT'S NO
DISTANCE AT ALL.

HE WAS A QUIET LITTLE GUY SOMEWHAT INTIMIDATED BY HIS
WIFE.

Primo   People seem strange to me, strangely aggressive in their
waking sleep, determined to go on living.

I WILL NOT GO SHOPPING ANYMORE. I REFUSE TO SHOP. NO
MORE RITE AID, NO MORE WALGREENS. THAT'S IT FOR ME.

Primo   Hostile to one another, in competition with one another,
and disappointed.
In one another.

So so so so

PRIMO MAKES A MOVE.

Primo   I wish for solidarity with the Jews,
For redemption of the Jews,
For an understanding of History
And peace in the holy land.

Let that be for me and for you.

Primo   Amen.

SO, EVERYTHING IN THE WORLD CONTINUES
AND ON AND ON IT GOES.

BURY ME IN LOS ANGELES IN A JEWISH GRAVE.

"EMILE BRASMAN, COMEDIAN," ON THE DOUBLE TRIANGLE.

ONE GOES UP, ONE GOES DOWN.

ONE WHAT?

ONE TRIANGLE GOES UP, THE OTHER DOWN.

WHO CARES?

I DON'T.

I DON'T CARE EITHER.

I DON'T.

SO, FINE.

Primo   A tiny bit of spittle forms in the corner of my mouth. Deep wrinkles cluster round my eyes and heavy bags lie beneath them. Lines of worry, bags of grief. What is this thing with feet and arms and two eyes? With holes for eating and shitting. That automatically grows decrepit and useless. In the grip of time, on the edge of a precipice. There we fall and we never return.

WE FALL.

I DON'T GIVE A RAT'S ASS.

ME, NEITHER.

NOT ME.

So, fine.

GREAT.

PRIMO SAYS GOODBYE
BECAUSE IT WASN'T ENOUGH TO HAVE WITNESSED
TO HAVE WITNESSED
WITNESSED THE HORRORS OF LIFE ON EARTH
LIFE ON EARTH

Primo   GOODBYE.

Stop!

Emile   Why?

Because there's a certain thing called determination.

Louis had it.

Louis had it and you have it.
It's called determination,
Sturdy determination.
You can see it in his face.

Louis Brasman had it,
And you're a Brasman,
So you have it, too.

It's called sturdy determination.

Emile   But for what?

Determination for what?

To survive.

But he's got that sly look,
He's got that sly and knowing look
Of a peasant Jew from the steppes,
Who knows about animal survival,
And sex.

That's right!

Unlike Primo, who had his mother and his wife
In the same apartment.

That's right!

Who more or less ran his life for him.

That's right!

You have him in you, too,
You have Primo,
The quiet gentle Jew and lover of words
Who bore witness.

And then there's another guy,
He doesn't want anything to do with anybody.
He just wants to stay home alone and watch television.

Who?

You.

Me.

You.

Emile   Oh.

So, go.

Emile   Go?

Go.

There, go into the audience, go on. *(EMILE goes)*

There you go.

Thank you.

Don't bother anybody, don't disturb anybody.

Emile   I WON'T.

Don't talk to anybody, don't touch anybody.

Emile   I WON'T.

Don't look at anybody, don't wink at anybody.

Emile   I won't.

You're always winking at people. Especially women. Don't do that anymore.

Emile   Okay!

It's social insecurity.

Emile   Stop talking to me. I'M NOT ON STAGE.

Get over it.

Give it up.

Drop it.

Let it go.

Surrender.

Emile   NOTHING TO IT.

Good.

Fine.

Great.

Mazel tov.

Emile   PAUL CELAN.

Yes?

No?

What?

Emile   A PLAY. DO A PLAY.

Who?

What?

Where?

When?

Emile   PAUL CELAN IN THE BLACK FOREST.

With Heidegger?

With Heidegger?

Emile   PAUL CELAN IN THE BLACK FOREST WITH THE GNOMIC NAZI
HEIDEGGER.

Begin.

Emile   No, you, you be Paul.
Fine.

Emile   Go.
Paul   So, you live in a hut? You live in this hut in the forest?
Heidegger   I do. Yes. This is where I live.
Paul   You are a stupid motherfucker if ever I saw one.

Heidegger	Excuse me?
Paul	I said you are a stupid, no-account, motherfucker.
Emile	STOP.

Why?

What's wrong?

Emile	You can't say stupid, no-account motherfucker. Start over.

Sure.

You bet.

Emile	Go.
Paul	I have come to tell you.
Heidegger	Speak.
Paul	Of your emptiness and falsehood.
Heidegger	I say only what I think. I think what I say.
Paul	You have no being.
Heidegger	Being speaks German. I speak German.
Paul	You are only the squawk of yourself in the dark.
Heidegger	I won't hear that.
Paul	Yes, you hide somewhere in your head where there is no reality.
Heidegger	And you?
Paul	I am a true poet.
Heidegger	Yes? What makes you so?
Paul	I know silence.
Heidegger	Silence you know, but me you will never know.
Paul	Because you are not.

Heidegger	I say I am.
Paul	It is a hollow statement, without meaning. Empty words.
Emile	STOP.

What is it?

What now?

Emile	HE SHOULDN'T SAY I KNOW SILENCE. WHY DOES HE SAY, I KNOW SILENCE? HE SHOULD SAY SOMETHING ELSE THERE.

All right.

Thank you.

Emile	START AGAIN.

Well.

Fine and good.

Heidegger	I heard you read your poems.
Paul	Yes?
Heidegger	Something insistent in your voice.
Paul	Yes?
Heidegger	A bit much, perhaps.
Paul	And something else also.
Heidegger	What else?
Paul	Silence.
Heidegger	Are you all right?

Paul	Ha, ha, ha.
Heidegger	What's wrong with you?
Paul	They do experiments on me. You are aware of this. Doctors.
Heidegger	I was aware.
Paul	And now?
Heidegger	And now?
Paul	Are you aware now?
Heidegger	Yes. And you?
Paul	I'm all right now.
Heidegger	Can you think?
Paul	I think in poems. I think with poems.

SILENCE.

Heidegger	Shall we go for a walk?
Paul	The true names of things.
Heidegger	In German.
Paul	I have saved the soul of the German tongue.
Heidegger	We should go for a walk.
Paul	Do you think so?
Heidegger	Yes, it will help you, brace you.
Paul	Oh.

OH OH OH OH OH

Heidegger	Nothing to be afraid of.

NO NO NO NO NO

Heidegger	Shall we?
Paul	Ha, ha. Please, ha ha.

They exit.

(To audience) We'll come back to this when they return from their walk.

Emile	REST IN PEACE, PAUL, REST IN PEACE.

PRIMO approaches the stairway.

PRIMO crosses the threshold of his apartment in Turin.

Primo	My wife interrupts me when speaking with others, sometimes on the phone, sometimes in my home. She lectures me about my duty and chastises me for my depression. The fact that I am a literary man, well-known to the world, an intellectual, a chemist—these make no impression on her. Nor that I am a survivor and have borne witness—this has no effect on the tension of daily living. My mother also, dying slowly, demands my complete devotion. Outside, on the streets of the city, people seem to be living for no reason at all except for sheer momentum. I'm no longer certain of how to greet them and I have lost touch with the sense of what they are thinking. Elsewhere, Jew-hatred grows unabated by intelligence or remorse, and, in fact, the Muslims have sworn death to us everywhere. What good then—what good is it then—what good...?

PRIMO pauses for an instant, facing the stairs.

Primo   They're coming back. Paul Celan and Heidegger are
               returning from their walk on the cold wet moor, and here
               they are.

Paul   I just have to tell you, sir, most of what you say is bullshit
               and the rest is empty rhetoric. The German spirit and all
               that crap.

Heidegger Let me have your coat. Yes. What did you say?

Paul   Nothing.

Heidegger Yes, it's cold. Let's make a fire.

*HEIDEGGER is pretending that he hasn't heard PAUL
CELAN. CELAN is talking out of the side of his mouth. He's
a nervous wreck.*

Make yourself comfortable, please.

*PAUL receives this comment with alarm. He is never
comfortable. Outside it is cold and grey and dusk is
coming fast.*

Paul   Thank you.

*He says he is frightened. They are deep, deep into the
Black Forest, in Heidegger's gnomic hut in the forest.*

Heidegger I was very impressed with your knowledge of flora and
               fauna.

Paul   I am a poet.

Heidegger	First there are flowers, you see, and everything follows from that.
Paul	I beg your pardon? No.

NO NO NO NO NO NO

Heidegger	First the flowers, and then the insects to carry the pollen. You see?
Paul	Insects. Yes, insects.
Heidegger	And then eventually trees, and animals.
Paul	Yes, animals.

He can't think of anything else to say. He wants to know about Rector Heidegger's Nazi silence. He wants to be asked forgiveness. He wants to strangle the man and throw him down the well. Instead, he says:

Paul	I wrote something in your book.
Heidegger	Tell me what you wrote.
Paul	"Into the hut-book, looking at the well-star, with a hope for a coming word in the heart. On 25 July, 1967 Paul Celan."
Heidegger	Thank you so much.
Paul	Please.
Heidegger	Are you all right?
Paul	Yes, of course.

But of course he's not all right. He feels intimidated and his heart rate is up. Heidegger is a cunning German peasant with a strong stare.

Heidegger	You know more than I do.
Paul	Yes, it's true.
Heidegger	About flora and fauna.
Paul	Yes, in five or six languages.

YES YES YES

Paul	In German, in English, in Italian, in French, in Hebrew and in Russian.

YES YES YES YES YES

Paul	Middle High German. Romanian.
Heidegger	Yes, of course.
Paul	The naming of things. As they are. Truly.
Heidegger	Have you a question?
Paul	A question?
Heidegger	Have you a question you wish to ask?

He must be joking, this evil philosopher. Why should Paul wish to ask a question? Paul Celan is more intelligent, and more sincere, than Heidegger.

Paul	The True Names. THE TRUTH SAY.
	Silence.

Silence.

AND PRIMO LEVI STANDS FACING THE ABYSS.

AND PAUL CELAN.

And Paul Celan in the cold and the wet of that stupid hut in the darkness of the Black Forest of unspeakable horror.

And he has to finish the conversation and get up to leave and finish the conversation and get up to leave in all sanity and go back to Paris and the Seine and finish the conversation and get up to leave in all sanity and go back to Paris and the Seine where he stands accused.

As if he could bear it.

As if it were bearable.

While Emile drools spittle onto the floor. Emile drools spittle onto the floor because he's gradually losing control of his functions and his heart rate is up and he's battling depression.

Emile   So so so so so

EMILE is drooling spittle out of the corner of his mouth.

Emile   G-d bless Paul Celan!

Who wrote, soon after:

ARNICA, EYEBRIGHT, THE
DRINK FROM THE WELL WITH THE

STAR-DIE ON TOP,

IN THE
HUT,

INTO THE BOOK
WHOSE NAME DID IT TAKE IN
BEFORE MINE?
THE LINE WRITTEN INTO
THIS BOOK ABOUT
A HOPE, TODAY,
FOR A THINKER'S
(UN
DELAYED COMING)
WORD
IN THE HEART.

I just have to say, Emile.

Emile   What?

We're not interested in this kind of thing in America.

Emile   Eh, what?
This kind of poetry or this kind of concern.

Emile   Say?

We like money and sports over here.

Emile	I like money, I like sports.
	We like a drama you can understand. That's okay.
Emile	I like drama.
	We like a funny situation, a snappy line.
Emile	So do I, so do I.
	We're not into a whole lot of grief here.
Emile	Me neither, me neither.
	Are you just going to stand there and imitate everything that happens? Is that your modus operandi? Somebody says something and you immediately agree?
Emile	No no no no no
	That's what you do continually.
Emile	Sure.
	You're intimidated. You have no mind of your own.
Emile	I see that.
	Don't agree with me so readily.

Emile	I won't.
	Thank G-d you're not six feet under. Rejoice!
Emile	That's why it's good to be young and run about.
	I'm so glad.
Emile	I'm so glad I knew Brooklyn alleys and rooftops and wires across the sky and vacant lots and the rumbling subway, and woke up in the country morning with birds singing in the summer of '45.
	I'm so glad.
Emile	I'm so glad I could play ball and play well and fight hard with my fists.
	Very good.
Emile	Because there were a lot of sadists and bullies in the neighborhood.
	Good, Emile.
Emile	I'm so glad—
	WHAT HAPPENED TO PAUL?
Emile	Paul?

WHAT HAPPENED TO PAUL CELAN?

Emile   SO SO SO SO

WHAT HAPPENED?

SO HE GOES BACK, HE GOES BACK TO HIS APARTMENT IN
PARIS, ON THE FIFTH FLOOR, NEAR THE PONT MIRABEAU, AND
TO HIS WIFE, GISÈLE.

Paul   What can you expect from people like that? They are
always right, always justified.

Gisèle   Who, darling? Who are you talking about?

Paul   You know.

Gisèle   No, I'm not so sure.

Paul   The German literary establishment, Gisèle.

Gisèle   They're being very nice to you, I thought.

Paul   Yes, I'm an alibi for them.

Gisèle   I understand, but don't let it ruin your life.

HIS LIFE HAD ALREADY BEEN RUINED, BECAUSE THE GERMANS
HAD MURDERED HIS PARENTS. ON THE STEPPES OF THE
UKRAINE.

CORRECTO, EXACTO.

FOR NO FUCKING REASON. BUT NOW IT WAS ADDITIONALLY
RUINED. IT WAS ADDITIONALLY RUINED BY AN ACCUSER,
WHOSE NAME WAS GOLL.

Gisèle	Goll?
Paul	What can you expect from a name like GOLL?
Gisèle	Not much, I don't expect much. You translated him, didn't you?
Paul	Yes.
Gisèle	You tried to help him.
Paul	Yes.
Gisèle	And now he turns on you.
Paul	Yes.
Gisèle	That's how it goes with people.
Paul	Yes.
Gisèle	Another case of literary envy, literary hysteria.
Paul	Yes.
Gisèle	Say something else, why don't you.
Paul	Yes.
Gisèle	Where are you?
Paul	My father.
Gisèle	You didn't betray your father.
Paul	He held my hand through the wire. And then I ran away.
Gisèle	What else could you do? (*He weeps*) Paul?

So so so so so

Anyway.
Don't cry, Emile.

What are you crying about?

Emile	My dad.

Dad, Dad, Dad

Emile   Matinee Joe. He don't know.

JOE takes a stance next to EMILE: arms crossed, feet straight, head up. A tough guy from Brooklyn.

Joe   Yeah?

Emile   He was restless and he was absent and he was prone to accidents. But I thought he was good-natured, basically, only there was something wrong with his head, and there was something wrong with his sex. So, anyway, I don't think we ever had a single conversation about anything at all. After a while, I felt superior, and he was afraid of me.

What else could you do? *(He weeps)* Emile?

Emile   And then I ran away.

What else could you do?

First you didn't finish school, and then you took drugs.
You became a DRUG ADDICT.
Is that correct? Even though the gnome, Louis, brought
you to Belmont Avenue so you could have a place to lie
down, and go to college, even then you failed.

Well, what did you expect?

I mean, come on.

Emile   He didn't say a single fucking word, Louis. Not one.

SO WHAT?

(He has no idea what NORMAL is. He has no idea of NOR-
MAL.)

Emile   Are we talking about me again? Are you referring to me?

You know we are, Emile.

And it didn't help Primo, did it?

Emile	What didn't?
	Drugs, stupid. DRUGS, DRUGS, DRUGS.
	So, anyway. It didn't help Primo one bit.
Emile	*(As PAUL)* What can you expect from these people?
	The drugs didn't help him, and people couldn't help him. So that's it. That's that. You get the impression the sun never shines over there. Don't you? You get that impression, of endless darkness, endless cold? In Europe? In eastern Europe? On the steppes of the Ukraine, where the sun never shines?
	So, anyway.
Paul	Perhaps I should live alone, darling.
	(Her name is Gisèle. What a beautiful name. Gisèle.)
Gisèle	But how will you take care of yourself? You don't know how to take care of yourself.
Paul	I'm hoping for hope.
Gisèle	But what do you mean by that? You don't know what you mean by that.
Paul	I need to be able to concentrate, to make my poems. Then everything is all right.
Gisèle	Nothing is all right. There is only a poem. And still they persecute you. It's not enough that you survived, now they

	must torment you.
Paul	Then what do you propose?
Gisèle	Let's go to America, or to Israel. Let's forget the European project altogether.
Paul	I can't do that.
Gisèle	Why not?
Paul	My language is German.
Gisèle	You know many languages. You are a translator.
Paul	It is the language of my being.
Gisèle	Well, that's fine, it's up to you.
Paul	I am writing many poems and they are beyond dispute.
Gisèle	Yes, but I can't live with you anymore. So, it's up to you. I can't make you happy, so I'll go.
Paul	No no no. I'll try.
Gisèle	You can't try. You say you try but it's impossible for you. You live in another world. It's not my world. There is a boundary there, there is a wall. You don't smile through it. You can't see through it. You can't hear. You say strange things.
Paul	What can you expect from these people, with their vanity and their jealousy?
Gisèle	There, you see. Like that.
Paul	I was speaking of the Golls.
Gisèle	Yes, but I wasn't, was I?
Paul	I mention them as an example.
Gisèle	The Golls. Stupid, mean-spirited, conscienceless Yids.
Paul	No, because there's so little happiness handed out they didn't get any, so they want some credit, they want some attention.
Gisèle	They want what's coming to you.

Paul	That's how they are. That's what I mean.
Gisèle	Senseless and stupid. You see one of these creepy European intellectuals and you run screaming into the night.
Paul	Which ones?
Gisèle	You know which ones. Why did you say that? Empty rhetoric, Paul, because you're frightened, and you say things.
Paul	I meant which ones, which intellectuals?
Gisèle	The ones who accuse you of plagiarism, who find fault, who are never happy about a Jewish genius.
Paul	And they don't get the facts right.
Gisèle	I know that, Paul.
Paul	My parents were not killed at Auschwitz, I do not have a sister.
Gisèle	I know that very well.
Paul	They were killed in a work camp on the Ukrainian steppes.
Gisèle	Yes, I know.
Paul	There were many nice Jewish boys in Chernowitz, and I was one of them.
Gisèle	Yes. You don't have to tell me that.
Paul	I only say it, because—
Gisèle	You're intimidated and you can't think. Isn't that so?
	CORRECTO, EXACTO.
Paul	Well, I don't know.
Gisèle	You DO know. I know you know.
Paul	I'm sorry.
Gisèle	No, you're not sorry. You're getting ready to have a fit. Isn't that so?
Paul	No, no, no, no.

Gisèle	Yes, it's true. You'll throw chairs. You'll scream and yell. Well, I'm not going to put up with it.
Paul	You're so beautiful it takes my breath away.
Gisèle	Just because mankind is so disappointing, and history has no meaning.
Paul	Yes?
Gisèle	That's no reason not to be nice, not to enjoy yourself and your family.
Paul	Did you hear what I said?
Gisèle	Yes. And it intimidates you, it paralyzes you, it stops you in your tracks, so you can't make love to me, because I'm too beautiful and rare. Beautiful and rare and flesh and blood, the stuff of life, more and more life. That's what Heidegger was immune to, wasn't it?, the flesh and blood messiness of life, yes, and that's what you're sick of, and I don't blame you, I just don't want to be part of it, so I'm going.
Paul	Go.

GO GO GO GO GO GO

Paul	I love you.
Gisèle	No, you don't. You love words and ideas. You love the German language. That's why you went to that old Nazi in his hut, to verify the words.
Paul	I do love you.
Gisèle	Yes, but you're broken. They broke you. I know what that means now. You're a broken man.

THEY GAVE THE MOTHERFUCKER SHOCK TREATMENTS.

They gave him electric shocks,
And he had a shrill nervous laugh.

HA HA HA HA

That startled his friends.

Paul   "The doctors have much to answer for, every day is a
burden, what you call, 'my own health' is probably never
to be, the damage reaches to the core of my existence...
they've healed me to pieces!"

FUCKING BARBARIANS!

So so so so, anyway, as I was saying.

Emile So I'm looking at this photo of Mom and Dad. And they're standing in a doorway in the cold, in the Catskills. They have no home exactly. They are on the verge of homelessness, they're always on the verge of destitution.

How could that actually happen?

There are people who are destitute all over America.

Why don't you write about that?

All over America and all over the world.

AND?

And there's nothing to be done.

WHY NOT?

Because people are here to serve the earth. People are here to serve the earth. They are not here to be rich or to be poor, they are here to serve the earth. But of course they're not doing it. That's not what they're doing. They're destroying the earth instead. Stripping it of life, of its air and its water, stripping it bare. So what do you expect? What can you expect from people?

WHO IS THIS PERSON?

Who cares if they're rich? Who cares if they're poor?

NOT ME.

Of course not. Because they're not doing their job. They are destroying nature. They are destroying nature and they die like dogs. They spaz out and they gurgle and they cough up blood. The blood turns black and the bugs eat it. Bugs like we've never seen before, with big mouths.

Emile　So, anyway.

Just drinking up the black blood.

TELL THIS PERSON TO SHUT UP.

Emile   As I was saying.

Big mouths with creepy teeth, and they munch and they munch. And they suck the blood up.

THANK YOU.

With, like, straws in their nostrils or something.

I'M LEAVING.

Which is the end of the earth as we know it. (*Pause*) Okay, I'll step offstage for a moment.

GOOD.

And then you can talk, Emile.

GOOD.

So long. *(Exits)*

Emile   I'm looking at my parents, at my flesh and blood, and my mother is grinning at the camera, and my father, the street guy, stands stolidly staring straight ahead into the camera also. I don't know who was holding the camera. It's the winter. It looks like winter in the fifties.

WHERE WERE YOU?

Emile   Don't know where I was. I was running around with a ball.

WHAT ARE THEY SAYING?
WHAT ARE THEY THINKING?

Emile   I don't know.

(Reentering) What's the matter?

IT'S HIM!

What's the matter with him?

HE'S HYSTERICAL.

Leave him alone.

TELL HIM TO STOP CRYING!

I can't do that.

WHY NOT?

It's his perogative. He can cry if he wants to.

SHUT UP!

Maybe you better go.

I'M GOING.

Go go go go go

I'M GONE. *(Exits)*

Okay. He *(she)* will be back. Don't worry about it.

(Off) HE'S NOT WORRIED ABOUT IT.

I just want to say, you know. You know. I hate to use that
locution. I'm sorry. Most people don't think about suicide.
They don't think about it at all. Maybe teenagers. I don't
know, really. Maybe not all teenagers. Anyway, most people, most people just live their lives and they think everything is okay. They have an idea about it and they think
it's okay. Is that right?

(Off) No!

I think it is. Emile?

Emile   Yes, I agree with you.

You all right?

Emile   I'm fine.

As I was saying, most people on the Earth are enjoying themselves.

(Off) Bullshit!

Emile   Yeah, I agree with him *(her)*.

I guess that's not true.

Emile   People suffer.

So, as I was saying. Paul had been in the river ten days maybe, floating in the river.

Paul   I read: the Open ones carry/ the stone behind their eye,/ it knows you,/ come the Sabbath.

Beautiful, very beautiful.

Paul   Heidegger was there. I said, "Pay attention, you. You have no attention."

And he?

Heidegger   Paul Celan is a sick man. He will never recover.

Paul, is there another world?

Paul   Yes, the world of poetry, the world of a poem, which I call, "actualized language." This means: there is another level of reality, touching another quality of attention. Which is what is meant by Being. It is in the Psalms. In the Book of Job. I tried to talk to Heidegger more than once. He didn't understand. He had no understanding. He had no real attention. It was all mental for him. He lacked sorrow, and couldn't help me at all. The world of a poem demands attention. The world of Being demands attention. Attention creates the world.

Primo   And so, and so. I stand. The body impulses. I go and go. I feel myself here, here in the present. I watch myself. I fall. I watch…

And so and so,

This must be the end now.

But no—

(Reentering) Hey! Where's Schwartz? What happened to Schwartz?

You're still wondering What happened to Schwartz?

(Who me? Not me!)

Tell! Tell!

So I go up to Vegas to see my uncle Saul

Schwartz,
My half uncle Saul Schwartz.

He's glad to see me
After sixty years or more—
He bought my baby carriage and a layette
When I was born.

"A layette"
Shaking his head
Like it was an unfortunate situation.

So so so
What happened to Schwartz?

Saul   I never wanted to know him,
          I never wanted to see him,
          And she wouldn't talk about him.

(Oh, no!)

Saul   But I heard he was a streetcar conductor
          In Brooklyn, Schwartz.

WHAT? AND YOU NEVER?

Saul   No, I never did.

So so so Why?

Saul	I didn't want nothing to do with him. Mama would never mention him. She would only cry. Until I was three I lived in one of those, what do you call them? Like a day care?
Emile	Orphanage?
Saul	In an orphanage. I remember, Mama would come and slip me candy through the bars.
Emile	What happened to Schwartz?
Saul	He came from a rich family. He was a Hungarian, from Hungary. Mama was a farm girl, from Pinsk, in Poland. He took her to Hungary to meet his family. They said, What are you doing? You can't marry this poor person, Celia Zabrowski! So he took her to America. And there he left her, in Brooklyn, and then came along Louis, three years later.
Emile	How did they get married?
Saul	Oh, it was brokered. Here was a woman, a beautiful woman, with a three-year-old, who was me. and she doesn't have a husband, who was Schwartz. And here comes Louis Brasman to Brooklyn, he's an illegal immigrant, he's a widower with my brother, Harry. My half brother, Harry. So, it was arranged. I'll tell you a story. There was a box of letters. Mama used to write to her father, and their next door neighbor there became the Pime Minister of Israel. I can't remember his name now.

Emile   Ben Gurion?

Saul   No, not him. But her father in Pinsk couldn't read or write, so the neighbor would do it and later he became the Prime Minister, this neighbor. So the government of Israel would like to have those letters. But Mama destroyed them, and she tore up some pictures.

Emile   You never saw them?

Saul   No, I never did.

(OH, NO!)

Emile   I'm sorry.

Saul   I'm not sorry. Mama cried a lot over it. She was very emotional. Very bitter. They had an apartment on West End Avenue, after the war.

Emile   Schwartz?

Saul   Yeah, the family, and I was going to see them.

Emile   And did you?

Saul   No, I never went.

(OH, NO!)

Emile	And Louis?
Saul	What?
Emile	What was he like?

Soft-spoken UNCLE SAUL *shrugs and smiles. He never wants to say a bad word.*

Saul	He wasn't much help to Mama. He was never home. He was always going someplace.
Emile	I heard he liked the ladies.
Saul	I think so. And he wore three pairs of pants. So you could never get any money out of him! *(Laughs)*
Emile	He was from a town called Tomashbele, in the Ukraine, am I right?

(TO-MOSH-BA-LEH.)

Saul	Yes, he had *Lansmen* from there, in the Catskills.
Emile	Aha!
Saul	Sure. People he knew from that town. *Tomashbele.* He was a very good coppersmith. He made a still, a copper still, you know? He was a bootlegger, he made vodka with that thing. Powerful strong vodka. And he was a very

good dancer. He could dance the Kazaktsky very well. Your grandfather.

(This is the end now, this must be the End.)

YES. DARK, VERY DARK.

WE HAVE TO LOOK
AT THE HUMAN SITUATION
AS IT IS, AS IT IS

ARMS AND LEGS AND BACK
DISINTEGRATING
AGING AND DEPRESSION

CAPABLE OF ANYTHING
MACHINES

WHERE IS THE GOOD?

SO SO SO SO SO

SO WHERE'S THE GOOD?

IT'S IN YOU, EMILE
EVEN THOUGH, EVEN THOUGH

IT'S HARD TO FIND

IT'S HARD TO FIND.

SPEAK.

Emile   Hail Czernowitz, home place of Celan (born Antschel), and of Aaron Applefeld (born on the same street)! Hail Turin, founder of Primo—great lineages of Praise—Praise and Bow.

PRAISE AND BOW

PRAISING AND BOWING NO MATTER WHAT

AT THE MOMENT OF TORTUROUS DEATH
UNDEFEATED

PRAISE G-D, MOTHERFUCKER
THEY CRIED,
PRAISE G-D, YOU PIECE OF SHIT!

THE GREAT LINEAGES OF MASTERS
BLESS THEM ALL
AMEN.

BLACKOUT.

The End

Temple Dog
by Wesley Walker

Temple Dog *was produced at the Lillian Theater by Padua Playwrights in July 2005, under the playwright's direction, with the following cast:*

Katarina: *Mari Ueda*
Randolph: *Andy Hopper*
Philip: *Gray Palmer*

An earlier version of the play was presented by Sharon's Farm at Wattles Park in Los Angeles in April 2005. The play was directed by the playwright, with the following cast:

Katarina: *Mari Ueda*
Randolph: *Corbett Ward*
Philip: *Seth Macari*

Characters

Katarina

Randolph

Philip

Scene

A park in Los Angeles, nighttime.

RANDOLPH, a young man, stands alone. Behind him,
KATARINA, a pale Japanese woman, covered in torn gauze,
rises from the earth.

Katarina You have some interesting feeling. This is good day for you. I'm no stranger. My name is Katarina Witt.

Randolph Katarina Witt?

Katarina The skater from so long ago. You see me on TV, cutting the Carmen, icy spectacle. My face is white to tell of shrinking soul.

Randolph Philip, my friend Philip... is looking... Is there a temple...?

Katarina Yes! There is temple.

Randolph He's been gone a while...

Katarina Yes! It's so yesterday here. So many good day, but all of them gone.

Randolph We're doing the Noir Tour... The Death Tour, whatever. Hollywood Forever, or... and... Black Dahlia...

Katarina So exciting all the dead people! *(Pause)* Well, I tell you, it really has been great!

Randolph I told him don't leave me here.

Katarina I try very hard to listen to you.

Randolph Yes.

Katarina Because what you say is difficult to hear. Is this true?

Randolph Yes.

Katarina That's what makes a friend. Anyway, I go. They want me under the world. *(Pause)* Katarina Witt, champion! Under the world, where everyone works hard.

KATARINA exits. Lights change. PHILIP, a slightly older man, appears.

Randolph	Hey, Philip.
Philip	I don't like you. I don't like you anymore, man.
Randolph	I got... scared. Sorry.
Philip	Timidity... and feebleness of purpose will... Eat this. *(Hands RANDOLPH a rice ball)* It's a rice ball. Stay here— I'll come back for you later.
Randolph	I'd rather...
Philip	You're a waste, man. Wait here.

PHILIP exits. Lights change. KATARINA appears.

Katarina	Hello again! You must know who I am.
Randolph	OK.
Katarina	They kick my leg; take my skate. Rearrange my apartment. So cruel! And for what? To scare an innocent person?

Sound of distant, distorted wolf howl.

Randolph	What's that sound?
Katarina	This is temple dog.
Randolph	I guess I never saw you skate, on account of I hate that shit, but your name, though, is kind of...
Katarina	Well under here there are many people... so tired. Because the assignment. We lift dirt. But we keep the sunshine demeanor. Else they tell us we are not who we want to be. I want to be Katarina, world skater, 1984.
Randolph	Yeah, well, we wanted to take some time, see the tragic— Philip did—of L.A. You know Kenneth Anger? So many people are famous and then what have you and they're

	dead. We went to the Ambassador. And now a temple—I hope so, anyway—Shinto, which is Japanese.
Katarina	I will not lie to you anymore.
Randolph	What?
Katarina	I will not lie to you anymore about your friend. About Philip. I know his boss, I met his boss. Very friendly man.
Randolph	Philip... Philip's all right...
Katarina	Philip, yes, and now where can he be? His boss—increasingly friendly. But I say just you wait. We have a river under here; it's black oil. We have a language just for television. If I'm famous, it's because in me you see something you wish for yourself.
Randolph	I wish I were a... larger... man.
Katarina	Sure! But this thing I cannot hide this thing I heard... It's a shame.

Sound of wolf howl.

Randolph	What's that sound?
Katarina	Temple dog. His boss say, "Hey, Katarina. I want you make me new religion." No, I say! But he's homosexual.
Randolph	Who's homosexual?
Katarina	Under here, each of us is famous. Who do you want to be? He says, "Make me religion, I bring you special gift." *(She begins to retreat)* Watch me! Katarina—famous, and her very long wrist! Auf Wiedersehen!

KATARINA *hides. Lights change.* PHILIP *enters.*

Philip	You're weak, man. *(Pause)* I wasn't trying to kiss you earlier.

Randolph	I know, Philip.
Philip	I was… showing you my mouth. And the emotion.
Randolph	*(Makes a few halfhearted feints toward unwrapping the seaweed from his rice ball)* Am I…? Am I supposed to…?
Philip	I thought I knew who you were. It's disappointing. Finish your rice ball and join us. *(Pause)* We're over there.
Randolph	Ok. Who's over there? *(No answer)* You said, "we're over there." *(Pause)* Is there a dog…?
Philip	Just a temple. And me, Philip. Your friend Philip. Philip.

Exit PHILIP. *Lights change.* KATARINA *enters.*

Katarina	Hello again from under the world. I just won competition! Competition who's most perfect. I'm most perfect again! But also I am spy. In Deutschland, there is gossip. You smell fish. The work—it's very tiring.
Randolph	For some reason, Katarina, I disappoint people.
Katarina	I skate in perfect circle. If the day get longer I explode. We dig under here—so many mound! Bury corpse head, bury corpse head. I can't feel sorry for myself.
Randolph	Here's a question: what's Shinto?
Katarina	It is believed that things have "kami" or spirit, if you love a tree, this tree has spirit or a solemn rock, but also there are ancestor and each year you come back. This is the festival Oban. You make a paper antelope. Wait! I hear singing! OK, underground is a feast! I must go! Auf Wiedersehen!
Randolph	'Bye!

KATARINA *exits. Lights change.* PHILIP *enters.*

Philip	Give me the rice ball, Randolph. *(RANDOLPH hesitates, then does so. Pause)* Let me have your shirt.
Randolph	Uh... I just want to be who I want to be.

PHILIP looks at him. RANDOLPH acquiesces. He removes his shirt, hands it to PHILIP.

Philip	Shoes.
Randolph	... In the end, a man is a man. And none of his acts diminish him. Right?
Philip	I was supposed to brandish my mouth. Let me have your pants. You were supposed to finish the rice.

RANDOLPH removes his pants, hands them to PHILIP.

Randolph	Well, you know what?
Philip	Here... Place the belt... Put the belt around your ankles.

RANDOLPH puts the belt around his ankles. PHILIP hands RANDOLPH the rice ball.

Eat the fucking rice ball!

PHILIP cinches the belt tight, knocking RANDOLPH to the ground.

I'm tired of this shit!

PHILIP exits. Lights change. KATARINA enters.

Katarina	It was a sad feast. Our hero died today. We celebrate him with the folding chair. His head was gone.
Randolph	Philip said yeah... Let's go out find the crime scenes, whatever, the various loci of pain. I was barely even into it!
Katarina	Philip, yes, I know his boss. His hands are very hairy. He wants to start a religion from me; I say no way.
Randolph	He doesn't have a boss, Katarina. Philip's on disability. For his foot.
Katarina	No religion; no figurine. I want to live here always. "Please," he says, "we worship you with bumble bees." No, I say. "Please, we bring you ripe encounters."
Randolph	Katarina?
Katarina	Yes?
Randolph	Katarina!
Katarina	Yes.
Randolph	Am I being held accountable for something? *(No answer)* We'd been driving, you know, in his old Camaro, he'd shown me the hotels, the famous bars, I was bored, he knew I was bored. Then—suddenly, I was by a hunger seized. Show me the death place of that handsome starlet, I said. The one without a name. Show me where her blood was spilt, her jewels taken. So that I may wear again the murderer's gloves and wear again his mind. I want to be the one who killed her. That grave man... see his hands upon the neck? Throttle... throttle... choke the life from this too pure thing. Live again in her tears. Where was she murdered, Philip?! Show me! Show me! And lo, I don her dangerous panties. And stride in regalia by her windowed outlook. Pride, fortune! The raiment of the victim: I look so good in it. That's what I said to him. That's what I said to Philip. And then, you

know, he touched my shoulder... tried to kiss me. So, as it were, I got out of the car. Something changed between us, I guess it's clear to you now. Yes, we all do things we're not proud of. Yes, we live our lives away without knowing even that one thing for which we hunger.

Katarina If you know who you are, friend, before you die, then there is no reason to do it. *(Pause. She turns)* I skate in perfect circle; no one knows me but ice. Every memory is my memory; every circle: me.

KATARINA exits. Lights change. PHILIP enters.

Randolph What's that, Philip?

Philip It's a paring knife.

Randolph It's a...? It's kind of small.

Philip Someone's asking for your foreskin. *(Pause)* I have to get your foreskin.

Randolph Wait.

Philip Yeah.

Sound of wolf howl. PHILIP lunges. They struggle. Blood.

Randolph Aghh!

PHILIP triumphs. PHILIP exits with foreskin.

Randolph Aggh!

KATARINA appears. Wolf howling continues.

Katarina	Great is the pity. Copious the tears. The man was not who he want to be. They tell me take the meager token, but I say no, for new religion this will not do.
Randolph	What's that sound?
Katarina	"Look," they say, "we circumcise." I say no. Kill the Christian, cut off head. In his mind are many flower. We kill these out with vinegar.
Randolph	Katarina… I'm going to be OK, right? I'm going to be OK.
Katarina	Cut off head, put vinegar. Make the world happen.

PHILIP enters. He carries a bloody sack, a human head inside. RANDOLPH, stricken with recognition, looks on.

Tears, tears, tears. For who among us pure?

PHILIP offers the sack to KATARINA. She accepts it, embracing it to her bosom as if it were a child. The men watch her. The wolf cries grow more frantic as lights fade.

The End

The Wasps
by Guy Zimmerman

The Wasps *was produced at the Lillian Theater by Padua Playwrights in July 2005, under the playwright's direction, with the following cast:*

Barbara: Niamh McCormally
Jenna: Annie Weirich

Characters

Jenna and **Barbara:** Marie Antoinette twins from Texas.

Scene

The great hall of an abandoned observatory/laboratory in the hills above an American city, after the end of the age of oil.

In black, the low, sinister rumble of an oil pump. Lights
slowly rise on JENNA *and* BARBARA, *wearing tattered*
evening gowns, their arms in chains. Around them is a
vast, dark space—a former ballroom or banquet hall. The
sound of the pump slowly fades. They look out.

Jenna	Hi, I like your crown
Barbara	Thanks, it's new
Jenna	Hi, I like your dress
Barbara	Thanks, it's new
Jenna	Hi, I like your pink earrings
Barbara	Thanks, they're new
Jenna	Hello, I like your shoes
Barbara	Thanks, they're new
Jenna	Hello, I like your red lipstick
Barbara	Thanks, it's new
Jenna	Hello, I like your silver broach
Barbara	Thanks, it's new
Jenna	Hi, I like your red ribbon
Barbara	Thanks, it's new
Jenna	Shall we begin?
Barbara	Let's begin

They commence dancing.

Jenna	Once we were American girls
Together	Now we're just celestial angels
Jenna	Hey, Barbara?
Barbara	Yes, Jenna
Jenna	There was a wasp in my bedroom

366

Barbara	Never tell lies
Jenna	An evil dagger of a wasp
	Patrolling my private bed chambers
Barbara	You have no private bed chambers
	You have no non-private bed chambers
	All you have is a blanket in the corner on the floor
Jenna	Well, I was over in the field this afternoon
Barbara	Stay out of that field due to outbreak of rabies
Jenna	Well, I was over by the lake
Barbara	Stay away from that lake
	Due to chemical warfare
Jenna	I climbed down into that dark hole in the field
Barbara	Fear is a beautiful flower
Jenna	Did you know there's a man living in that hole?

They pause abruptly.

Barbara	I don't believe you
Jenna	A young man barely a man at all
Barbara	He looks like Peter Pan
Together	Only black as night
Barbara	Black as night is right
Jenna	He says he knows you
Barbara	It used to be one of Poppa's oil wells, that hole
Jenna	No, no; it was formed by falling metal from the heavens
Barbara	It was the last of Poppa's wells
Jenna	A falling metallic visitor formed that hole
Barbara	I don't believe you
Jenna	A young man barely a man at all and ageless
	He says you go see him every night

	With no clothes on
Barbara	I could be nursing him toward adulthood
	With fluids from my body
Jenna	Well, that explains it
Barbara	Well, that explains it

They resume dancing.

Barbara	Jenna?
Jenna	Yes, Barbara
Barbara	Are you able to keep a person's confidences?
Jenna	No
Barbara	Do you recall the night of our ball?
Jenna	How could I forget?
Barbara	I forget all the time
Jenna	It had to be cancelled
Barbara	Our ball had to be cancelled due to lack of light
Jenna	Lack of precious resources on behalf of the population
Barbara	You couldn't sleep the night of our ball
Jenna	The night our ball was cancelled, I was rudely awakened
Barbara	By a marauding dagger of a wasp
Jenna	The countryside was crawling with the wayward and the lost
Together	Don't think back
Jenna	I won't think back

They pause abruptly.

Jenna	Barbara?
Barbara	Yes, Jenna

Jenna	Oil in the ground...
Barbara	What about it?
Jenna	It was like a kind of blood, right?
Barbara	It was the residue of dead things, yes
Jenna	Dead tiny plants and things
Barbara	Dead little sea animals that floated down
Jenna	Down down to lie in the mud at the bottom of the sea
Barbara	The mud at the bottom of the sea
	That folded its warm arms around the dead
Jenna	Fields and fields of dead things and things
Barbara	Cooked forever inside the soft arms of the warm earth
Jenna	Oil Petrol Gasoline
Barbara	Cheapest fuel there is in the universe
Jenna	All gone now
Barbara	All gone now

They dance.

Jenna	Hey, Barbara
Barbara	Yes, Jenna
Jenna	My arm swelled up from getting wasped
Barbara	Musta hurt like the dickens
Jenna	It felt like jagged glass digging in
Barbara	I imagine it would
Jenna	I woke up the sheets were wet
Barbara	Musta thought it was that young man from the hole
Jenna	I got stung I ran out into the field
Barbara	You musta heard him singing
Jenna	Yes, I heard his sad, sad voice in song
Barbara	Under the shadows of the trees

Jenna	I noticed his whole hairless body tastes like iron
Barbara	He fell to earth in a cloud of fire and ash
Jenna	I don't believe you
Barbara	Two sisters never shared such a young man before
	And survived
Jenna	We should roll our dice for him
Barbara	Whoever loses has to leave town on the next train
Jenna	Or else fly off like a migratory bird
Barbara	And go live in cities
Jenna	And die broken and abandoned
Barbara	We'll arm wrestle with him as the prize
Jenna	Eyes gouged out, cheeks bit to ribbons
Barbara	We'll fight like Lady Macbeth
Jenna	Like Calamity Jane
Barbara	Like the last of the Apaches
Jenna	Like Theodore Roosevelt

They pause.

Barbara	Shhh...!
Jenna	*(Hushed)* What is it?
Barbara	*(Hushed)* I thought I heard that scraping sound again
Jenna	Stone on stone?
Barbara	It's those slabs I think
Jenna	Those two big stone slabs
Barbara	Are they listening?
Jenna	Safe to say they're always listening

They resume.

Jenna	We were born in the back of a car
	Isn't that so, Barbara?
Barbara	Yes, that's correct
Jenna	On the interstate, the turnpike, the route?
Barbara	Yes, our Poppa loved to drive—who knows why
Jenna	The highway the freeway the road
Barbara	Back and forth on the land he loved to drive and drive
Jenna	Meeting his brethren in wealth, his supporters
Barbara	We were born that way we grew up that way
Jenna	Seventy, eighty miles an hour
Barbara	Hustling along
Jenna	But we don't drive anymore
Barbara	No no no
Jenna	We don't go anywhere we don't leave
Barbara	There's nowhere to go
Jenna	Nowhere left
Barbara	But when we were young
Jenna	Always a city at night as we hurtled along
Barbara	Dallas Houston Tulsa lit in the night
Jenna	Revolving slowly as we sped by on the plain
Barbara	Always the rush of the wheels
Jenna	First invention of man they say
Barbara	The rush of the wheels
Jenna	The song of the engine
	RumRumRumRum
Barbara	Whoever falls asleep first loses out on the man in the hole
Jenna	The gorgeous youth who fell from the black black sky
Barbara	The scrumptious youth whose body tastes like iron
Jenna	I don't think girls from Texas are ever supposed to act the way we do

Barbara	Sleep will never come again to this observatory/laboratory
Jenna	What if I were to hang eighteen of my closest advisors in a fit of pique?
Barbara	Or else castrate thirty-two prisoners out of sexual greed?
Jenna	Or burn sixteen villages in the rural outback?
Barbara	I've got a better idea
	Let's graft our bodies together along the midline
	And fuck him together
Jenna	Let's do it right now tonight out in the field
Barbara	Oh it's so wild
Jenna	So wild and wild
Barbara	It's as beautiful as outer space between the stars
Together	Ha ha ha
Barbara	*(Looking up)* Shhhh...!
Jenna	Are they watching?
Barbara	Safe to say they're always watching *(Pause. Whisper)* I saw him first
Jenna	*(Whisper)* I smelled him first
Barbara	*(Whisper)* I dreamed him first in a burst of white feathers
Jenna	*(Whisper)* You'll die in convulsions
Barbara	*(Whisper)* You'll die in emotional turmoil
Jenna	Oh of course
	I am gripped by an emotion
Barbara	What is the emotion?
Jenna	It is anger, it is sadness

Resume.

Barbara	I tell my stories
	You tell your stories

| | We laugh we laugh |
| Jenna | Pretty soon we hate each other |

Pause.

Barbara	Listen, sister
	You try to fuck me
	I'll fuck you twice as hard
Jenna	That's lesson number one

Resume.

Barbara	It was the night of our ball
Jenna	Everyone who was anyone was on their way
Barbara	Come see the stars...!
Jenna	Poppa leased our own observatory/laboratory
Barbara	Come see the galaxies and the stars...!
Jenna	We had our own telescope
Barbara	Our own astronomical genius
Jenna	An old geezer was gonna guide us around the galaxies
Barbara	With his thin and reedy voice
Jenna	He was going to teach us about the genesis of light or love
	But then in the city below
Barbara	All the lights went out
Jenna	You could hear it get real quiet
Barbara	The grid the grid they shut down the grid
Jenna	We always knew it would happen
	We just didn't know when
Barbara	No more oil no more light
Jenna	No more oil no more light

Barbara	Ah what the hell
Jenna	We'll just fly over to New York
	Sorry, no lights there
Barbara	We'll fly to Boston, Chicago
Jenna	Sorry, sorry
Barbara	Dallas, Houston, Atlanta
Jenna	Dark dark dark
Barbara	Dark, like dead jewels
Jenna	Barbara?
Barbara	Yes?
Jenna	Why us?
Barbara	Why did this happen to us?
Jenna	We are evil
Barbara	Vile
Jenna	Lucky
Barbara	Blessed
Jenna	We are blessed, yes
Barbara	We are a blessing
Jenna	We are *the* blessing
Barbara	Through us the world will continue
Jenna	We were practicing with Henry
Barbara	He was our dance instructor
	Young and handsome an ex-Marine
Jenna	Our own private dance instructor
Barbara	An old friend of Poppa's
Jenna	I'll be right back Henry said
Barbara	And then he left
Jenna	Henry left
Barbara	I'll go see what's happened he said
Jenna	She means Henry

Barbara	In the city below
Jenna	He said
Barbara	Something's gone wrong Henry said
Jenna	A short while later the lights went out
Barbara	The lights went out all over
Jenna	That was precisely five years ago today
Barbara	How could all the lights go out all at once?
Jenna	That never happens no no no
Barbara	People need light to see
	To read
Jenna	To dry their hair
Barbara	In the end we proved indispensable to Henry
Jenna	A precious resource to Henry
Barbara	Don't kill us, Henry!
Jenna	Don't take our lives!

They pause.

Barbara	There is no more oil
Jenna	Only a few can live on
	In that old way live on
Barbara	Only a few will survive

They resume.

Jenna	It wasn't so bad
Barbara	It could have been worse
Jenna	We laughed on the terraces
Barbara	Ah, not to worry
	They'll figure it out

Jenna	We kicked up our heels
Barbara	They always do—
Jenna	We tossed our empty bottles off the balconies—
Barbara	Figure it out
Jenna	Into the burning streets—
Barbara	Always they figure it out
Jenna	The fires, the screaming crowds
Barbara	Ahh, they'll figure it out
Jenna	No need to worry
	Ha ha ha
Barbara	You know what I think?
Jenna	I wish you'd tell me
Barbara	I think the poor deserved their dark fate for one simple reason:
Together	THEY HAD NO MONEY.
Jenna	Ha ha ha
	That's what I always say
Barbara	We sat atop a huge black boulder of wealth
Jenna	Guilt
Barbara	No I said wealth
	A huge black boulder of
Jenna	Guilt
Barbara	It rolled along, the black ball of guilt and shame
Jenna	Smothering the oceans
Barbara	Crushing the forests and the mountains
Jenna	You can't stop a thing like that
Barbara	It can't be guilt that fills us now
Jenna	Whoever heard of anyone dancing
	Out of guilt or shame
Barbara	We were born

	We did not want to die
Jenna	It's dialed into the heart of things
Barbara	Of things that live
Jenna	That movement that dance
Barbara	Ha ha ha does that sound harsh?
Jenna	The poor had no taste
	Is the other thing
Barbara	It was obvious from the cars they drove
Jenna	Among so many other signs
Barbara	Crappy little tin cans
Jenna	In the best of times it was such a drag to be rich in America
Barbara	You couldn't simply enjoy yourself
Jenna	You hadda gussie up a career
Barbara	Pretend to be part of the middle class
Together	Fuck the middle class
Jenna	That's my campaign slogan

They pause.

	Oh but the cities at night
Barbara	The cities and the towns
Jenna	Oh the glittering lights
Barbara	The tall silent buildings far far away
Jenna	Glistening as they turned
Barbara	As they turned as we passed
Jenna	As we passed at seventy or eighty miles per hour
Barbara	On the road the dark road

Resume.

Barbara	What's wrong, Jenna, are you feeling bored tonight?
Jenna	Yeah, I just feel, you know, a little restless
Barbara	Wherever you would like to go
	We can go there right now
Jenna	Well, what if I want to visit Graceland, Tennessee?
Barbara	Fine by me
	We'll take the highway
Jenna	Well, but, what if I want to visit Niagara Falls?
Barbara	Fine by me
	We'll take the interstate
Jenna	Well, but, what if I need to run an errand in the Inland Empire?
Barbara	Fine by me
	We'll take the turnpike
Jenna	The car is right outside
Barbara	The tank is full and when it runs down
Together	We'll just pull up to the nearest pump
	Ha ha ha.

Pause.

Jenna	I can feel that other place
Barbara	That other time?
Jenna	I can feel it right now
	It's like I'm halfway there already
	No it's like I never left
	But then I've never been there
	So it's like traveling into the future
	Where that other place
	Is still waiting for me

Resume.

Barbara	We're still practicing
Jenna	We want to be ready for the ball
Barbara	When things start up again
Jenna	We want to be ready for the invitation to the ball
Barbara	When things kick in again
Jenna	Sometimes I pause and feel dizzy with sorrow
Barbara	When we were young our mother one day came to us
Jenna	Come with me she said
Barbara	And she drove us to a strange place
Jenna	Many cars parked forever in rows
Barbara	At the center of the cars a great rising windowless building
Jenna	The mall...!
Barbara	The mall...!
Jenna	She took us inside
Barbara	Showed us some girls
Jenna	Act like that she said
Barbara	Talk like they talk
Jenna	Eat like they eat
Barbara	Wear those same clothes and feel Those same feelings
Jenna	Call each other lesbos and laugh
Barbara	Otherwise one day they'll rise up and kill you
Jenna	And so it came to pass
Barbara	They rose up and now they will kill us

Pause.

Jenna	And now today

	The sun is out
Barbara	The guns are all quiet
Jenna	The pines below the terrace so wet with dew

They dance.

Barbara	It's the perfect day to launch a conspiracy
Jenna	A prison break...!
Barbara	A revolution from above...!
Jenna	My spine is electric
Barbara	My mind is a machine churning out
	Mischief mischief mischief
Jenna	To hear that our ball is suddenly on again
Barbara	On the schedule again
Jenna	To be attended by multitudes
Barbara	They must have discovered a vast new deposit
	Of oil
Jenna	The cities will light up one by one
Barbara	With a subsonic whir the party will restart
Jenna	The party will gather itself out of the gloom of night
Barbara	The party will descend upon our spinal columns
Jenna	And everything will return to normal
Barbara	Even better then normal
Jenna	And they brought in two blocks of beautiful stone
Barbara	Two slabs of beautiful stone for us to dance on
Jenna	In front of the adoring crowds
Barbara	The adoring screeching crowds
Jenna	Crying in unison for a crimson encore
Barbara	Give us our crimson encore...!
Jenna	It's what we'll be famous for

Barbara	Our crimson encore…!
Jenna	Our heads lopped off and falling
Barbara	The blood gushing up
Jenna	Those who adore us must not be disappointed
Barbara	They'd lose faith in history
Jenna	The mercy of their betters
Barbara	We don't mind
Jenna	We embrace our dark fate with cheerful faces

They pause.

Barbara	I wish we didn't have to dance
Jenna	To the music of the screams
Barbara	I personally plan to retain exclusive possession of my sexual organs *always*.
Jenna	Is that odd?
Barbara	Is that extreme?
Jenna	Sometimes I feel as if the world might end if we
Barbara	For a single moment
Jenna	Truly stopped
Barbara	If we were for one moment to tire
Jenna	It is just beginning, isn't it?
Together	Just beginning just beginning just beginning

Resume.

Barbara	But it's hard to be patient
Jenna	It's not like it used to be
Barbara	No, it might take days for the crowd to arrive
Jenna	They can't just climb into their cars anymore

Barbara	They have to be driven
Jenna	They have to be driven on foot
Barbara	Driven by soldiers who are properly trained
Jenna	Who know how to inspire...
Barbara	Obedience
Jenna	That's right, obedience
Barbara	Soldiers who know how to inspire obedience
Jenna	And crush crush crush all opposition
Barbara	Nothing must be left to creep around
Jenna	No creeping around
Barbara	Crush crush crush
	And of course meanwhile
Jenna	We have to wait here and be patient
	For our guests to arrive
Barbara	We have to be patient and we have to prepare
Jenna	Barbara?
Barbara	Yes, dear
Jenna	Heard a funny joke the other day
	Two birds walked into a bar
	ha ha ha
Barbara	It's funny already
Together	Ha ha ha!
Barbara	People say we talk a lot
Jenna	I don't buy it
Barbara	We let our actions do the talking
Jenna	Get off it, man
Barbara	Get over yourself

Pause.

Jenna	How could we be the ones
	Who are punished?
Barbara	We knew nothing
Jenna	Nothing at all
Barbara	We were born
Jenna	We did not want to die

Resume.

Jenna	It's odd
Barbara	What's odd?
Jenna	We have our own killer trapped in the next room
	And now we're falling in love with him
Barbara	Anything less would be anticlimactic
Jenna	It's terrible to be amorous
Barbara	To want to consume everything you've ever heard about
	Or thought
Jenna	Most people don't lap it up quite like we do
Barbara	Of course we're also defiant
Jenna	We run out a little ways and then we fall
Barbara	It's all we can manage
Jenna	Poppa?
Barbara	*(Texan accent)* Yes, dear
Jenna	Barbara and I made a new friend the other night
Barbara	*(Texan accent)* Oh, that's nice
Jenna	We call him Peter Pan
Barbara	He lives in a ditch
Jenna	Well, more like a hole
Barbara	He only emerges by moonlight
Jenna	I must say he is unusual in the requests he makes

Barbara	The things he asks us to do
Jenna	We don't like to refuse
Barbara	To refuse would be rude when he's our treasured guest
Jenna	Our treasured guest, Poppa
Barbara	*(Texan accent)* Yes, dear
Jenna	Have you been listening, Poppa?
Barbara	*(Texan accent)* Of course, dear
Jenna	We've got someone we'd like to introduce you to
Barbara	A friend we'd like to introduce you to
Jenna	He's not very reputable
Barbara	He never learned the secret of well mannered behavior
Jenna	He's a bit on the savage side
Barbara	A bit bloodthirsty
Jenna	A bit brutal
Barbara	More than once he's served time for violent crime
Jenna	He never confesses
Barbara	Even when caught red-handed
Together	He denies the whole caper
Jenna	He's one of those terrifying creatures
Barbara	Who refuse to age
Jenna	One day he just said to hell with this aging bullshit
Barbara	He's so macho that way
Jenna	That was years ago now
Barbara	To hell with the passage of time
Together	That was years ago now
Barbara	He's still wearing the same beard
Jenna	I begin to think he threatens your survival
	Dear Poppa

Pause.

Barbara	Death is terrible
Jenna	A horror a horror
Barbara	*(Falls to her knees)* We confess it
	We abjure it
	We disavow it down on our knees
	With our hands raised we beg and grovel
	We're prepared to roll around with whoever
	We're prepared we're more than prepared
	We need that kind of attention right now from you
	From you
	Whoever you are
	Whatever you like think like feel like
	Hello? Hello?

JENNA helps BARBARA to her feet. They dance.

Jenna	Barbara?
Barbara	If we dance long enough
Jenna	And with a pure heart
Barbara	We might wake up to find ourselves in the bedroom
	With the wasp
Jenna	And the field outside
Barbara	And the lake beyond the field
Jenna	And the hole with the young man at the bottom
Barbara	The barefoot young man whose body tastes of iron
Jenna	It would be meaningful
Barbara	In a very small way
Jenna	We won't be in this frightening observatory/laboratory anymore
Barbara	Waiting for the killers of our beautiful world

Jenna	Which has heretofore been so kind to us
Barbara	Isn't that strange
Jenna	That we could get it so backward in our memories
Barbara	They were so kind to trap us in this abandoned observatory/laboratory
Jenna	With the deep freeze locker
Barbara	And the room of empty cages and the slabs out front
Jenna	Beside the long trumpets
Barbara	And the drums
Jenna	And the women in the robes
Barbara	Their eyes rolled back
Jenna	What will they keep in those cages?
Barbara	Why weren't we consulted?
Jenna	They could have asked for our permission
Barbara	We might have agreed
Jenna	We might have said yes
Barbara	"Yes," we might have said
Jenna	"You may have this dance," we might have said
Barbara	"You may have this one dance if you behave," We might have added
Jenna	Instead they come at us with these threatening requests
Barbara	These commands
Jenna	Involving cages and slabs of stone and sacrificial knives

They stop.

Barbara	As far as I'm concerned they'll have to take it up with Henry
Together	He's our dance instructor
Jenna	He brought us up here and said practice makes perfect

386

Barbara	He said it with such conviction we decided to comply
Together	We've been dancing ever since

They resume.

Jenna	You've got to go along to get along
Barbara	That's what I always say
Jenna	Any minute he'll tell us we can stop practicing
Barbara	And besides no one should mess with us ever
Jenna	We have friends in high places
Barbara	Places on high
Jenna	We have friends in the heavens
Barbara	Powerful swift
Jenna	They control the very sky
Barbara	You wouldn't be laughing if you really knew
Jenna	Not a snicker nor a chuckle if you only knew
Barbara	He's always watching
Jenna	He's a choreographical genius
Barbara	He knows just how far he can push us
Jenna	Henry?
Together	The chains don't get in the way
	The chains scarcely matter at all
Barbara	Henry?
Jenna	Henry?
Barbara	He's not inherently cruel
Jenna	He'll say you can stop now
Barbara	We'll fall down in a heap on the floor

Pause.

Jenna	This terrible rushing all the time
Barbara	Which takes such a toll
Jenna	Rushing like water
Barbara	White water
Jenna	Down through the years, a cascade
Barbara	Shimmering
Jenna	Falling

Resume.

Barbara	I'm savoring this moment
	Because I know it won't last

Pause.

Jenna	Uh, what was I saying...?
Barbara	You were talking about our black-as-night friend, Peter Pan—
Jenna	He's more than a friend
Barbara	He's a lover
Jenna	A lover a lover a lover
Barbara	Your plans to unleash Peter—
Jenna	And then I...
Barbara	Faltered, yes.
Jenna	It's the progression of the disease

They resume briefly, then pause abruptly.

Barbara	Our own private Peter Pan
Jenna	Our own traveling minstrel

Barbara	In his sad hole singing his sad songs
Jenna	Across the field by the lake
Together	Under the shadows of the trees
Barbara	"He looks like Peter Pan," you said
Jenna	"Only black as night," I said
Barbara	If Peter Pan were here I'd ask him a question
Jenna	Would you?
Barbara	Yes, I would *(Pause)* "Peter Pan," I'd say
Jenna	"Yes, Wendy?" he'd reply
Barbara	Do you think the world is real?
Jenna	In what way real?
Barbara	If we stopped dancing
	Would the world implode in a fever?

Long pause.

Jenna	When I don't talk
	Terror overwhelms me
Barbara	Talk down to me I'll give you a kiss
Jenna	Talk down to me I'll follow you anywhere

They resume.

Jenna	We could be dancing like this till the end of all time
Barbara	This is the end of time
Jenna	The very things we cling to
	Are the things that kill us
Barbara	Sad to say
Jenna	We must become other than we are
Barbara	We must recreate our childhood

Jenna	Images unfaded by time
Barbara	Landscapes of perfection
Jenna	Which at the time almost ruined us
Barbara	But which have since acquired
Jenna	The most heart wrenching beauty
Barbara	The amber light of memory
Jenna	How we long and pine away
Barbara	For the house by the field by the lake
Jenna	The house by the field with the hole
Barbara	We should have had that young man arrested for safe keeping
Jenna	Way back when
Barbara	While his crimes were still fresh on our bodies
Jenna	Instead poppa left him so hurt so wounded
Barbara	His black body strung up that way
Jenna	Strung up at the edge of the field
Barbara	Strung up with a view of the lake
Jenna	Strung up above the hole
Barbara	The man of oil
Jenna	His body sucking up all the oil in the world
Barbara	Turned so black that way
Jenna	That's how he turned black, yes
Barbara	So beautiful strung up that way in the air
Jenna	From the limb of a tree
Barbara	From the limb of a tree
Jenna	Didn't they know he'd exact his revenge?
Barbara	Didn't they know he'd ruin the world?
Jenna	Step by step
Barbara	It was even kind of fun
Jenna	He destroyed the world

Barbara	But right away it came back again
Jenna	His black body strung up that way
	And now he comes back to haunt us
Barbara	You mean save us
Jenna	To torture and torment us
Barbara	You mean to nurture and caress us
Jenna	The mystery goes on and on like music
Barbara	Top 40 radio
Jenna	STOP EVERYTHING RIGHT NOW!

Pause.

Barbara	Look at that
Jenna	He reaches into the heart of every atom
Barbara	STOP EVERYTHING RIGHT NOW!

Pause, then slowly resume.

Jenna	See there?
Barbara	How remarkable
Jenna	Watch out watch out watch out
Barbara	He's on his way right now
Jenna	He's on his way to your little town
Together	Riding his rabid bear
Jenna	Watch out watch out watch out

They pause abruptly.

Jenna	The tears of angels
Barbara	The compartments of heaven

They resume.

Jenna	Afraid to love
Barbara	Afraid to lose

They pause abruptly.

Jenna	Every moment wild
	Long-haired and tilted
Barbara	Riding on skinny legs
Jenna	Dog-faced and greasy
Barbara	Reptilian to the core

They resume. They pause abruptly. They resume. Pause.
Tableau. Lights slowly fade to black.

The End

Vagrant
by Guy Zimmerman

Vagrant was produced at the Electric Lodge by Padua Playwrights in February 2006, under the playwright's direction. The set was designed by Jeffrey Atherton, with original music and sound design by Don Preston.

With the following cast:

Meyer: Christopher Allport
Larkin: Patrick Burleigh
Patty/Pauline: Niamh McCormally

Los Angeles is the capital of forgetting.

R.J. Smith, The Great Black Way

Characters

Meyer *An ex-convict, now running a small business in Los Angeles, 50s.*

Larkin *A member of the LAPD, late 20s.*

Patty *Meyer's wife, a part-time seamstress.*

Pauline *Meyer and Patty's daughter, also a seamstress. (*NOTE: *to be played by the same actress as Patty)*

Scene

An audio equipment repair shop somewhere in South Los Angeles. Downstage, the suggestion of a picture window looking out on the parking lot of the mini-mall and the boulevard beyond.

Act One

In black the sound of traffic. Lights up on Meyer, *wearing a flashy track suit. He stands looking out the front window. Beside him is* Larkin, *in a policeman's uniform and carrying a worn-out duffel bag. Upstage is the door to the stock room.*

Meyer	*(Looking out)* No one's there.
Larkin	Could be hiding.
Meyer	Behind a car…?
Larkin	*(Pointing)* You watch that way.
Meyer	I don't see him.
Larkin	I'm crossing the parking lot, he comes up behind.
Meyer	What is he, uh…
Larkin	Sonofabitch is right behind me.
Meyer	*(Beat)* You never saw him.
Larkin	Never laid eyes on him.
Meyer	So how do you know he was there?
Larkin	I felt him.
Meyer	In your bones…
Larkin	He walks up behind, I duck in your door…
Meyer	Either way we're alone now.
Larkin	Sonofabitch.
Meyer	*(Inspecting* Larkin*)* Let's have a look at ya.

Larkin	Sneaking up on an officer of the law...
Meyer	*(Inspecting LARKIN)* Your face has a familiar...
Larkin	No, I don't believe we ever met.
Meyer	*(Pointing at LARKIN's duffel bag)* I bet you got something for me in that ruck sack.
Larkin	*(Hearing something)* Woah...!
Meyer	*(Whispering)* What now?
Larkin	*(Then, relaxing)* Heard someone cough.
Meyer	Cough?
Larkin	Choke.
Meyer	A choking sound? *(Pause)* Calm down, Christ.
Larkin	I forgot about this neighborhood.
Meyer	What about it?
Larkin	Horrific and tense down here.
Meyer	Yeah, well, hey.
Larkin	Electricity in the air down here.
Meyer	When the work dries up, the streets take on a kind of a negative charge. You should know all that.
Larkin	Why should I know all that?
Meyer	You're no rookie, that's why. *(Pause)* Have an olive.

MEYER holds out a plastic dish. Smiles.

Larkin	Little snack... five PM...

LARKIN selects an olive. Hesitates.

Meyer	It's well known I like to pamper my patrons.

MEYER selects an olive and eats it. LARKIN eats his now too.

Larkin	*(Chewing)* Various pickled goods and so forth...
Meyer	*(Pointing)* There's the pit bowl...

Both men drop their pits in a second dish. A pause.

Meyer	You're no rookie. You must have transferred in.
Larkin	Never served 'cept here in the precinct.
Meyer	You've been on leave.
Larkin	*(Nodding)* This is my first day back on the job.
Meyer	*(Offering)* Have another.
Larkin	So I'm a little rocky.
Meyer	A little green around the gills.
Larkin	Two olives, I bloat up.
Meyer	No way.
Larkin	You too, huh?
Meyer	Like a fucking dead whale on a hot beach.

Pause.

Larkin	Yeah, I came up in the precinct, but since the last riot I've been on leave.
Meyer	*(Beat)* That was five years ago now.
Larkin	Feels good to be back on the beat...
Meyer	Five years back is when I opened shop. How it is I never saw your handsome face before? Oh, it was a mess down here after those riots. This mini-mall was a burned-out shell. You guys learned some things since then, am I right? About clamping down?
Larkin	This part of town almost exploded again last week.
Meyer	You don't say.

Larkin	After a certain incident out on your center divider.
Meyer	That crazy bum they dragged away?
Larkin	Homeless man gets leaned on a little hard... could be the spark that sets it off.
Meyer	Hey, police have to be careful. There are always malcontents hanging around on the edges of society without a fixed identity. When enough of them gather, ka-blam—it's a powder keg.
Larkin	You witnessed the entire episode, did you not?
Meyer	*(Nodding)* Other than that I had nothing to do with it.
Larkin	When you filed the original complaint, you said: "there's this old man out on my center divider exposing himself."
Meyer	Young man.

LARKIN pulls a notebook from his hip pocket, flips to the last page.

Larkin	*(Reading)* "There's this *young* man out on my center divider, *harassing* my customers and *exposing* himself to women."
Meyer	Without mercy, wreaking havoc.
Larkin	"And I want him removed," you said.

LARKIN pockets the notebook. MEYER crosses to the front window and looks out.

| Meyer | It was cold that day and raining and the streets were slick. He didn't put up much of a fight. For Los Angeles it was very cold and I think the cold and the rain had weakened him. He looked... weakened. He was bent over and sort of |

rocking back and forth and I believe he had defecated and was possibly feverish and certainly very tired. They stuffed him down into that cruiser and drove off and that was that.

LARKIN gets the notebook out again.

Larkin (*Reading*) "I want him sorted out once and for all," is what you said.

LARKIN pockets the notebook.

Meyer Hey, I'm just trying to run a business here.

Larkin People across the neighborhood have been asking about that young man. They have gifts for him, some of them.

Meyer What he'd do, he'd throw up all over his shoes.

Larkin Mrs. Delblanco at the dry cleaners, one day she looks out, white doves are perching up and down his arms. (*Pointing out*) Look. Already there's a little shrine for him out on your center divider.

MEYER slowly peers out.

Meyer That's just his high-top sneaker.

Larkin It's a shrine.

Meyer Must have fell off in the ruckus.

Larkin They're putting little flowers around it.

Meyer Who's in charge of this investigation?

Larkin Dishes of sweet water.

Meyer Lieutenant Kilkelly?

Larkin Imagination.

Meyer	What about it?
Larkin	You need more than you got.
Meyer	I can draw faces from memory.
Larkin	You can't even see yourself in another guy's shoes.
Meyer	I can see myself in your shoes walking right out of my shop!
Larkin	How your own life could turn.
Meyer	I don't need a sermon, neither!
Larkin	You want him "sorted out once and for all...!"
Meyer	Last thing I need is a goddamn sermon!

MEYER raises his hand to strike LARKIN. A pause.

Larkin	Don't we get fussy.
Meyer	Little fussy, yeah. *(Lowers his hand)*
Larkin	No harm done.
Meyer	Relieved to hear it.
Larkin	We're just talking, right?
Meyer	Probably you'll be going now.
Larkin	Nah, I got some time.
Meyer	It was very nice to make your acquaintance.
Larkin	Stored up some downtime.
Meyer	Got a little problem with my temper, that's all.
Larkin	We'll have to work on that.
Meyer	*(Beat)* We?
Larkin	We.

Pause.

| Meyer | Hell, I was looking for someone to talk to. My mind has been clouded all day long with dark and troubling thoughts. |

We don't perceive things as they truly are, is what I've been thinking. We walk around, we're stuck in the past, I've been thinking. Our minds are infected with dreams, I've been thinking. It's that homeless beggar who brought all this to mind. I have thoughts due to him that I didn't have before. Standing out there all day long, calm and patient as the Pope.

Larkin   For that homeless guy, every moment was what it was.

Meyer   Without connection to what went before or came after.

Larkin   Time just moved right through that homeless man.

Meyer   Let go, I learned.

Larkin   Let go of the wreck.

Meyer   Don't drag the wreck with you everywhere you go. Just now, you and me, we're having a pleasant conversation, all of a sudden I fly off at the mouth. And it has nothing to do with you!

Larkin   I had that same issue back when I joined the force.

Meyer   What set me off was the memory of some deadbeat fuckhead long gone now! Oops, look at the time.

Larkin   Time to go swim your laps.

Meyer   You bet.

Larkin   Down at the Y.

Meyer   Exercising all the muscle groups at once. *(Then, with suspicion)* Someone must've told you about me, I guess. About my daily swim down at the Y. Someone at the station house must have brought that up in conversation. My swim. The Y.

Larkin   I could smell it on you.

Meyer   The chlorine?

Larkin   Noticed it right away.

Meyer   *(Relieved)* No kidding.

Larkin   Public pool, they use a lot.

Meyer	They use a lot. But never enough for me.
Larkin	Most people dislike chlorine.
Meyer	Not me, I love it. I love the smell of it. I love the feeling on my skin, that coating of chalk and lime. Sometimes I think it gets right into my bones.
Larkin	I said to myself, this man's a lap swimmer.
Meyer	I am, I'm a lap swimmer! It's one of the bonuses of this location—proximity to the Y. After those riots my wife didn't want to come down here, but I know a good deal when it crosses my path.
Larkin	So that homeless bastard stood out front week after week, correct?

MEYER *turns and stares out at the street. A pause.*

Meyer	*(Bitter)* Like a virus lying dormant. Sometimes I'd hardly notice. Then he'd act up. Make some new attempt to get inside.
Larkin	Some new attempt to get in *here*?
Meyer	Yeah, he was always pressing to get in.
Larkin	Here you are, making a saint out of the guy...
Meyer	Sometimes he'd sneak around back. Other days he'd rush the front door.
Larkin	What in God's name did he want from a miserable shop like this?
Meyer	Well, I'm waiting to find out, aren't I. I'm waiting to learn. You walk through that door, I figure you'll have all the answers.
Larkin	His heart must've hungered for what you peddle.
Meyer	*(Beats)* That's just simple logic. That's just basic inference with a little deductive reasoning tossed in on the side.

Larkin	What is it you peddle here, anyway?
Meyer	You had him up there all week long, for fuck's sake.
Larkin	What's your stock-in-trade?
Meyer	You oughta do better than basic goddamn logic!
Larkin	What commodity or service do you render?
Meyer	*(Beat)* What, you mean, like, *here*?
Larkin	Here in the store.

Pause.

Meyer	We sell audio gear.
Larkin	I don't believe it.
Meyer	New and used.
Larkin	You're making a joke.
Meyer	I also do repairs. Solid state, digical.
Larkin	Digi*tal*.
Meyer	As I said.
Larkin	You said digi*cal*. It's digi*tal*, not digi*cal*.
Meyer	*(Shrugging)* Digital, digical…
Larkin	Digi*cal* refers to nothing in the known universe.
Meyer	We fix it all, we sell it all.
Larkin	This is one of those shops you see in Los Angeles, you wonder how in God's name they survive.
Meyer	We got high hopes for the future.
Larkin	We?
Meyer	My wife and I. She's a seamstress. Works there in back.
Larkin	Oh, I get it. You sell audio equipment out here, she stitches fabrics there in back. That explains everything. Here's a guy couldn't fix a broken light bulb, how's he pay his rent? Turns out there's another revenue stream on the

premises. To contribute to the bottom line. It's all making a bit more sense to me. In fact, amigo, I'm starting to see the upside of a little shop like this. A man could do worse, no? In Los Angeles. I'll have to look into it. As an option for my retirement. Here's a question: would you sell me this shop right now? How much would you charge to vacate the premises in the next five minutes? I'll tell you what I'd like to do, I'd like to talk to your wife in person.

LARKIN turns toward the stock room; MEYER blocks his way.

Meyer	She's away from the premises at the current time.
Larkin	You're lying.
Meyer	Yes, I'm lying.
Larkin	Stock room back there?
Meyer	Stock room, yeah.
Larkin	Got an exit to the rear?
Meyer	Never use it. Keep it locked.
Larkin	Nothing hid back there?
Meyer	Nothing hid.
Larkin	I'll tell you what I begin to think.
Patty	*(Off)* Meyer...?

Both men freeze at the sound of footsteps. Numerous locks are undone and the door swings open, revealing PATTY in the doorway. She stands there for a moment, then enters, crossing downstage. LARKIN stares at her, mesmerized. A pause.

Meyer	Officer, say hello to my good wife.

Patty	I'm sitting there in back, I thought I heard a woman's voice.
Larkin	You must have been dreaming.
Patty	Sure, I while away the daylight hours, but then I remember. Do I need to remind you? Okay, I'll remind you: four foot, eleven inches high, eighty pounds. Blue and white jumper. You'll want to write this all down. Five brass buttons down the front, or maybe six. Couple simple hair clips. Take some goddamn notes. Soft hearted. Quick to laugh. A rushing, kinda loose-hipped kinda walk. A little stooped, a little slope-shouldered. Overly fucking trusting. Overly fucking credulous. Naïve in the mind, am I right, Meyer? Funny word, doncha think? NAIIIIEVE?

Pause.

Meyer	Patty's a graduate of the liberal arts. With that graceful neck. Isn't her neck graceful?
Patty	*(To LARKIN)* Turn away. Don't look at me.
Meyer	Patricia's haunted. Hasn't slept for weeks.
Larkin	Without sleep you lose track of who you are.
Meyer	That homeless beggar haunts her fragile mind.
Larkin	Is he correct?
Patty	About what?
Larkin	About that homeless guy out front. Does he haunt your fragile mind?
Patty	I just asked you not to look at me.
Larkin	I'd like to know how come you're hiding out in an unlit stock room.
Patty	Oh, I'm not hiding back there.
Larkin	A woman like you.

Patty	I'm waiting back there.
Larkin	Waiting for what?
Patty	Waiting for you.

PATTY crosses to MEYER. He embraces her protectively. A pause.

Meyer	Now we get to the heart of the matter, yes indeed. The soul of the heart of the matter. You can tell things are not what they seem here in our humble repair shop. You're enough of a detective to sniff that out.
Larkin	I'm really not sure what that's supposed to mean.
Meyer	Around here it can be difficult to see things as they truly are.
Patty	It's in the air down here.
Larkin	What's in the air down here?
Patty	A forgetfulness that comes and goes.
Meyer	A murk.
Patty	A fogginess of the mind.
Larkin	I-I need to sit.
Patty	You know a thing one moment...
Meyer	... the next moment it's gone.
Patty	The fog sets in.
Meyer	The clarity slips away.
Patty	I look at you...
Meyer	... I know exactly who you are.
Patty	A moment later I forget.
Meyer	Down here in South L.A....
Patty	... things are too much for our fragile minds.
Meyer	We walk around, our tender hearts hang open to the world.

Patty	We love and need each other too much for our fragile and delicate minds...
Meyer	Life is too much...
Patty	We take one look at life, we tumble back into a fog.
Larkin	I feel sick.
Patty	We can't see. We can't see. We topple back into darkness.

LARKIN falls to his knees.

Meyer	Yes, well, in any case, as I was saying... Ours is a family afflicted by tragic events.
Patty	A family on which the past weighs heavy as stone.
Meyer	Happiness was ours, but happiness has departed.
Patty	We had a daughter.
Meyer	Pauline was her name.
Patty	Never a brave girl, Pauline.
Meyer	Beautiful, but never brave.
Patty	And overly trusting.
Meyer	Disappeared five years back, our Pauline.
Patty	Right before that riot is when she vanished.
Meyer	L.A. reared up its angry mouth, swallowed her whole.
Patty	Swallowed up by Los Angeles, who knows where.
Meyer	The whole city went nuts.
Patty	For five long years we've been waiting.
Meyer	Patty hears a voice, she thinks it's someone bearing news. Even that homeless guy out front.
Patty	He knew something, Meyer.
Meyer	She thought that vagrant had information. Ha ha ha.
Patty	You had him dragged away.
Meyer	Drove her crazy, like you see her now.

Patty	Hope is not crazy.
Meyer	Look at those tears. How they tumble down her perfect cheeks.
Patty	Meyer loves to talk like I'm not here.
Meyer	She heard your voice, she thought you'd come with glad tidings.
Patty	Like I died long ago.
Meyer	Glad tidings about our sweet missing girl... *(Weeps)*
Patty	What is it, Meyer? You think I'm afraid of you? I was never afraid. A mother's heart is fearless. *(To LARKIN)* Pauline and I, we went over all this at various times. What to do in case of personal abduction or theft. The moves that can be made. The countermeasures. Escape. Flight. I gave her pointers, any mother would. But something must have happened to her memory. It'll come back, once she gets home. Once she gets home and things settle down, she'll recall the life that was ours and that remains ours. I sit there in back, I see her shuffling along, bent over, like I taught her. If I hold the image long enough, she'll come knocking on that door.
Larkin	I arrived. I'm here right now.
Patty	You?
Larkin	I'm not Pauline, but I'm here all the same.
Patty	Yes, you arrived.
Larkin	I could be here to rescue you.

PATTY crosses to LARKIN.

Patty	You had that homeless bastard up there all week long! He must have told you something!

Meyer	*(Drying his eyes)* I'm warning you, Patricia!
Patty	Where he took her! Where she's locked up, cold and hungry, crouching in the dark! *(To MEYER)* This goddamn cop's got answers, Meyer!
Meyer	They won't be the ones you want to hear!
Patty	I CAN SEE IT IN HIS EYE!
Meyer	It's been five long years!
Patty	I CAN SMELL IT ON HIM!
Meyer	I'M WARNING YOU, PATRICIA!
Patty	THE STENCH OF IT POURS OFF HIM IN WAVES!
Meyer	LOCK IT DOWN! LOCK IT DOWN!
Larkin	She's right. I do have answers.

Pause.

Patty	You hear that, Meyer?
Meyer	I heard it.
Patty	*(To LARKIN)* Let's have your answers one by one.
Larkin	Your daughter's very much alive. She's alive. She's safe. She's on her way here at the present moment.
Patty	These things you want. And you dream and you want... They *can* come true. You see that, Meyer? *(Then, pointing)* I just saw something...!
Meyer	*(Looking)* In the parking lot?
Patty	A shadow...!
Meyer	Out by the curb...?
Patty	Out there between the cars.
Meyer	*(Looking)* Nothing out there now...
Patty	Might have been a young woman. A young woman in a dress.
Meyer	*(Looking out)* No... girls... visible...

Pause.

Patty	I guess I maybe felt it more than saw it.
Meyer	In your bones.
Patty	In my bones.
Meyer	Either way, we're alone now.
Patty	I'm never alone. That's not how it is with me.
Meyer	It was your own reflection in the glass.
Patty	*(Beat)* My own reflection in the glass...
Meyer	Must have been.
Patty	*(Shrugging)* After five long years, what's a few minutes more? We'll straighten up. Lay out some presents. *(To LARKIN)* I need an estimated time of arrival.
Larkin	*(Lost in thought)* Estimated time of arrival...?
Patty	For Pauline.
Larkin	Right, the missing daughter...
Patty	When they'll bring her by. I mean, that's what you just said.
Larkin	*(Looking out)* Yes, but, have you ever noticed how the world...
Patty	My daughter.
Larkin	*(Gesturing out)* The telephone wires...
Patty	My little girl.
Larkin	... the sun-blasted buildings...
Patty	"She's on her way," is what you said.
Larkin	The whole world is trying to... wake up...
Patty	You said exactly that.
Larkin	*(Shifting)* Then it must be true. Look, you can relax, because they'd call first, wouldn't they?
Patty	*(Softer)* Before sending her over, they'd call...
Larkin	To check it's okay.
Patty	The front desk would call.

Larkin	Make sure someone's here to receive her.
Patty	"Is this Patty?" they'd say. "We've got good news," they'd say. "Your daughter's on her way." "Fine," I'd reply. *(To MEYER)* Are you getting all this, Meyer?
Meyer	All of it.
Patty	"I'm here," I'd say.
Meyer	*(To LARKIN)* You certainly took your sweet time getting around to the big revelation.
Patty	"I'm waiting."
Meyer	Why not come right out with it?
Patty	Oh, Meyer, what does that matter now?!
Meyer	Why all this beating around the bush?
Larkin	You gotta be careful with runaways, that's why.
Patty	Make sure it's safe back in the home.
Meyer	Why wouldn't it be safe?
Patty	No danger on the homefront.
Meyer	What exactly is the accusation?

Pause.

Patty	Are you really asking me that question?
Meyer	Okay, calm down.
Patty	'Cuz if you'd like me to delve into the grim details…
Meyer	No need to delve.
Patty	But it's a miracle. My Pauline. First thing, she'll shower, have a hot meal. But look at me. Such a mess. I'll go change.

PATTY runs out. A pause. MEYER regards LARKIN with great suspicion.

Meyer	Well, it certainly is quite exciting. The mystery solved after all these many years. A promising young woman reunited with her loving parents. Excitement indeed. *(Beat)* I hope you're not lying to my wife. She couldn't take it. She'd fall apart. Other cops, they've dangled similar hopes before. I'm not sure what they wanted. It's better I never find out. That's why I have to ask for some specific details. You know, with that vagrant. Back at the stationhouse. Did he explain his behavior? Did he confess? Did he beg for mercy on his knees?
Larkin	I'm not from the stationhouse.
Meyer	Come again?
Larkin	I've been lying.
Meyer	I see.
Larkin	Making things up as I go along.
Meyer	Let's have that badge. *(MEYER grabs the badge off LARKIN'S shirt)* This is no policeman's badge!
Larkin	Oh, I went over there the other day. To see my old pals.
Meyer	THIS BADGE IS MADE OF CHEAP PLASTIC!
Larkin	We tossed around the idea I might return to the force.
Meyer	IMPERSONATING AN OFFICER OF THE LAW! TAKING ADVANTAGE OF A MOTHER'S BROKEN HEART! YOU'RE NOTHING BUT A CON MAN OF THE VERY WORST KIND!
Larkin	*(Indicating Off)* What's she keep back there anyway?
Meyer	*(Shifting)* Back in the stock room?
Larkin	By way of furnishings.
Meyer	Well, I'm never all that sure. *(Off LARKIN'S look)* Oh, I'm not allowed back there.
Larkin	Not allowed in your own stockroom…?
Meyer	That stock room has been off limits for many a moon now.
Larkin	Harsh.

Meyer	Very harsh. And I'm unsure exactly how she's fixed it up.
Larkin	Go ahead and take a wild frickin' guess.
Meyer	I'd guess she's done it up real nice.
Larkin	She keep a cot back there...?
Meyer	More like a bed, I'd imagine. *(Beat)* I'd guess she's done the whole place up nice with, like, red and stuff.
Larkin	Lots of satin and cushions to put the visitor at his ease?
Meyer	Little canopy. She sleeps back there. *(Pause. Whispering)* Officer...? Can I still call you that?
Larkin	I don't see why not.
Meyer	Sure, I mean you're dressed like one. Officer...?
Larkin	Yes?
Meyer	I have opened every corner of my life to this woman. There's no place left for me to hide.

Pause.

Larkin	You know what they told me, don't you?
Meyer	Down at the stationhouse?
Larkin	When I stopped by the other day.
Meyer	Tell me what they said.
Larkin	They said your wife Patty, she'll offer it up to any man who puts you six feet under.
Meyer	That's what they said?
Larkin	That's what they said.
Meyer	Down at the stationhouse.
Larkin	I went over there, it was like nothing had changed. All my old pals gathered around. We discussed the international arena. Developments in microbiology. Before long our discussion drifted to this fine establishment. That's when

	they told me about your wife Patty. How she'll offer it up to any man who puts you six feet under.
Meyer	So you came down here to test out the proposition.
Larkin	Thought I'd investigate around some.

MEYER *slowly crosses, standing close to* LARKIN.

Meyer	I saw that vagrant up close one time, did they mention that too?
Larkin	The topic never came up, no.
Meyer	Saw him real close one time, yeah. Early on. Close as we are now. Came home early from my daily swim, he's at the stock room door working that lock with a shiv.
Larkin	What sort of visage did he offer up to the light of your inspection?

MEYER *studies* LARKIN'S *face.*

Meyer	Grimy. Panicked. Rabid. Scared Patricia half to death. One look at me, that vagrant hobbled off in his high-top sneakers. That's when I called in my initial report, got Kilkelly on the horn. "John," I said—he and the boys were playing mahjong, so it must have been a Tuesday—"John," I said, "I just got back from the Y," I said, "there's a goddamn vagrant in my store, wreaking havoc with the wife." "We'll take care of it," I'm told. "Don't give it another thought," he says. Frickin' guy's back out front by fall of night!
Larkin	They manipulate the legal system at will, these vagrants.
Meyer	By fall of night he's prancing around out on my center divider! I felt let down!

Larkin	After all you've done for them over the years!
Meyer	Oh, they've been treating me like dirt.
Larkin	Like some Johnny-on-the-spot!
Meyer	Hey, I know where the goddamn bodies are buried!
Larkin	They should take care of you!
Meyer	Damn right, they should take care!
Larkin	Instead all you get are threats and innuendo!
Meyer	A thick fog of lies!
Larkin	Next time you wanna go take your dip...
Meyer	Goddamn vagrant on the loose...
Larkin	Your wife stuck there in back...
Meyer	All open to the skies...
Larkin	Terrorized...!
Meyer	Even at night, she never leaves. *(Woman's voice)* "I'm not leavin'. He'll follow us home. He'll see where we live." *(Normal voice)* Oh, it's been a trying time for Meyer. A very trying time... *(Wipes his brow)* On the other hand, every era is subject to change, as I've learned many times over the course of my long life. Every era is subject to change, and looking back, well, even some of the very worst patches get tinged with a certain nostalgia. *(Pause)* Let me tell you, that whole time he was out there... it was... well... *(Then, smiling)* In the mornings, what I'd do, I'd escort Patty out for little walks.
Larkin	Just to the edge of the parking lot.
Meyer	She'd smoke a cigarette or two, run back inside and hide.
Larkin	One look from that hungry vagrant...
Meyer	One look is all it ever took.
Larkin	The general seediness of the guy.
Meyer	The lack of prospects.

Larkin	The whole way he carried himself was contagious.
Meyer	Ah, but it was cute the way she scampered.
Larkin	It was. It was very cute.
Meyer	It rained that day they came and got him. Did I mention? And the streets were slick.
Larkin	Yeah, we went over all that.
Meyer	Oh, good. *(Pause)*... he seemed so weak, so tired and cold... sad, really... young man like that... *(Pause)* It wasn't so bad, all in all. Having him out there, come rain or come shine. All and all I was adjusting to his presence. Have to admit being a little surprised by the viciousness of the sudden snatch-'n-grab. I'd been complaining for months. Why now?
Larkin	They were just reaching out to help a good friend.
Meyer	You mean me?
Larkin	Because it was an unworkable situation.
Meyer	A little help from the boys in blue...
Larkin	For your long years of service.
Meyer	Once in a great while they do choke out some meager token of respect...
Larkin	Cough up some spare officer to keep your wife company...
Meyer	Cover that loose hour...
Larkin	That loose hour here or there...
Meyer	I go swim my laps knowing things are copacetic back at the ranch...
Larkin	Everybody benefits...
Meyer	Where's the harm?
Larkin	Speaking of which, lap swim time's come and gone almost by now.
Meyer	*(Checking watch)* The evening session, almost gone!

Larkin	Why not head on over to the Y, stroke off a couple quick 800s.
Meyer	You'd keep an eye on things here?
Larkin	I'd be happy to.
Meyer	Stay here, guard the missus?
Larkin	I'll keep her safe and sound from every menace.
Meyer	Let me get this straight. You'd take an hour out of your very busy day just to help me out? Me, a total stranger? That's... I don't know how to put it... that's remarkable is the only word for it. Remarkable. In this era. In this time and place. And I am... touched. No, let me finish. I am deeply moved. That you would take my concerns, my issues, my worries, that you would take them to heart in such a selfless fashion. On the other hand, since they came and got that vagrant, what the hell do I need you for?
Larkin	Good point.
Meyer	There's no danger now.
Larkin	You don't need me at all.
Meyer	You could fuck off right out of my store.

Pause.

Larkin	Guess I could just fuck right off.
Meyer	I leave my front door swinging open in the breeze, there's no problem now.
Larkin	No danger day or night, unless... what if he escaped?
Meyer	*(Beat)* Escaped? That young man?
Larkin	From the stationhouse, yeah. What if he broke loose?
Meyer	Scarecrow like that, he'd never break loose. Through all those hundreds of cops? Never.
Larkin	He'd hustle right back down here, looking for a way in.

Meyer	They'd cuff him hand and foot like a fucking goat.
Larkin	They might undo the cuffs and turn him loose.
Meyer	They'd never dare! To me? Not a chance. *(Beat)* WHY IN GOD'S NAME WOULD THEY DO ME THAT WAY, THOSE MOTHERLESS—
Larkin	Could've been some kind of connection between them.
Meyer	BETWEEN A BUNCH OF LAPD COPS AND A HOME-LESS, STINKING— Maybe he himself is an ex-cop.
Larkin	An ex-cop wanting to rejoin the force.
Meyer	Wanting to prove himself after a long absence. *(Beat)* Hell, he could be you—IN FACT, I THINK HE IS YOU! I THINK YOU'RE THAT YOUNG MAN THEY DRAGGED AWAY! I THINK THEY SHAVED YOUR FACE, TOSSED YOU IN THE SHOWER, STUFFED YOU INTO A UNIFORM AND SENT YOU DOWN HERE TO END MY LIFE! BE HONEST! WHAT DID I DO? WAS IT MY WIFE? HAS SHE THREATENED SOMEONE? IS SHE BEING IN ANY WAY DIFFICULT? IS THAT WHO YOU CAME FOR?!
Larkin	Calm down, pops, you'll freak yourself out.
Meyer	Okay.

MEYER sits. Long pause. LARKIN chuckles.

Larkin	You thought I came here to kill you!
Meyer	I did. That's what I thought. And now I love you. I love you dearly and tears of joy pour down my face. On the other hand, I'd like you to leave right now and never come back. I don't want you in my store.

The phone rings. Both men stare at the phone. It rings again. MEYER *grabs it.*

Meyer   *(Into phone)* Lo-Cost Digical Repair... Yeah, John... *(To* LARKIN, *cupping phone)* It's the Lieutenant... *(Into phone)* What's that? *(Long pause)* Oh, well sure... *(A beat.* MEYER *hands the phone to* LARKIN*)*

Larkin   *(Into phone)* Hey, boss... Sure, I can do that... No, not a problem...

LARKIN *hands the phone back to* MEYER. MEYER *hangs it up. A pause.*

Meyer   Did he say anything? What did he say?

LARKIN *picks up the bowl of olives.*

Larkin   *(Offering)* Have an olive.

They regard each other.

BLACKOUT.

End of Act One

424

Act Two

*LARKIN holds the pit bowl out for MEYER. MEYER spits a
pit into the bowl.*

Meyer   *(Looking out)* Who's that...?!

Larkin   Who's what?

Meyer   Thought I saw someone...

Larkin   In the parking lot?

Meyer   Moving sideways past the cars...

Larkin   Coulda been a customer.

Meyer   *(Incredulous)* For *my* shop?

Larkin   Could've been heading for the dry cleaners.

Meyer   *(Beat)* Delblanco, sure.

Larkin   Could've been your own nightmarish reflection in the glass.

Meyer   This has been one of the worst days on record.

Larkin   It's not over yet, pops. *(Looking around)* Not a bad idea at all. For an ex-policeman. Shop like this.

Meyer   Has its advantages.

Larkin   I mean, do I really want to recommence with the daily grind? Is that my big dream in life?

Meyer   I had a dream once. About Kilkelly and the guys. They surprised me in the shallow end, is what I dreamed. I'm swimming my 800, I look up... the whole stationhouse is standing there. They grab my ankles. Hold me under. Listen to me, officer, there's a way you can rule over them. From a position like this. Knowing where the bodies are buried, that's leverage. Oh, sure, at one time or another, they've all come to me and kneeled down. But I got tired of their petty disputes. And during my war with that vagrant I grew... inattentive. I let the reins slip from my hand. And now all I want to do is sit alone somewhere, warmed by the sun. It could be like an occupation. The sad majesty of it all. This time and place. The beauty all around us... *(Then, calling off)* Patty...?! *(To LARKIN)* I miss her when she's away. *(Calling off)* PATTY...!?

Silence.

Larkin	I went back to Simi this morning. To get my old uniform. There was a parade. I thought it was for me. It wasn't for me. Didn't have anything to do with me. In fact, they chased me out of there. Couldn't even march in my own parade! Then I couldn't find my old house. All the houses looked the same. Finally, they chased me out of the whole goddamn valley. Like I was... I don't know... unclean. *(Indicating uniform)* I had to buy this in a secondhand store.
Meyer	Oh, that really is too frickin' bad.
Larkin	The glow is gone. The glow has definitely faded. *(Moves to the stock room door and stares off. A long pause)*
Meyer	Tell me something, officer.
Larkin	What is it?
Meyer	Are you the jealous type?

Larkin	Not at all, no.
Meyer	I'm the jealous type. Always have been. Patty and I, we joke it wasn't love at first sight, it was jealous at first sight. Oh, I obsess about her constantly. In my mind she's like a planet, weighing everything down. When we first met, she looked like Joan Baez. The magnificence of that face...! I brought her out here via the Panama Canal. I'd drag her up to the prow of that freighter just to watch her shining beauty light up the dark waters all around. Everyone else on board could have dropped dead of the plague, I wouldn't have noticed. Thing about Patty, though...once she worms her way into your heart you need an axe to hack her out!

The door to the stock room swings open. Both men step back in fear. A pause.

Meyer	Can you make out what she's up to back there?

LARKIN crosses. Looks around the door. Returns.

Larkin	*(Low)* She's gotten all undressed...
Meyer	She does that sometimes, I'm told. Takes off all her clothes.

Pause.

Larkin	*(Looking off)* Now she's climbing into a yellow dress.
Meyer	A yellow sundress?
Larkin	*(Looking off)* Bright yellow sundress...

Meyer	I know the one. Haven't seen it for years. Very flattering to her comely figure. You should feel honored.
Larkin	Maybe I should go, you know, lend a hand.
Meyer	Over my dead body you step one foot in that stock room, pal! *(Pause)* She'll come out. Not to worry. She'll come out, she'll say, "I thought I heard voices." "Patty's a graduate of the liberal arts," I'll say. "With that graceful neck. Isn't her neck graceful?" *(Laughing)* She'll say, "I thought I heard a woman's voice."
Larkin	Maybe she's been dreaming.
Meyer	Oh, sure. She whiles away the daylight hours.
Larkin	About that missing daughter, most likely.
Meyer	Someone's a part of your world, suddenly they're gone. Swallowed up by Los Angeles, who knows where. Trust me. She'll come out. She'll tell you not to look at her. "Turn aside," she'll say. Here's another thing she'll tell you: "Meyer's in love with failure." That's what she'll say.
Larkin	Is it true?
Meyer	Sure it's true. Meyer loves to fail.
Larkin	Failure can be... liberating.
Meyer	Winning chokes the life out of you! Nobody knows that better than Meyer. *(Beat)* Meyer was a melon farmer. One of the very best. Had a house out there in Topanga. Couple kids sprouting up among the weeds. He'd go scuba diving down by Portuguese Bend. Take his spear gun, walk right out into the waves. He wasn't afraid. The sea was his friend. He'd come back loaded down with lobster and abalone. Net fulls he'd shake out across the kitchen floor. It was a quiet time for Meyer, a good time for Meyer...
Larkin	What ended it?

Meyer	What? Oh, jail time. What else? Prison. Obispo. *(Beat)* Look at you, wondering—what was he in for? Bad. The very worst. Murder is what I was convicted of. My wife, they say. They say I killed my Patty in a melon field... as if she wasn't in back right now helping out with the rent, God bless her...!
Larkin	I begin to think you're an extremely violent man.
Meyer	No excuse for that. Violence. Not ever. And it's a mystery to me. Remains a mystery to me. Where that violence comes from. When it seizes my shoulders and locks onto my brain. Am I repellent, do you find? Am I a deeply repellent man, or, here's another question: can deeply repellent men like me, can we redeem ourselves? Is that even possible? And what would it look like, if we could redeem ourselves? What in God's name would that look like?
Larkin	If you redeemed yourself you'd become somebody different.
Meyer	I would, wouldn't I. I'd be somebody different. *(Beat)* No more Meyer.

PATTY enters wearing a sundress from the 1960s. The dress has long gashes in it. She crosses, moving close to LARKIN.

Patty	Sorry it took so long. As I was dressing an image came to mind. I saw myself standing in a melon field, only I didn't look like myself. "Who is this woman," I asked myself. "Who is this woman in my memories?" *(Crosses center)* Well, I'm ready for my Pauline. Call whoever you need to call. Have them send her in.
Larkin	I can't do that.

Patty	Why not?
Larkin	There's something wrong with that dress, that's why.
Meyer	Little tears in it?
Larkin	LITTLE RIPS AND TEARS IN THAT GODDAMN DRESS!
Patty	This is the dress I wore when Pauline was taken from me.
Larkin	LITTLE GASHES IN THAT DRESS!
Patty	I looked up and said goodbye and then I got dragged down into darkness.

PATTY freezes.

Larkin	*(To MEYER, breathless)* Sorry I went off like that... It's just... I had a female friend once... I let her move into my cabana... but then we got... over-involved... and that was unhealthy.
Meyer	Are you okay?
Larkin	Just... catch my breath...
Meyer	You don't need to feel ashamed. We know how it is. You can wander into these relationships where you spiral downward, and everywhere you turn your way is blocked, and all the walls of your prison are on fire and closing in on you, consuming oxygen.
Larkin	*(To PATTY, calm now)* Tell me something, missus. What's it like being married? Do you enjoy it?

PATTY crosses to LARKIN. She leans in, kissing LARKIN on the mouth. MEYER looks on.

Meyer	*(To PATTY)* Go ahead. Tell him. *(Pause)* Okay, then, I'll tell him.

PATTY and LARKIN separate, looking at each other. They kiss again.

Meyer   Thing about marriage, see… there are always little tensions. Also, it can be easy to take each other for granted. It can be easy to forget how special one's partner is, given the mind-numbing routines of daily life.

MEYER crosses, grabs the bag LARKIN brought in and unzips it. He rummages through the bag, pulling out a filthy overcoat. He shakes the overcoat in the light, staring intently.

Larkin   Pauline—that was my friend's name.

Hearing the name, PATTY recoils.

Meyer   Hey, now. I've been looking for a coat like this.

Patty   Did you hear that, Meyer?!

Meyer   I could wear this down to the Y like a kind of housecoat.

Patty   This officer had a girlfriend. His girlfriend's name was Pauline.

Covering herself with her hands, PATTY crosses toward MEYER.

Patty   GET MY ROBE, MEYER! CAN'T YOU SEE I'M ALMOST NAKED?!

PATTY turns and sees MEYER in the coat. He raises his arms, scaring her.

Meyer	Raaaa!!!!

Patty screams and runs toward the door. She stops before exiting. Meyer laughs.

Meyer	Ha ha ha, did you see that?! Did you see how she scampered?!
Larkin	Cute. Very cute.
Meyer	Heh, heh... Thinking I'm that homeless guy back from the dead...!
Patty	*(Turns and speaks)* That's not what she thought.
Meyer	No?
Patty	Larkin knows where Pauline is right now, is what she thinks.
Meyer	*(Sobers)* She's not as crazy as she seems, because I think so too.
Larkin	Well, I know where to find my old friend Pauline. But I also know your wife can't be her mother.
Meyer	You'll need to explain that little puzzle.
Larkin	Pauline's mother died when Pauline was very young.
Meyer	That's terrible.
Patty	She was killed.
Meyer	No!
Patty	A case of murder.
Meyer	Murder!?
Larkin	In a melon field when Pauline was five years old.
Meyer	Murder is a serious offense!
Patty	Very serious!
Meyer	And traumatic! For a five year old?!
Larkin	She and her kinfolk were out on a picnic.
Meyer	A family picnic?
Larkin	I'm afraid so.

Meyer	How terrible!
Patty	A picnic in a melon field.
Meyer	With a checkered cloth?
Larkin	And a wicker basket.
Meyer	Death among the melons for Pauline's ma!
Larkin	Poor little tyke!
Meyer	Sad little creature in her tiny blue dress!
Patty	Witnessing the terrible event!
Meyer	Ancient history now.
Patty	Few remember it.
Meyer	Maybe you should go investigate that crime!
Larkin	It was investigated in its day.
Meyer	Well, I'm greatly relieved to hear you say that...!
Larkin	The offending party was tried and punished, put away for many years.
Meyer	The filthy bastard...!
Patty	Turns out it was the poor woman's husband.
Meyer	All too often is in such cases, sad to say!
Patty	She'd fallen for another man, is what he believed.
Meyer	Oh, she was very cruel, that woman!
Larkin	He had the same name as you, the man who killed Mama.
Meyer	Well, then, I should change my name!
Patty	Meyer was his name.
Meyer	I'll have to change my name to Natches or Dougherty after learning that! I'll need to get down on my knees and do hard penance! With each breath I'll need to choke on a black smog that clouds my eyes! And still it won't be enough! It'll never be enough unless you forgive me! YOU, YOURSELVES! RIGHT HERE, RIGHT NOW!

MEYER falls to his knees at LARKIN'S feet. PATTY turns and crosses to the shelves, stage right. LARKIN crosses to the stock room door and peers off.

Larkin   She okay?

Meyer   *(Looking off)* She's just upset. She'll get over it. She generally does. You're the problem. You get on her nerves. A husband can tell these things.

Larkin   Maybe I should go... lend a hand.

Meyer   *(Despondent)* Ah, she'll come back out. Any minute now she'll come out, she'll say, "I thought I heard a woman's voice."

Larkin   Maybe she's been dreaming.

Meyer   *(Distraught)* Oh sure, she whiles away the daylight hours.

Larkin   About that missing daughter, most likely.

PATTY takes a worn jewelry box from the shelves and sits on the floor with it. It's the kind of box that might belong to a small child. She opens it, taking out small beads and trinkets.

Meyer   Can you blame her? Someone's a part of your world, suddenly they're gone. Swallowed up by Los Angeles.

Larkin   *(Standing)* I think I'll go talk one-on-one with your wife right now.

Meyer   *(In tears)* No, please...! I won't let you...! There must be a way...! For me to explain...! How these things persist and—and—and get passed down.

Larkin   From father to son...

Meyer   From father to son...

Larkin	I already know that.
Meyer	You do?
Larkin	My name... I'm Larkin.

Hearing the name, PATTY *clutches the jewelry box protectively.* MEYER *looks up, stares at* LARKIN.

Meyer	Officer *Larkin?*
Larkin	I know.
Meyer	Your fellow officers, they hear your name, they light right up.
Larkin	Good cops everywhere do.
Meyer	You were a legend on the force. With your daring. Your indifference to danger.
Larkin	I believed.
Meyer	They hear your name, they light right up. But then straight away the light kind of... dies.
Larkin	Kind of fades away.
Meyer	And you ask 'em why and they point to a certain spasm of civic violence that brought the entire city to its knees.
Larkin	I'm the one that set it off.
Meyer	The riots, yes. You lit the spark. Beating that black man in the street like you did. And the news channels replaying the footage for days on end.
Larkin	The poor black bastard.
Meyer	He was a blind man, if I remember correctly. Come to think of it, before she disappeared our Pauline took up with a black guy blind in both eyes. Hakim was his name. Oh, he was well known about town, Hakim. What he'd do, he'd access the spirits of the dead. In order to locate

missing relatives. He took a special interest in Pauline. Because her case was so unique. She'd lost touch with her cherished brother, that was the thing. Hakim was making progress too. Claimed he'd found the guy, a member of the LAPD.

Larkin I'll tell you how it started. I was just sitting at my desk smiling softly in my usual manner. Here comes blind Hakim, walking right up to my desk, tap tap tap. Says he wants to talk about some "personal matter." I tossed my coffee in his face. Then, later, I tracked him back to his crappy little bungalow. And see, well, swinging a police baton, after a while your arm gets sore up near the shoulder. So I give myself a breather. A little downtime. That's when I see Pauline in the doorway, watching me with those spooky eyes. In that first glance I know she and I have something to give each other over the long haul. Hakim feels it too, I can tell. Kneeling there on the asphalt, he looks up at us with shining eyes, clear eyes... the man is free. No name, no past, no history at all.

Meyer What happened to Pauline?

Larkin I took her home.

Meyer Out to Simi Valley.

Patty Little ranch house out in Simi.

Meyer Little pool house in back...

Patty Nestled up against the hills.

Meyer Way back off the street.

Larkin For a time we were happy out there, Pauline and I.

Patty But we were...

Larkin ... too much alike...

Patty ... and we...

Larkin	... fell into each other.

A pause. MEYER *moves close to* LARKIN.

Meyer	*(Soft)* You don't need to feel ashamed. I know how it is. You can wander into these relationships where you spiral downward and it becomes—
Larkin	*(Cutting him off)* Fortunately I had some friends, they intervened.
Meyer	Your buddies on the force, looking out for one of their own. *(Sits close to* LARKIN*)*
Patty	They came and took Pauline.
Meyer	They knew where she belonged.
Larkin	They came and took her, they wouldn't tell me where.
Meyer	They knew I'd keep her safe and sound.
Patty	*(Looking around)* They brought her here, it seems to me right now.
Meyer	Little girls, how they long for papa's steady hand! And the police, they're sensitive to that need. And maybe even her father had, you know, put in a special request to his friends on the force, and made certain promises regarding services he would render in return. And for you too, maybe this was best. Knowing how confused things can become in your fragile mind.
Larkin	I let it get me down.
Meyer	You wandered off.
Patty	Across the city at night...
Meyer	Your head bent low toward the surface of the streets...
Patty	Never looking left or right...
Meyer	Following a thread only you could see...

Larkin	I came down along the boulevards.
Meyer	Your clothes fell away.
Larkin	My beard grew long.
Meyer	People stepped away on your approach.
Patty	The months turned into years.
Larkin	I hobbled along in my high-top sneakers. And then one day, there she is...
Patty	Out for her morning walk to the edge of the parking lot.
Larkin	I stand in silent wonder until the birds fly down and settle on my outstretched arms.

Long pause.

Patty	Here's what you could have done: you could have taken him with you.
Meyer	Who's that?
Patty	That young vagrant.
Meyer	Lurking out front in his cloud of flies...! No good for business...! No good at all...!
Patty	You could've taken him with you down to the Y.

MEYER crosses down, staring out at the street.

Meyer	*(To himself)* Young man like that... probably hadn't had a good scrub for ages...
Larkin	You could've taken him with you to the Y, tossed him in the shallow end, let him paddle to and fro with all them other youngsters.
Meyer	*(Smiling)* He could have been like a son to me.
Larkin	Patricia stays here, parades around without a care...

438

Meyer	I had a son once. For all I know he's still out there, rattling around in the world... but let me tell you something, pal— there is nothing in this world like a good lap swim. *(Paces the shop now, limbering up)*
Larkin	Exercising all the muscle groups at once.
Meyer	And the chlorine...!
Larkin	Public pool, they use a lot!
Meyer	They do! They use a lot! But not enough for me!
Larkin	Most people dislike chlorine.
Meyer	Not me, I love it! I love the smell of it! I love the feeling on my skin, that coating of chalk and lime—it's like you're dead already! Sometimes I think it gets right into my bones!
Larkin	I can smell it on you right now.
Meyer	No kidding.
Larkin	Noticed it right away. I said to myself, this man's a lap swimmer.
Meyer	I am! I'm a lap swimmer! It's one of the bonuses of this location, proximity to the Y. Patty didn't want to come down here, but I know a good deal when it crosses my path. My friends at the stationhouse, they helped us relocate, did I tell you that? They said they needed help with the troubled population of this district. I didn't argue. I do pretty much what they say. If you can't trust the police, who can you trust? I learned that in the pen. Oh, I was the darling of the C.O.s. I'd snitch off my best friend for a pack of smokes.
Patty	Why don't you go grab yourself a couple laps right now?
Meyer	Oh, it's long past lap swim time by now.
Patty	Maybe they'll let you in anyway.
Meyer	They keep that building locked up tight.

Patty	Not tonight.
Meyer	No?
Larkin	Tonight the locks on that Y are all open.
Meyer	All open to the skies... !
Patty	The locks are all open, the water glows!
Meyer	Oh, I love it when the water glows!
Larkin	All around you the water glows!
Meyer	What time is it? You could stick around a while?
Larkin	Not a problem.
Meyer	Couple quick 800s, be back in sixty minutes tops. *(Starts out. Pauses in the doorway, then turns and looks back at LARKIN)* Let's say I left right now to swim my laps.
Larkin	To the Y?
Meyer	Leaving you here to guard the missus.
Larkin	I'd keep her safe and sound from every menace.
Meyer	Well, but... what all would happen next?
Larkin	After you left?
Meyer	Lay it out for me in black and white.
Larkin	Well, uh, you're gone five or ten minutes, probably your wife would sidle on out all slinkified and beautiful.
Meyer	Sidle on out for a chat...?
Larkin	And to socialize.
Meyer	*(Turns to PATTY)* Honey? Our friend Larkin here, he's saying that if I left right now, you'd slink on out for a little chat.
Patty	And to socialize.
Meyer	You'd sidle on out through the stock room door just to chat this young fucker up?
Patty	I'm cooped up sewing all day long.
Meyer	What kind of wicked things would you two chat about?
Patty	Tough to tell.

Meyer	Take a wild frickin' guess.
Patty	Oh, I might say something like: "It's very cruel what they're planning to do. To my husband. Down at that Y."
Meyer	You'd just lob that right out there, huh.
Patty	"It's cruel what they're planning to do... your fellow officers." That might be my opening line. "Grabbing his ankles that way. Holding him under."
Meyer	*(To LARKIN)* Assuming she said all that about the Y, how would you respond?
Larkin	I'd probably be a little staggered back.
Meyer	I can see how you might be.
Larkin	I'd shake my head once or twice, ask her to repeat that hurtful statement.
Meyer	*(To PATTY)* Would you repeat it for him? Would you clarify?
Patty	"It's very cruel what they're planning to do to my husband. Don't think I don't know."

Pause.

Larkin	I bet he's upset now. I bet he's very upset.
Patty	That right, Poppa? You upset?

MEYER watches, silent.

Patty	Is he gone?
Larkin	Gone to the Y to swim his laps.
Patty	I hope he never comes back.
Larkin	He'll never come back, and we won't miss him.
Patty	*(Moving up behind LARKIN)* What's the first thing we'll do when they're finished and he's dead?

Larkin	We'll wander the streets.
Patty	Free at last.
Larkin	Free at last.
Patty	You'll ask me questions all day long.
Larkin	You won't be married anymore.
Patty	What kind of questions will you ask?
Larkin	For starters I'd ask something about your age.
Patty	Do I seem young to you?
Larkin	To have raised a full grown daughter. A full grown daughter who then left and disappeared and all of that.
Patty	Oh, well, my Pauline and I are the same age.
Larkin	You and your daughter are the same age...?
Patty	Born at the very same moment.
Larkin	Listen, sweetheart, your speech apparatus, it's in need of repair. Each time you talk you spit out broken words. They're broken when they come out and crooked.
Patty	What if I actually am Pauline?
Meyer	You gotta admire the way she lays it right out there!
Larkin	No... woman... can be... her own... daughter! *(Then, calmly)* Something slips when you speak. "What if I am Pauline?" Hear that? That little slip beneath the words?
Patty	Would you be happy or sad...

The character previously referred to as PATTY *will now be referred to as* PAULINE.

	... if I really were your Pauline?
Meyer	She's asking you a big question now, boy! Would you be happy or sad?!
Larkin	I feel... not so good on my feet.

PAULINE backs away upstage. She pauses in the doorway, turning to LARKIN.

Pauline	Why would I want to occupy Patricia's life?
Larkin	Oh, well, she was our mother.
Pauline	And you know this?
Larkin	But then it slips my mind again. Should it be like that?
Pauline	Where you can know something and not know it at the same time.
Larkin	I don't think it should be like that.

PAULINE moves up behind LARKIN, close.

Pauline	Do you remember, Larkin, when we were kids together in the mornings we'd walk to school in Topanga and the air would be wet on our faces with mist from the sea?
Larkin	Down that winding, long canyon road…
Pauline	Do you recall that white dog, he would wait for us?
Larkin	Little stray pup waiting for us beside the road…
Pauline	Little white dog turning flips on the shoulder of the road, remember that?
Larkin	And we'd feed him table scraps and he'd run around attacking shafts of sunlight? No. No, I don't remember that at all.

PAULINE touches LARKIN'S cheek. MEYER groans, gnashing his teeth.

Pauline	Will you stay with me a while? There's nothing wrong. I'll teach you things. How to be alone.

Long silence.

Meyer   Okay, okay, what would happen next? If I were to head off to the Y and then come home dripping from my swim?

Larkin   Our friends from the force didn't meet you there?

Meyer   *(Touching the coat)* Didn't see me. In my new disguise, I passed unnoticed. They let me swim my laps thinking I was some homeless beggar. They let me climb out and leave again, heading home dripping from my swim.

Larkin   Back from your swim.

Meyer   Refreshed from my swim, finding the two of you here and me none the wiser.

Larkin   None the wiser, but refreshed in your extremities.

Meyer   Nothing happened while I was gone? No sign of that vagrant?

Larkin   All quiet on the center divider. And you? See anything on your way home?

Meyer   The whole city's quiet. No one's around. The streets are devoid of cars. And the stars hang naked in the sky, have you noticed? The entire world holds its breath, can you feel it? There's no wind. The wind is sick. The wind is sick and stayed home, up off the streets. And the sky got sucked out into space. And there's nothing to be done. *(Pause)* Would it be okay if I just stayed out there?

Pauline   Out on our center divider?

Meyer   Stayed out there warning of dangers?

Larkin   And never came in?

Meyer   And never came in.

Pauline   And never begged for favors or scraps.

Meyer   Never begged for favors or scraps.

Larkin	And always blessed the store and all its commerce.
Meyer	And approved in advance new floor displays and blessed them.
Pauline	And blessed the customers streaming in.

A Pause. The sound of rainfall.

Larkin	Well, if you don't have any more questions for us today...
Meyer	I think that about settles it.
Pauline	I'm relieved to hear you say that.
Meyer	You thought I came here to kill you!
Larkin	I did.
Pauline	That's what I thought.
Larkin	And now I love you.
Pauline	I love you dearly and tears of joy pour down my face.
Larkin	On the other hand, I'd like you to leave right now and never come back.
Pauline	We don't want you in our store.

Pause.

| Meyer | I'll let myself out. |

Nobody moves. Lights slowly fade to black.

The End

The Apple Juice Man

by Sarah Koskoff

A reading of **Apple Juice Man** *was performed at the Tamarind Theater in October 2006, under the direction of Guy Zimmerman, with the following cast:*

Dad/Sol: Brian Cox
Dan Sackiss: Arye Gross
Miranda: Angela Goethals
Ghost: Shannon Holt

Characters

Dad/Sol *A pissed-off former actor and Miranda's father, 50s.*
Dan Sackiss *A movie producer, also former actor, 40s.*
Miranda *A precocious, neurotic girl, 15.*
Ghost *The ghost of Miranda's mother.*

Scene

The backyard of MIRANDA *and* SOL'S *house, overgrown from lack of care. The woods encroach on the stage, right. A door to the house, left. Also an entrance to the backyard from the front of the house, center left.*

Act One

Lights up briefly on the hazy, pale face of a woman, upstage center. Her arms are crossed over her chest, hands by her neck. Pause in black. Lights up on SOL, fifties, dressed in outdated clothes, his shirt awkwardly tucked into his khakis.

Sol   *(Hands out like he's just rolled dice)* So the lights come up on me, right? And I'm standin' out there and I got these robes on, 'cause I'm the king, right...? Ha-ha-ha-ha-ha-ha— And Sackiss—Sackiss was the fool...

Lights up on DAN SACKISS, forties. He wears an expensive, beige linen suit with pleated pants and carries a soft leather overnight bag and shoulder bag. SACKISS looks at SOL, stone-faced. Frozen moment. SACKISS then purses his lips, a smile, then a laugh. He opens his arms, and they both burst into loud laughter.

Both   Ah-ha-ha-ha-ha-ha-ha-ha...

Lights up on Miranda, fifteen, gawky, in shorts, looking upstage at SOL and SACKISS.

Miranda	*(Covering her mouth and laughing along, eagerly)* Hm-hm-hm...
Sol	*(Shaking his head)* You motherfucker...
Sackiss	*(Shaking a finger at* SOL*)* No no no...
Sol	You lousy motherfucker... *(To* MIRANDA*)* This is a guy...
Sackiss	Ha-ha...
Sol	*(Finger at* SACKISS*)* Shh... This is a guy who...
Sackiss	No no... *(To* MIRANDA*)* Your father is the kind of guy....
Sol	No, no, no, no...
Sackiss	Ha-ha. Yes.
Sol	*(Hand up)* Hold on, hold on...
Sackiss	No, no—outta my way—Ha-ha...
Sol	I'm trying to tell a story over here. Ha-ha!
Sackiss	Outta my way, you fuckin' prick! Ha-ha. *(To* MIRANDA*)* You shouldn't believe a word he says, you know.
Miranda	*(Covering her mouth, forcing a laugh)* Hm-hm-hm...
Sol	So this is the story...
Sackiss	Jesus...
Sol	I'm standing out there on stage...
Sackiss	He doesn't give up this guy...
Sol	And the lights come up on me—and I got these robes on see... Ha-ha...
Sackiss	Jesus Christ...
Sol	And I'm the king, and—
Sackiss	Put a sock in it, would ya? *(Turning to* MIRANDA*, bending forward)* Ha-ha-ha-ha!
Sol	Wait-wait-wait—So I'm standing out there, like I said, and I got these robes on, right?
Sackiss	Hey—We know! We know you got the robes on, okay? *(Rolling his eyes)* Jesus...!

Sol	Well—it's the truth!
Sackiss	Enough with the, with the robes...
Sol	No no no...
Sackiss	Oy—He rewrites history, this one... Ha-ha!
Sol	My memory's like a fuckin' diamond...
Sackiss	Nuh-uh... *(Pointing at MIRANDA, knowingly)* See, she knows, she knows... Ha-ha....
Miranda	*(Covering her mouth in a forced giggle)* Hm-hm...
Sol	You know this story, Dan....
Sackiss	*(Shaking his head)* I don't know it...
Sol	Let me tell it, let me tell it. Come on...
Sackiss	Ha-ha.
Sol	What—still feel guilty? About leaving me out there, leaving me out there on stage? About missing your entrance completely! Still feel guilty?

Beat.

Sackiss	*(Dismissive gesture)* Nah.

SOL and SACKISS and MIRANDA burst into laughter.
Laughter fades as they recover.

Sackiss	Well, look at you, huh? I don't believe it.
Sol	I don't believe it.
Sackiss	Look at what's happened to you! Huh? You've gotten gray.
Sol	Fuck me—I've gotten more than that!
Sackiss	Nah...
Sol	Look at you, though.

Sackiss	Yeah... *(Patting his belly)* I've thickened. *(To MIRANDA)* Like a tree. Ha-ha...
Sol	*(Dismissive gesture)* Noooo....
Sackiss	Yes I have, yes I have. It's what men do. It's okay.
Sol	Well—whatta ya know—You're like an apparition. Like a ghost.
Sackiss	Nah... *(Comic beat, then)* Ghosts aren't hung like me! Ha-ha-ha-ha-ha-ha.
Sol	Ah-ha-ha-ha-ha-ha. *(Beat)* This is my daughter, Miranda.
Sackiss	Oh, excuse me.
Miranda	It's okay.
Sol	She doesn't care.
Sackiss	Hello there. Hello there.
Miranda	Hi.
Sol	What's the point in keeping her protected?
Miranda	I'm sophisticated.
Sackiss	And my name's Sackiss nice to meet you. Ha ha.

SACKISS holds out his hand. MIRANDA shakes it. She tries to take her hand away. He won't let go.

Sackiss	Ha-ha...
Miranda	*(Covering her mouth with her free hand)* Hm-hm-hm...
Sackiss	Ha-ha— I'm just kidding. *(Lets go of her hand)* Oh, here's a good one. So this actor comes home and finds his house burned down. He says, "What the hell is goin' on here?" Neighbor says, "Oh, man it's terrible," he says, "your agent came by and raped and murdered your wife and daughter and burned your house down." Actor says, "My agent came by?!" Ah-ha-ha-ha-ha!

Sol	Ha-ha-ha-ha-ha...
Miranda	*(Covering her mouth)* Hm-hm-hm...
Sackiss	*(To* MIRANDA*)* So your Dad tell you about me?
Miranda	I—
Sol	Course I did...
Sackiss	He tell you I was funny?
Miranda	Well...
Sol	Course I did, Miranda.
Miranda	I don't think so.
Sol	Jesus Christ. Course I did! This is Sackiss, Mir! Jesus.
Miranda	Okay!
Sol	I told you! We acted together!
Sackiss	Jesus—that was us? Ha-ha...
Miranda	That's amazing...
Sol	I haven't seen you in what? Twenty-five years. Something.
Sackiss	Incredible. *(Putting his bags down and looking around)* Wooooowwwww... Look at where you live. I don't believe it. I don't believe it.
Sol	This is it. Home sweet home. This is where it all happens. Ha-ha...
Sackiss	It's not like Hollywood... *(Looks up)* The sky's so small...
Miranda	Don't look up.
Sol	Miranda...!
Miranda	What?!
Sol	Do ya have ta—?
Miranda	There's an eclipse today!
Sol	*(Muttering)* Do ya have ta make such a big deal?
Miranda	You can't look directly at the sun or you'll go blind.
Sol	That's all I need.
Sackiss	I didn't know that.

Miranda	Yeah, they don't happen very often—these eclipses.
Sol	"These late eclipses of the sun and moon portend no good to us," right Sackiss?
Miranda	That's from *Lear*.
Sol	Don't show off, Miranda.
Miranda	You're the one!
Sol	You hear that? She's always contradicting me.
Miranda	No, I'm not!
Sol	I taught her Shakespeare. I taught her all the parts. And then she turns on me.

Awkward pause.

Sackiss	Oh. Well. Look at this. The real suburbs, huh? The real thing.
Sol	It's not so bad.
Sackiss	*(Pulling his shirt from his chest)* No? Kinda humid, though, huh...? Ha-ha...
Sol	You feel secure. Solid.
Sackiss	So this is your mom's house, huh?
Sol	And kids. Well. There's nothing like that. Nothing like that. To watch a child grow. It's the most incredible thing there is. Until they turn on you. Yeah. You never had kids did you?
Sackiss	No.
Sol	Too bad.
Sackiss	Poor me. Ha-ha!
Sol	I feel sorry for you there.
Sackiss	I did get married finally, though.
Sol	You did not.
Sackiss	I did.

Sol	Whattaya know!
Sackiss	I know. Who'd a thunk it?
Sol	Not I.
Sackiss	You gotta settle down sometime. And you meet that special someone. You lose interest in playin' around and all that stuff. Basically—when I met Debbie I stopped looking.
Sol	Well, who is she?
Sackiss	*(Dismissive gesture)* Some shiksa.

They both laugh, crouching forward towards each other.

Miranda	What's a shiksa?
Sackiss	Oh, in this case, a former cheerleader.

They both laugh.

Miranda	*(Nervous laughter)* Hm-hm-hm...
Sackiss	No, not really. There is no Debbie. Only in my, in my private moments, if you know what I mean. Ha-ha-ha-ha-ha.
Sol	Ha-ha-ha-ha-ha. You're still the same aren't ya?
Sackiss	Well. I hope not! Ha-ha-ha-ha-ha....
Sol	Ha-ha-ha-ha-ha. No. You're still the same.
Sackiss	I'm not actually, Sol. I'm not the same. I've changed. *(Pause)* Well I can't believe. Who would have thought? Who would have thought you'd end up in the suburbs. *(To MIRANDA)* Your Dad always got the big parts.
Sol	Tell her.
Sackiss	Your Dad always got the lead.
Sol	She doesn't know.

Miranda	You tell me enough...
Sol	You hear that? I taught her Shakespeare. I taught her all the parts. And this is how she treats me!
Sackiss	I always got the clown, the fool.
Sol	And now you're a producer!
Sackiss	Yep.
Sol	Whattaya know!
Sackiss	Not much. Ha-ha!
Sol	At least you can't miss your entrance! Ha-ha-ha—being a producer...!
Sackiss	Ha-ha-ha-ha-ha—
Sol	You don't have to worry about that! Ha-ha!
Sackiss	Nope—Ha-ha!
Sol	Don't have to worry about leaving any one stranded out on stage! Ha-ha-ha!
Sackiss	Ha-ha-ha!
Sol	Well isn't that great!
Sackiss	It is. I love my job. I guess I'm lucky.
Sol	Television, huh?
Sackiss	Yeah...
Sol	Wow. What kind of pussy works in television? *(Beat)* Ha-ha-ha-ha-ha!
Sackiss	*(Fake thinks)* Oh, let's see, um... The kind of pussy that makes a million and half a week!

SACKISS laughs. SOL laughs. MIRANDA laughs too loudly.

Sackiss	Well I started out in TV, Sol. But now I'm doin' movies.
Sol	I saw that movie that you made.
Sackiss	You did?

Sol	Yeah. About the talking dog?
Sackiss	Yeah.
Sol	Yeah. A real piece of art, huh? Ha-ha-ha....
Sackiss	Ah-ha-ha-ha-ha.
Miranda	Dad...!
Sol	A real cinematic accomplishment! Ha-ha-ha.
Sackiss	Ah-ha-ha-ha-ha-ha.
Sol	No—good for you. Good for you and all that. But, you know, the stage was my first love. You know how the stage, it was my first love.
Sackiss	Yeah. *(Gesturing to the yard)* So is this your stage now? *(Beat. Pointing a finger at SOL)* Ah-ha-ha-ha-ha-ha...
Sol	Ha-ha-ha-ha-ha!
Miranda	So are you gonna give my Dad a job?
Sackiss	Whoa...!
Dad	*(Out of the corner of his mouth)* Miranda...
Miranda	What? You need a job!
Sol	Will you shut the fuck up! *(To SACKISS)* Ha-ha-ha-ha.
Sackiss	What about you little lady?
Miranda	Nothing.
Sol	She's fine.
Sackiss	You married? Ha-ha...
Miranda	No.
Sol	He's kidding!
Miranda	I know that!
Sackiss	*(To MIRANDA)* You like to act too, sweetheart? Are you an actress?
Miranda	Yes, I—
Sol	She's not an actress. She stopped acting with me. When her mother died.

Miranda	When's the audition gonna happen, Mr. Sackiss?
Sackiss	Call me Dan.
Sol	*(To* MIRANDA, *out of the corner of his mouth)* Miranda...
Miranda	What?!
Sol	*(To* SACKISS*)* Don't listen to her.
Miranda	But that's why he's here, for your audition...!
Sol	I'm sure he wants some lunch first.
Sackiss	I wouldn't mind a shower.
Sol	Ha-ha-ha-ha-ha...
Sackiss	Ha-ha-ha-ha-ha—no really—this humidity—I wouldn't mind a shower...
Sol	Ha-ha-ha-ha-ha...
Sackiss	No, really, I—
Miranda	Do you have the script?
Sol	*(To* MIRANDA, *out of the corner of his mouth)* Will you shut up...
Sackiss	It's at the bottom of my bag.
Sol	You don't have to get it.
Sackiss	Hey, you hear the one about the Polish actress? She thought she could make it in Hollywood by fucking a writer. Ha-ha-ha.
Sol	Ha-ha-ha-ha.
Miranda	*(Covering her mouth)* Hm-hm.
Sol	Oh, God. Sackiss, you're hilarious. Come on. Why don't you come in the house?
Sackiss	Are you sure it isn't some trap for Jews? Ha-ha.
Miranda	No...! My Dad's Jewish.
Sackiss	No, no. I'm kiddin' I'm kiddin'... That's what my father always thought things were: a trap for Jews... ha-ha...
Miranda	Oh...

Sackiss	Ha-ha-ha-ha-ha...
Sol	Hey, Miranda, give the guy some space, would ya?
Sackiss	She's fine...
Sol	Right this way. I'll take your bag.

SACKISS enters the house. SOL picks up the bag and follows. At the door he stops and turns to MIRANDA.

Sol	*(Hushed)* You gotta... look a little better. Could you look a little better? Look a little less shlumpy.
Miranda	Dad...!
Sol	Can you do that? Could you look a little less shlumpy? Can you straighten up...?
Miranda	My posture's perfect.
Sol	You're fuckin' shlumpy!
Miranda	Mr. Salatory says my posture's perfect—
Sol	That fag.
Miranda	He calls me the consummate actress...
Sol	He doesn't know the first thing, the first thing about acting!
Miranda	Well, I'm just saying!
Sol	You always gotta stick it to me, don't you?
Miranda	*(Under her breath)* Well, It's not my fault...
Sol	What?
Miranda	Nothing.
Sol	What did you say?
Miranda	Nothing!
Sol	What?
Miranda	It's not my fault that you got fired! *(Beat)* I mean... *(Beat)* Dad? I shouldn't have...

Sol	You don't care about me. You only care about yourself.
Miranda	You haven't worked! You haven't worked in fifteen months...!
Sol	Little bitch. Ever since your mother died you turned on me. When I needed you the most!
Miranda	Other people work, Dad! I see them. They carry briefcases and things. With papers in them. From jobs. And pens. And other things. And they get dropped off at the train. And they say, they say "see you at dinner" and stuff like that. And "I'll pick you up at soccer and..."
Sackiss	*(Off)* Hey! What is this—a trap for Jews?! Ha-ha!

SOL glares at MIRANDA. He enters the house. MIRANDA watches him leave. She turns front. Lights reveal the foggy face of the woman. Pause. MIRANDA stays facing front, frozen.

Miranda	I mean all great people in history have had hallucinations. So it makes sense I would have them. I mean, Moses. For one. Had hallucinations. And also—um... *(Pause)* Well, Moses. I mean—that's a big one, isn't it? *(Pause)* I read the Bible and there's all kinds of weird stuff in there. I like to read about all this stuff. Like paranormal things and stuff like that. Untimely child deaths. *(Beat)* So it doesn't affect me that much is what I'm saying. You know, maritime disasters. *(Beat)* I know it's just imaginary. I have an active imagination. It's a sign of intelligence. I, I don't get freaked out. Is what I'm saying. Like lots of girls do in my school. They're always getting freaked out. They don't ask the big questions. You know? That have been passed down

through history. *(Beat)* But I do. I ask the big questions. *(Beat)* That have been passed down through history. *(Pause)* You know like how did we get here. Anyway? And why... here? You know? Why... here? *(Swallows)* And where do we go? Anyway? After we die?

Ghost Miranda...

Miranda God, it's really humid! *(Laughs nervously)* Childhood isn't really good the way they say it is. Is it? *(Beat)* Anyway—I gotta go. I mean, I'd like to stay, 'cause this is fascinating, really...But my Dad will really mess things up without me. See people from Hollywood, you know, they don't tolerate any kind of awkwardness or weakness or anything. I mean, I heard that even if you're crossing the street in Hollywood you only get like five seconds to make it and then the cars will just run you over. And that weeds out anyone who's slow or lame in any way. *(Beat)* I don't know even know why I'm talking to you. You're not even really here. "You're just a vision proceeding from the heat-oppressed brain." Oh that's a line from *(Makes air quotes)* "the Scottish play." You have to call it *(Makes air quotes)* "the Scottish play" you know because it's bad luck to say the name. Especially in a theater. And if you accidentally say it then you have to say all these lines from *Hamlet* afterwards. The lines he says when he sees the ghost, you know? Of his father. You have to go like this... *(Turns to the left)* "Angels and ministers of grace—"

MIRANDA *stops when she sees the* GHOST.

(Quietly) "Defend us..."

MIRANDA *and* GHOST *stare at each other.*

Ghost	Miranda...
Sol	*(Off)* Miranda!
Miranda	Mom...? *(Turns slowly back front, swallows)*
Ghost	I heard you calling and I came. *(Laughs, astonished. Beat)* See, I left the bed where I was dying, when I saw you last. I left that bed... *(Beat)* And I walked down to the sea and that took seven years! And I found a ship. And they gave us their hand... *(Beat)* I didn't know the other people... but everyone seemed nice. There was an acrobat and she did flips. Oh, Miranda! *(Beat)* And we all got on this ship. *(Beat)* We didn't speak. We just stood there. Oh my God! We just stood there on the wooden ship. With all those sails... *(Beat)* And we wasn't afraid. Miranda. That's the thing. None of us wasn't... Because we knew. The place. That we were going. It's a place gloriful. And holy in its being without capture. And alone. In its peace. Perfect. See we're separated by a sea of death. And the sea just reveals and conceals us briefly...
Miranda	You don't speak correctly...
Ghost	I'm sorry. *(Beat)* In the act of speaking-doing, there's some difficulty. The words, I guess they strain from un-use. That's all—they strain from un-use...
Miranda	Listen...
Ghost	I was on this boat. I was on my way to dying. And then I heard you. I think: she's never called for me before. She just always wants her father. I have to go to her. So I just dove into the water.
Sol	*(Off)* Miranda!

Sarah Koskoff The Apple Juice Man   463

Miranda	That's my Dad. See, he's in the house with Sackiss...
Ghost	What...?
Miranda	I have to go...
Ghost	Did you say Sackiss? Dan Sackiss?!—
Miranda	He's a producer. He makes movies.
Ghost	I know Dan Sackiss...! *(Beat)* I was in *King Lear* with them. I played Cordelia... *(Beat)* He left your father there onstage. It was his last performance.
Miranda	Well, I called him here from Hollywood. To help us.
Ghost	Why would you call him to our house?
Miranda	It's not your house!

Pause.

Ghost	You used to play Cordelia. With your Dad. You played all my roles. The two of you, always together, leaving me out...
Miranda	No offense, but I really really don't want you here...
Ghost	But I heard you calling me. Miranda. *(Beat)* Miranda. Look at her. Why don't you turn and look at her. Your mother.

Lights disappear on the GHOST *as* SOL *emerges from the house.*

Sol	There you are. Jesus. Always hiding. Always sneaking around. Don't you know who's in there?
Miranda	I do, but...
Sol	Jesus! *(Then hushed)* Jesus. Take a knife! Just take a knife and stab me! Right here! Why don't you? Just do it! Don't you know what this means to me, Miranda?

Miranda	I know, but—
Sol	Well, I've been calling you for how long?—how long does a person?—how long?—God damn it! I'm screaming my head off! They'll call the police! Our neighbors! Dick Stein will call the police. Jesus H. Christ. *(Beat)* Don't look at me that way. You think I don't know what I'm talking about? Huh? You think I'm chopped liver? Is that what you think?
Miranda	I didn't say that...!
Sol	What do you think I am? Chopped liver? *(Hushed, looking behind him at the house)* Sackiss played the fool, you know. He played the clown. He didn't get the parts I got. He didn't get those parts.
Miranda	I know, I know! You were the king!
Sol	That's right, that's right. I was the king.
Miranda	And Sackiss was the fool.
Sol	Sackiss was the fool. *(Beat. Looks to the house; then, hushed)* But don't be a snob, Miranda. It's not always a bad thing to be. The fool. Sackiss got some speeches. He got some speeches. Sackiss. And he didn't get jealous. Nah. He didn't get that way. He looked up to me. He... He remembered me. That's the point. That's the point I'm making. He remembered me. From the stage. *(Beat)* That's why he's here. I haven't seen the guy in what? Twenty years. Something... then he calls, then he calls and says he's comin' over. And says he'll be in town. Says he wants me to read for something. Some part. In some movie. Who cares how big the part is—even if it's small—who cares? Work begets work, Miranda. Work begets work. That's the thing. I'm not gonna do this anymore, live this stultifying

life. Next to Dick Stein, that clown. If he had any idea what an actor I was—he'd look at me little differently. Yes, he would. Take me a little more seriously. So would you, for that matter. You little so and so. You little cunt. Bossing me around, since your mother died. Just standing there in your pajamas. Wanting apple juice all the time. What am I just a man who gets you apple juice? Just the apple juice man? *(Pause, looking at her)* I'm asking.

Miranda   No!

Sol   No, what?

Miranda   I don't think of you that way, Dad! As the apple juice man!

Sol   Oh, you just gotta, you just gotta twist the knife, don't you! Every chance you get... *(Beat)* Well what am I to you then? Huh?

Miranda   I don't know!

Sol   That's perfect.

Miranda   My father?!

Sol   Is that all you have to say?

Pause. MIRANDA stays frozen. SOL enters the house. Lights reveal the GHOST.

Ghost   Miranda... *(Pause)* Why don't you turn and look at me? *(Pause)* Mirand...?

Miranda   Because you're not really here. *(Beat)* You died.

Ghost   Yeah, I know. *(Pause)* I try to be like all the other mothers. But I'm not. *(Pause)* I don't have a body.

Miranda   I saw one.

Ghost   Well. I'm forcing myself to be seen.

466

Miranda	That doesn't make any sense...
Ghost	You should call me mom.
Miranda	I don't feel comfortable with that. See, I don't know if you, if you realize but you've been dead a while. And see I'm quite intelligent. I'm quite sophisticated for my age...
Ghost	And you're, what now, seven?
Miranda	I'm fifteen... *(Beat)* And what I'm saying, what I'm saying is I understand this. I know that I'm hallucinating. And I know that you're not really here.
Ghost	Well, my body has been... how do they say it, resurrected. But I'm dead. I hate that feeling. They tell you there's some peace in it. There isn't. *(Beat)* I hate it here. It's cold.
Miranda	Well don't you think you should be leaving then?
Ghost	You're the one who brought me here...
Miranda	I didn't bring you...
Ghost	Well, I heard you calling...
Miranda	*(Under her breath)* You're deluded...
Ghost	I'm deluded?! Gads... *(Beat)* I mean, It's not as if I want to be here. It's not as if I want to. If I could go to the beach I would. I would go to the fucking beach instead. If I could see the things there. I would go there in a second. Instead of being here. Instead of being the woods. Instead of wandering out there. Instead of bothering you. *(Beat)* Trust me. I would just stare at the kelp. I would. And I'd be fine. The way it washes up after a storm and looks like arms. Like limbs. From the sea. The wildness of it. *(Beat)* I would just drive to the fucking beach. Like I used to—with you in your car seat. You in the back looking at me from there. Oh, you were fine. They say don't do that, but come on. You were fine. Then I would take my shoes off. Oh, Miranda.

How I long to feel my feet in the sand again! The sand underneath my toes! And I would say the speeches out loud. I would say them on the beach and feel the tears roll down my face. I would do that again if I could. Trust me. *(Beat)* Miranda, Look at her! Why don't you turn and look at her? Your mother! *(Beat)* I can't be in these woods. Do you hear me? The end of my nose. It's frozen. I stand very crumpled up in the woods, you know. Tightly hunched to stay warm. And the trees seem mean. You know me, Miranda. I'm not a woman who ever went in the woods. I can't sleep out there. I'm cold.

Miranda You told me...

Ghost The end of my nose. My hands. I stand with my eyes open like this. I don't like the sounds of things out there. Miranda. I don't like the way things sound. I hear. Growling. I see crows.

Dad *(Off)* Miranda!

Miranda I have to go in there...

Ghost You think he's gonna help you? Sackiss. He's the cause of all these problems.

Miranda I have to go.

Ghost Passed out in the car. That Jewish prick. That kike.

Miranda God!

Ghost Oh, I'm so terrible, your dead mother, oh I'm the worst.

Miranda You're bitter. Because something's gonna happen for us and you're not here. That's why they say the dead come back. I know all about it. I read that stuff. They come for retribution.

Ghost You got that wrong. You're the one who dragged me back. You're the one who did it. Life is filled with hate,

Miranda. Death is nothing. The sea. The steel grey sea. The sails. See I don't care about retribution. Because I'm dead. Remember Mir? I was lying there. And I was dying. And they were about to put the morphine patches on. And I called out to you to say good-bye...

Miranda   *(Covering her face with one hand)* I know that you're not really here.

Ghost   Well... What difference does it make? *(Beat)* I'm here to you... *(Beat)*

Miranda   That's a good point....

Lights disappear on the GHOST as SOL emerges from the house. SOL and SACKISS emerge from the house laughing.

Sol   Ha-ha-ha? I can't take it...

Sackiss   There she is...

Sol   God dammit, Miranda...

Miranda   What? *(Takes her hand from her face)*

Sol   Whattaya think? We can't see you if you cover your face? What are you? Three years old?

Miranda   *(Flustered)* Um...

Sol   Huh?

Miranda   I was... just... looking at the sky for the eclipse.

Sackiss   We were looking for you... Okay—Listen... Guy's on a bridge, about to jump off, kill himself, you know, commit suicide. This other guy walks up to him, says, "Buddy— Jesus—get down from there—whatta you doing?" Guy says, "I'm killing myself." Other guy says, "Why?" Guy says, "I was an architect. A great architect, designing the most beautiful buildings and museums. But do they call me Dan the Architect? *(Beat)* And I composed, in my life, music, symphonies and operas performed all over Europe but do they call me Dan the Composer? *(Beat)* And a poet—I put the most beautiful words in the most perfect order, but do they call me Dan the Poet? *(Beat. Raises a finger in the air)* But suck one cock...!"

He laughs. SOL laughs. MIRANDA laughs a little but too loudly.

Miranda	So's the audition gonna happen now?
Sol	Jesus!
Sackiss	*(Looks around)* Oh, There it is—my bag. *(Goes to the bag)* Left it out here with the script inside it... *(Takes the script out)* Here it is...
Sol	God, remember doing Shakespeare, Dan? Remember *Lear*? What a time we had back then, huh, Sackiss? And touring with it. Before you left, that is. Out in the middle of God knows where. That little company? Just for the love of it. Those towns, one of those towns with a church smack-dab in the middle—those little towns with big fuck-ing churches just smack-dab in the middle.
Miranda	He says it was the greatest time.
Sol	She doesn't know.
Miranda	Well, that's what you say...!
Sol	But you don't know, you don't know...
Miranda	But he knows, right? Sackiss knows.

Pause.

Sol	Give the man some space, Miranda... remember, Dan? Just doing it for the love of it. Just for the love of it. We made no money remember? We didn't even have any understudies. The company—we couldn't afford 'em. Right, Dan?
Sackiss	See. It isn't good for me. It isn't good...
Sol	What isn't good?
Sackiss	It's not a good idea for me. To dwell. To dwell upon the past like this.
Sol	Not to reminisce? What—still feel guilty?
Sackiss	It just doesn't help me. See. To dwell... *(Pause)* See, I, uh, I, uh, I let go of the past, Sol. I have this teacher... *(Beat)* He's a sort of... a... spiritual teacher. His name is Kevin. *(Beat)* Look—I know what you're thinkin'—California. But it's not like that. It just helps a lot. It keeps me clear. It helps me from getting too bogged down in life. *(Beat)* And I exercise a lot. You know, it's a proven fact: cardiovascular exercise improves your sense of self. *(Pause)* It releases a lot of stress. And all that shame, you know, that deep, deep shame. It really does. For all that guilt and stuff. Stuff that haunts you. *(Beat)* See. Last time I saw you. I remember that. Something bad happened. Something really bad. We were together when it happened. *(Pause)* But after that bad thing, I left there. That's why I missed my so-called entrance. I haven't seen you since. Right, Sol? *(Pause)* From there I drove. I bet you didn't know this. I drove. And then I stopped in a place. A hotel. A motel. One of those deals right off the highway. No restaurant, nothin' in there. Guys walkin' around. And I double bolted the door. 'Cause fear set in. *(Beat)*

Fear set in, Solly, I... *(Beat)* I didn't sleep. And later on, I don't know what time, but at night, in the thick of night, as they say, in the so-called thick of the night I heard footsteps coming down the hall. Slowly down the hall. In this hotel, motel, whatever the thing was. I hear them coming. And they get closer. *(Beat)* And they stop. They stop outside my door. *(Beat)* These footsteps. These so-called footsteps. *(Beat)* And my heart. My heart. I think I could hear it. I mean looking back, looking back I hear it. And that's all we have, isn't it? Who knows what really happens in our lives. Any of it. All we have is what we recall right now. And I would spill my own blood, I mean it, about this—to swear I heard it. My heart. I fucking hear that thing that muscle fucking beating in my chest like to be let out, pounding, in the room, in this hotel. *(Beat)* Echoing with this sound not me anymore—me just fucking lying there, lying there sweat sliding down my cheeks, down my head, sliding, and I think I will die now from this—cause I will fucking welcome it—death, compared with this thing—to get this thing to stop, well if that means to die then— *(Pause)* Unable to breathe that's what I'm talkin' about, I'm talkin' about—

Sol   I don't want to hear any more of this...

Sackiss   No, but see—I stayed like that. I don't know how long. But then suddenly it lifted. The clamp from my chest. It lifted. Do you understand what I'm saying? The elephant on my chest. It got up. And walked away... *(Beat)* And I left that place and I went to Hollywood. I took a bus to Hollywood. The seat in front of me was broken. And the man's head was bald and sweaty and the seat fell back so it was in my lap basically, the man's head. Yeah it was in my lap for, I'd say, oh, the whole trip. But I just smiled. Because I was different, Solly. From that day on. They say it can happen. They say—I've read about it—this lifting of the thing. The "SOMETHING" is lifted. It lifts off of you. And you experience directly a kind of love—a kind of love for everything. For yourself even. A kind of opening to everything. And the world shines with it maybe.

The light shifts a shade darker.

Miranda   *(Overlapping)* It's the eclipse...

Sackiss   This man's head. The TV on this bus to Hollywood, blaring—some loudness, some laugh track and flatness and it shines too. And the old woman next to me—they say this can happen and this is what happened. This is what happened to me. This old woman. The way she glimmers suddenly. Even though she stinks of cigarettes. And the age spots on her hands and the blue polyester knit pantsuit laying on her bony thighs. And the mole on her eyelid. The most wasted life, is what you would normally feel, being next to her. And I don't like the smell of her, you'd normally feel. But now... the way she glimmers...

Sol   I don't want to hear this anymore. Did you hear me?

Sackiss   Well. This is what happened to me. This is what I remember. You asked what I remember. Well this is it.

Pause. SOL stands up. He takes the script.

Sol   I'll go inside. I'll go inside and read this.

Sol exits into the house. Awkward pause.

Sackiss   I have a tendency to go on and on...

Miranda   So do I. My dad says I talk too much when I get nervous.

Sackiss   We spoke on the phone...

Miranda   I know don't tell my dad...

Sackiss   I won't...

Miranda   He wouldn't like it...

Sackiss   I won't tell him.

Miranda   He wouldn't like it. *(Beat)* It's just... We saw your movie on TV. They showed it on TV. The one about the talking dog. That runs for president and...

Sackiss   Yeah—I could tell he didn't like it. But you know what? He has no idea, okay? People act like they know all about it. They're so judgmental. But they don't know, they don't know how hard it is to make a movie. *(Beat)* It's the hardest job there is.

Miranda   I didn't say...

Sackiss   I mean—we had meetings about the dog. And then at these meetings, we talk about the dog for hours. *(Beat)* You know—If I were the dog... we ask ourselves—in this situation in that situation...

Miranda   Well, I thought it was a social commentary. Your movie. That you were saying that, um, language has lost all its meaning. You know? That the thing that makes us human beings doesn't even matter anymore. To the point where a dog can be president. Is that what you were saying?

Beat.

Sackiss	*(Eyes darting)* Yeah.
Miranda	See that's what I told my dad.
Sackiss	I'm glad you picked that up...
Miranda	Yeah. I'm smart like that. And I have a really high intelligence level. I mean, it's like, whew, off the charts. But I'm stifled at school. Because it's an institution, you know? It's stifling to be people who are really smart. I mean, Einstein didn't even do well in school because he thought fours were noses. *(Beat)* No, that's Picasso. Anyway—all the girls, they walk by me like I'm nothing. They laugh against the lockers, stuff like that. And those fluorescent lights, they're just flickering all day. Acting is the only thing... And I'm like the best person there, I really am. The best actor. I'm the best. *(Beat)* Yeah. If it weren't for acting I wouldn't even go to school. But there's an acting teacher there who loves me. Mr. Salatory. But I just call him Bob. He lets me. You know? He lets me call him Bob. He says "call me Bob" when I forget. *(Pause)* He wears an ascot. His wife's a clown. She has a drinking problem. But he says I have a gift. You know? And we have this special... this special kind of.... He calls, me, um the consummate actress. He says that that no one, that no one can enunciate like I can. And think that quickly. 'Cause it requires you to think that quickly. To think as fast as he does.
Sackiss	Bob?
Miranda	No, Shakespeare. His mind was so incredible. That if you get a chance to think like him you're lucky. Because you become that smart. And you think as fast as light. It makes it be like there's no time. Or something. Maybe only for when you're speaking it. Maybe only then. But still. You become it. And your mind gets bigger from it...

Pause.

Sackiss   Oh.

Miranda   Yeah, I'm his star pupil. We talk on and on about it—
Shakespeare. All the meanings. *(Beat)* So you played the
Fool in *Lear*.

Sackiss   Yeah, I always played the Fool, the clown...

Miranda   The Fool in *Lear* is kind of weird. You know? He's not that
funny. First of all. He's creepy. And he disappears at one
point in the play. And he's just gone. And at the end Lear
says, "and my poor Fool is hanged," but he's not saying it
about the Fool. He's saying it about Cordelia. 'Cause she's
been hanged by Edmund. But where's the Fool at that point?
We don't know? So maybe he's a part of her. Or something.
Of Cordelia. *(Pause)* And Cordelia is a part of Lear. *(Pause)*
Mr. Salatory told me. "Coeur" means heart in French. And
"de" is of. And "Lia." Lear. "Cor-de-lia." "Heart of Lear."

Sackiss   Yeah, I never liked that play.

Miranda   What do you mean?

Sackiss   There's nobody likable in it. I can't get behind it.

Pause.

Miranda   Anyway. what was I saying? Oh, my Dad. He saw your
name. At the beginning of the movie. He saw your name
up there. Dan Sackiss. And he told me that he knew you.
From when you were onstage. In Shakespeare plays. He
kept on saying, "I can't believe it. Sackiss." Just like that.
And I knew that you'd lost touch and everything. So I just
had to call and see if you'd remembered him.

476

Sackiss	Of course I did.
Miranda	So I thought you'd have a part for him.
Sackiss	How could I forget him?
Miranda	An acting part. And he's so good at acting.
Sackiss	I might.
Miranda	You'll hear him read and see.
Sackiss	I'll hear him read. He's in there reading now. He's reading the script in there right now. *(Pause)* Yeah—I had a lot of problems back then. You know. When I knew your dad. But I've changed a lot. Now I'm happy. I didn't like myself back then. I like to stay upbeat and positive about things. And Kevin says it's good to let it go. The shame. To, you know, to cut the rope that's carrying this armor, this heavy armor up the mountain. The deep, deep shame. That's what Kevin calls it. He even wrote a book about it.
Miranda	What's it called?

Beat.

Sackiss	*Deep, Deep Shame. (Beat)* He asks, you know, in the book, he asks, isn't it time to love yourself?
Miranda	Yeah, but, if everyone just took that approach, then the world would never change. We would just, we would all be these sort of weak nothing people just loving ourselves and fat and... Anyway. You should definitely put him in your movie. My dad. He's really good at acting. See, we're a really special family. We ask the big questions. You know? That have been passed down through history.

Beat.

| Sackiss | You want a piece of gum? |

Beat. She shakes her head.

| Miranda | No, thanks. |

He pulls the gum out of his pocket.

Sackiss	*(Holding it out to her)* Come on, have one...
Miranda	No that's okay...
Sackiss	It's really good. It's minty. *(Pushing it out toward her)* Here.
Miranda	*(Turning toward him)* Okay.

She slowly and awkwardly crosses upstage left to him and stops. She laughs nervously. He laughs along with her.

| Sackiss | *(Handing her the gum)* Well, take it... |
| Miranda | Oh... |

They both laugh. She takes the gum. She unwraps the gum and puts it in her mouth. She chews. He watches her. Pause.

| Sackiss | Don't... don't chew so hard you get a headache. |

She smiles and chews. They both chew, loudly. Awkward. Pause. Then the light changes, getting grayer.

| Miranda | Did you feel the light just change? |

Sackiss	I did.
Miranda	There's an eclipse today...
Sackiss	You said that.
Miranda	It's already started. The eclipse. You can see a bite out of the sun but—

He starts to look up—

Miranda	DON'T LOOK AT IT!!!

SACKISS holds his chest.

Sackiss	Jesus Christ...!
Miranda	Sorry, but you're not supposed to look at the sun like that. Or you'll go blind...
Sackiss	At least I wouldn't be dead from a heart attack...
Miranda	It burns your retina... And you don't feel it—that's part of why it's dangerous. You don't even feel it—and then you're blind. *(Laughs nervously)* What was I saying? *(Beat)* Oh, I heard that, there's this story. That when God created things. He tried to make the moon and sun be equal. But the moon said you shouldn't make us equal. You should make it so that one of us is stronger. And God said—okay—you be less. *(Pause)* So—the eclipse is the moon's one revenge. When he gets to come back and beat the sun for once.

Pause.

Sackiss	I'm in the entertainment business... *(Pause. He breathes deeply through his nose)* Yeah, it's good to be around this

	stuff. All these woods and stuff. And all this air. It's so beautiful...
Miranda	No—it's all a big facade, you know? Things are hidden here. Underneath there's all these creepy things.
Sackiss	Like what?
Miranda	Like murderings....
Sackiss	I don't believe it.
Miranda	You don't know what goes on here. It looks really normal and everything. But it's not. You wouldn't believe this town. I mean. Just go to the library. You can read about all kinds of deaths there. That's what I do. I like to read about all kinds of deaths. *(Pause)* Like the Indians they slaughtered just right near here. The motel's named after 'em. And so's the library where I read the stuff. After the whole tribe of Indians that was slaughtered. And so's the diner. They even have a special on the menu named for them. Some kind of corn dish. *(Beat)* And they killed a witch right near here.
Sackiss	No...
Miranda	Sure. They killed a witch. She was pregnant by some guy but they thought it was the *(Making air quotes)* "devil's spawn" or something. You know. Those Puritans. The way they talk. Like they never say "big" they always say "large." *(Pause)* Anyway, they tied her to a chair, this witch. This girl, I mean. And they put this wooden stake into her mouth to keep it open. *(Beat)* And they took her to the river. And they unleashed this dam. And all these people watched while she exploded. *(Pause)* And all those people, Mr. Sackiss.
Sackiss	Call me Dan...

Miranda	Those men in their tall hats. And those women in their bonnets. With their children. After it was over, after they saw her die, the girl... They just walked back in total silence. *(Pause)* Just the sound of crunching leaves. See they had this theory: If you're a witch you float. And if you're a human being then you drown.

Pause.

Sackiss	I don't know anything about that. You know—I like to stay positive and not dwell on this kind of stuff. It's nice to me. So, so... woodsy. *(Gets on his knees)* Ahhh... I love it. Nature... *(Takes a deep inhale through his nose)*
Miranda	What are you...?
Sackiss	It's so generous. So yielding!

He leans forward with eyes closed and puts his hands into the ground. Then, suddenly, he opens his mouth and eyes and screams at the top of his lungs in agony.

Ahhhhhhh!

He pulls his left hand from the ground and shakes it.

	Fuck...!
Miranda	What is it...?!
Sackiss	I was fucking stung...!
Miranda	Oh my God...
Sackiss	*(Sucking on his finger)* Jesus!
Miranda	It happened so fast, I just—

Sackiss	Gotta get some ice—

SACKISS enters into the house. Lights reveal the GHOST.

Ghost	I'm back.
Miranda	I have to go inside...
Ghost	What did you think? I wouldn't come back?
Miranda	No...
Ghost	Did you think I wouldn't come back?
Miranda	I knew you'd come back, but...!
Ghost	I'm back.
Miranda	I can't talk to you right now! Sackiss got stung!
Ghost	That fucking drunk...!
Miranda	He's changed! You don't know!
Ghost	Well, what am I supposed to do out there? Tell me that? What the fuck am I supposed to do out there? You know a big piece of dust flew in my eye. It hurts. And it's getting darker. And I'm getting scraped by twigs. I have mosquitoes buzzing in my ears. I hear owls...
Miranda	We don't have owls...
Ghost	Well something makes that sound. That who who who. Maybe they're not owls fine but something makes that sound. How would you like to be resurrected?
Miranda	I wouldn't...
Ghost	Huh?
Miranda	I wouldn't!
Ghost	I didn't ask to be. I don't have followers. Or, what d'ya call it... disciples. It's loud out there. I hear crunching. Who-ing like I told you. Do you have any more gum?
Miranda	No...

Ghost	Fine. You bring me here and then abandon me. It's perfect. I don't know why I trusted you. Just like your father. He couldn't be onstage. So I gave it up for him. I gave up everything for him. Because I wanted to dissolve in him. To die with him. To kill him dead. To have him kill me dead, together dead. That's love, Miranda, what it is to love. To love is bad. It's only bad.
Miranda	Thanks for the advice...
Ghost	And he drags me to this town. This town. All these women with their, their hair that flips up at the bottom. And their kelly green shirts. Their white smiles. Their shining lying eyes. Looking at me like I'm strange.
Miranda	You didn't have to come here. It was your choice to come here.
Ghost	And then to have to watch you. Acting. With your father. I had to watch you playing all my roles. Cordelia. Desdemona. Viola. Rosalyn. Beatrice. Kate. Lady Anne. Miranda. You stole my parts Miranda. How do you think that felt. Listening to you. The two of you. Having to listen to that all day. The two of you acting. I have feelings too you know.
Miranda	You always ruined everything. Like now. You have to ruin everything for me.
Ghost	Why you deceitful—I didn't ask to be here. You little deceitful... You drag me from my fucking grave for this. You ungrateful—
Miranda	Why don't you get out of here?! Why don't you leave?
Ghost	You're always turned away from me.
Miranda	We have a chance for something now! Don't you see that?
Ghost	Always looking at the back of your head...
Miranda	We have a chance. To leave this town... To do something else.

Ghost	Not your eyes, Mirand... always turned away from me...
Miranda	My father has a chance to be an actor...
Ghost	You wanted me to die. *(Pause)* So you could have him to yourself... *(Pause)* Do you know what happens? To the things that we keep hidden?
Miranda	I don't want to know!
Ghost	They don't disappear, Miranda. They go up in the hills. And they feed on bugs and tree bark. They form strange alliances. Separate customs. And religions. And they pick oleander. And they appoint a leader. And many days they just sit up there and wait. And they listen to their breathing. The sounds of their breath becoming one. And they wait. And they wait. For the day that they'll come down. I promise you. Come down into these empty fields. Brandishing their sharp objects, their sticks they've fashioned into knives. And metals—calling their calls long forgotten. And they'll take back what's theirs. They'll take by force what they've been— they'll take by force their fields....
Miranda	This is my least favorite...
Ghost	Miranda...
Miranda	Of our conversations so far...

The light shifts a little darker.

Ghost	The light.
Miranda	It's shifting.
Ghost	Can you feel it?
Miranda	Yes...
Ghost	It starts with just a bite out of the sun..
Miranda	It's gotten gray...

484

Ghost	Events proceed from there...
Miranda	It's the eclipse...
Ghost	Narrow bands of shadow and of light will race across the ground...
Miranda	It's coming faster...
Ghost	And all the speed you can imagine can't outrun it.
Miranda	I know all about it...
Ghost	And the shadow of the moon will rush in quickly...

Light quickly fades.

End of Act One

Act Two

Lights up on Miranda *and* Sackiss. *Everything in shadow.*

Miranda	It's the eclipse...
Sackiss	What...?
Miranda	The bees, they burrow from it...
Sackiss	Oh.
Miranda	In the ground. They hide. *(Beat)* Is my dad still in there reading...?
Sackiss	He's almost done. *(Looks out front)* Look at that American flag. Waving...

Miranda *looks front.*

Sackiss	I remember, I remember when the American flag used to come on at the end of TV programming. Waving like that. It was comforting. Something out there deciding for you it was over.
Miranda	But it's so ridiculous he has a flag. That guy. Dick Stein. He's Jewish! And he has a flag. I read the Bible. They're not supposed to do that. Have a country.
Sackiss	Whattaya gonna do—hold onto things forever? Huh?
Miranda	He also skis and sails and golfs...

486

Sackiss	Let's wipe the slate clean, Kevin says. People should just love themselves...
Miranda	I don't think so...
Sackiss	It's all you have, yourself.
Miranda	It's selfish.
Sackiss	Selfish? To do something for yourself is selfish?
Miranda	It's not good for people... when people let themselves off the hook, you know, they say, well, I tried, and things like that. Because, well, because how can they not want to be better, want to be better than they are?
Sackiss	But to really dig down deep. And make peace. With all the things you've done. Don't you think that's good?
Miranda	Well look at what happened to Jesus. I mean he loved himself. Look at what happened to him. You look at those old paintings of him. With his white light coming out of his soul. And, and, and all those people standing around with their mouths open. With their jaws dropped. *(Beat)* And then with his palms open, too. God. Like a flower. Or a girl. Loving himself. Just begging for it. Open. And soft. And raw. Well that's why they hammered the spike in...
Sackiss	You don't have to think about that stuff, Miranda. That's what I'm saying. The past. You don't have to. You can let it all go. You have a choice. Where I live, in Hollywood. You don't have all these things reminding you all the time. You know? All these things reminding you constantly about the past. The past weighing you down. 'Cause things are new. And people don't obsess about Jesus. Or if they do it's in kind of a relaxed way. They don't get so intense about it. 'Cause you can just can let go there and just be free to love yourself. You can just drive around. And wonder. About yourself.

What else can I accomplish? What else can I think of doing? How do I feel about this and that? And am I hungry? And do I feel like maybe resting? *(Beat)* And sometimes I look out from my office building. And it's all glass, you know. And I look out and from there I can see the sign. And it says Hollywood. And no matter how dirty the air is, how polluted, the sign stays white. Like the whitest smile you can think of. And I just look at it. And I disappear into that whiteness.

SOL emerges from the house holding the script and stops. Pause. MIRANDA and SACKISS look at him.

Sackiss   Well.

Pause.

Sol   Ha-ha-ha-ha-ha.

Pause.

Miranda   *(Forcing a laugh, nervously)* Hm-hm-hm!

Pause.

Sol   Ha-ha-ha-ha-ha-ha-ha-ha...

Pause.

Sackiss and Sol   HA-HA-HA-HA-HA-HA-HA

Sackiss,	Ha-ha-ha-ha-ha-ha-ha-ha-ha-ha-ha-ha-ha-ha-ha
Sol, and	
Miranda	

Laughter crescendos and then dies out. Pause.

Sackiss	So...?
Sol	So.
Sackiss	You read the script.
Sol	I did.

Pause.

Sol	Well.
Sackiss	Well, well.
Sol	Well-well-well.
Sackiss	Ha-ha...
Sol	It isn't Shakespeare, is it?
Miranda	Dad...
Sol	It isn't the Bard, now is it?
Miranda	It doesn't have to be.
Sackiss	I never made that claim.
Sol	And it's a good thing... Ha-ha...
Sackiss	I didn't claim it to be Shakespeare.
Sol	And it's a good thing, now isn't it?
Miranda	Everything can't be Shakespeare, Dad!
Sol	Yeah, yeah—lots of ideas in this piece. Lots of language. That's what I like about it. The complexity was just astounding. Gives me the chills just thinking of it. Not even a movie. It's more like a long commercial. Only the

product is elusive. The product is... what? Lack of meaning? Numbness?

Sackiss Well it's a living.

Sol I guess it better be.

Sackiss Well, it is.

Pause.

Sol Awww. I'm just joking. I'm just joking, Dan.

Miranda He was joking...! He's gonna read for it...

Sol For what?

Miranda A part.

Sol Let's see... *(Thumbs through the script)* Now what part would I play in here...?

Sackiss You could play a number of 'em.

Sol That's right. Ahhh. Here. I could play this guy. I see. Here's a part. The guidance counselor. I could play this part...

Miranda Dad...

Sol Shut up, Miranda...

Miranda It doesn't matter what the part is!

Sackiss Sol...

Sol Or I could play this cop here at the end... first or second cop. Well—with all my training—I could really make it sing this part. I could, I could make it soar... boy—they'll never see a second cop like my second cop...

Miranda There are no small parts, Dad.

Sol Not the same as doin' Shakespeare, is it?

Sackiss It is what it is, Sol.

Sol Not the same.

Sackiss It is what it is.

Miranda	Dad, you have to read. We don't have a choice.
Sol	Why don't you stay out of it, Miranda!
Sackiss	Why don't you read? Huh, Sol?
Miranda	We're running out of money!
Sackiss	It's just a formality.
Miranda	You don't have a job!
Sol	*(To MIRANDA)* Why don't you put a fucking sign up on the lawn?
Miranda	Well you have to get a job, Dad.
Sackiss	It can lead to other things. It will. I'm sure. Lead to other jobs...
Sol	There's nothing in this script!
Miranda	People don't always like their jobs!
Sackiss	It will lead to other things, Sol.
Sol	Traveled all this way to humiliate me... is that it?
Sackiss	Sol, I hate to say it, but you could drop your pants for all they care, all anybody cares. I mean Jesus Christ. All your standards. They don't mean a fucking thing.
Miranda	They get onto the train and go there... they don't think about it. They do it 'cause they have to do it. They don't think so much about it...
Sol	What about my needs? Huh? You ever think of that?
Sackiss	All you need is one big break, Sol...
Sol	Traveled all this way to humiliate me... is that it? You planned this didn't you? The two of you!
Miranda	You have to do it, Dad! You have to!
Sol	Traveled all this way...
Miranda	Work begets work.
Sackiss	Work begets work, Sol.
Sol	But we were doing Shakespeare...
Miranda	I can't hear about it anymore...

Sackiss	Let go of the past Sol...
Sol	Jesus Christ. I was playing Lear...
Sackiss	Well, I don't like to think about that time...
Sol	For fuck's sake! Lear...
Sackiss	That time in my life, I'm saying, Sol...
Miranda	That time is over...
Sackiss	I was in the darkness back then, Sol...
Sol	I was the only one.
Sackiss	I was suffering.
Sol	They said I had that thing. People work their lives to get that thing.
Sackiss	But I hadn't found myself yet...
Sol	I had that thing at twenty, Sackiss, twenty.
Sackiss	Well you're very lucky.
Sol	I was the king.
Miranda	I know you were the king...
Sackiss	Some of us it takes a while.
Sol	I was the king. And you were the fool.
Sackiss	You can change, Solly—I promise—you can... if I can change...
Sol	Oh—You haven't changed...

Pause.

Sackiss	But I have. I have changed.
Sol	Nah...

Pause.

Sackiss	Why don't you let go of all of it...? Huh? Why don't you let go...?

492

Sol	You haven't changed one bit...
Sackiss	I let go of more each day, more baggage...
Sol	You're the same stinking slime bag you always were...

Pause.

Sackiss	You could let go of all of it...
Sol	The same drunken fool...
Sackiss	Well, I haven't had a drink since I last saw you...
Sol	You never took it seriously...
Sackiss	I haven't had a drink since then.
Sol	You never studied like I did.
Sackiss	I've changed, Sol.
Sol	We don't change. People are what they are...
Sackiss	Some terrible things...
Sol	You can't hide from me...
Sackiss	I had no self-respect. No self-love. But I'd hope you'd find it in your heart... To forgive me, Sol... For your own sake. Not for mine. For your own sake. You're the one who's carrying the burden of your anger.
Sol	You left me there onstage. *(Pause)* You left me out there.

Pause. Lights reveal the GHOST.

Ghost	You can feel the light begin to change, Mirand...
Miranda	Not now...
Sackiss	If not now then when, Miranda?
Miranda	That's not...
Ghost	You can hear the earth get quiet.
Sackiss	Then when?

Miranda	I didn't...
Ghost	The birds have stopped. You notice?
Sackiss	When? He has to look at things. To let things go.
Miranda	I know.
Ghost	The crescent of the sun has shrunk. It's just a tiny sliver...
Miranda	Yes...
Ghost	So beautiful like that. It breaks. So many points of light. Oh, Mirand.
Sol	Coming to my house like this...!
Ghost	See the sunlight. It shines through the valleys that surround the face of her, the moon.
Sackiss	See he doesn't want to change, Miranda... He doesn't want to let go.
Ghost	There's only one point of light that's left.
Sol	There's something else.
Ghost	The brilliance of that light. It just outlines the moon.
Sackiss	What?
Ghost	It's like a diamond ring.
Sol	There's something else that happened.

Pause.

Sackiss	It shouldn't be said, Sol.
Sol	It happened.

Pause.

Sackiss	You should let go, Sol.
Sol	Didn't it happen?
Sackiss	You shouldn't hold onto things...

Miranda	What happened?
Sackiss	Kevin says...
Miranda	I don't know about it.
Sol	We were doing it, the play...
Ghost	I was Cordelia.
Sol	I was young.
Sackiss	You can be yourself right now, Sol.
Sol	We were in some, we were... some godforsaken town, we were... working in, remember? Some godforsaken place... Out in the middle of bum fuck, out in the middle of God knows where, some town with a church, with a church smack-dab in the middle of it. You know those towns, with a church smack-dab in the middle? Miranda...?
Sackiss	He has a choice, Miranda. He can relieve himself of the burden...
Sol	And I was having the show of my life. Goddamnit. I was having the, the run of my life.
Sackiss	Of the weight of this armor...
Sol	The show of my life. I floated out of myself. I floated out...
Ghost	Miranda...
Miranda	Yes...
Sackiss	If you could let go of all of it...
Ghost	I was very sick with cancer.
Sol	I pushed out of myself...
Ghost	My esophagus. You remember?
Sackiss	Just cut the ropes that hold it. Sol...
Ghost	And your father.
Sol	And how I, how I rode the light. How I...
Ghost	He sits by my bed.

Sackiss	Cut the ropes. And be clear. And step in that lake.
Sol	And Sackiss,
Ghost	He starts to shake.
Sol	And one day Sackiss he,
Ghost	And I'm lying there. I'm helpless. I don't know what he wants from me. What does he want from me? I'm dying. It hurts to die.
Sackiss	You can let it all go.
Sol	He wants to get a drink before the show. Why did I go?
Sackiss	I can see all the pain in you, you know? The pain.
Ghost	And people look at you. And you feel far away from them. How I long to put my feet in the sand again! Mirand...
Sol	If I could not go.
Ghost	You haven't even talked to me in weeks. You haven't. You've stayed outside the door...
Sackiss	I can feel it in you...
Sol	I think about it, I think about it.
Sackiss	The pain...
Sol	I imagine it. And I, I... it comes from somewhere. It doesn't have words is what I'm saying. What I need to tell you. I don't know the words...
Ghost	I've tried to talk to you. And you won't look at me, will you? You won't look at me. Or talk to me. Miranda, why won't you talk to me?
Sackiss	And you don't have to feel it, Sol. You have a choice. In life. And I know that you can change...
Sol	We go into this bar because it's the only place in town. And there's no one but this, this, this girl... *(Pause)* ... and she's sitting there. And she's too young for this. And she's too young to be here. In this place.

Miranda	I don't know...
Sol	She's a...
Miranda	I don't know if I can hear this...
Sol	She's a... She's a...
Miranda	I don't know if I can...
Sol	A prostitute. *(Beat)* You can tell. *(Beat)* She was young. Her bones... were small. She has a gap between her teeth...
Miranda	I think I...
Sol	See this guy comes out of nowhere and propositions us. He asks us if we want a ride with her. The girl. *(Beat)* We get into his car. The car was green, a faded green, like peas. The inside of the car was cold. I stretch my hands. They tingle. And all my joints are stiff. I don't know why. *(Beat)* My breath comes out in clouds. Sackiss looks ahead. He sits in back. I sit in the front. The guy is driving. *(Pause)* The guy is tall and thin. But you can tell the work he'd done was physical. You can tell he doesn't like us. He... He stinks of scotch. And smelly aftershave. The two scents mingle. The scotch and sweet perfume. And cigarettes. I look over to him. I'm a young man still. I... I can feel it still. His hair is greasy. I can see it. Combed over to the side. His nose is flat and looks like it's been broken. And his face is red from drinking. His face is wide and clumsy. His face... He isn't smart, this guy, he isn't bright. But he thinks he knows more than me and Sackiss. He... hates us I can tell. And... Suddenly I wake up... See... I've been asleep. Who knows how long, Miranda. I don't know. See... I look at Sackiss sleeping like a kid in back. I'm suddenly awake. I guess I fell asleep because the guy has made some crazy turn. We're driving over ground, like

	grass and holes, and this car was not the kind of car for this. He says. I'll take you to a place you won't forget. A place you won't be seen by folks. *(Beat)* And then I see this thing off in the distance. *(Beat)*
Miranda	The sun, it burns my eyes.
Sol	*(Beat)* This giant thing. I hate the sight of this. An empty field. And there's some kind of structure there. *(Beat)* A dilapidated structure. More. A structure... A skeletal structure. Gutted. And shaped... for no use anymore. It can't be used for anything anymore. All the use has been taken from it. More. Pieces of wood blow when the wind blows. Pieces of useless wood. Hanging by rusted nails. With splinters you would get, I'm sure. Splinters that would burrow up the bottom of your foot like some terrible bug. This giant thing. With its terrible swinging. The sky beats down on it. In this clearing. It towers above me. God I can't tell what it was ever for. A terrible ripping of some kind. And what is it doing out here...?
Miranda	Dad...?
Sol	A terrible anger made the world, Miranda...
Miranda	No...
Sol	A terrible anger...
Miranda	It's not true...
Sol	At nothing.
Miranda	It can't be true...
Sol	At the towering nothing. And in that rage, I think, we were conceived. And we were born, I think, Miranda. I never believed in protecting you...
Miranda	I know...
Sol	Miranda.

Miranda	I know, Dad...
Sol	Forced into being...
Miranda	Yes, Dad.
Sol	He killed the girl. *(Beat)* The man. *(Beat)* In the cold, Miranda. With his hands... *(Beat)* And we just stand there watching. Why are we just standing here? Why's he doing it?
Sackiss	I don't know, Sol...
Sol	He kills the girl. In front of us. He kills her. He... *(Beat)* But we just watch in silence. *(Weeps)*
Ghost	I see you at the door. And Sol—he sees it in my face. And looks behind him. He sees you standing there in your pajamas. They're going to put the morphine patches on me. And it's time to say goodbye. *(Beat)* I look for something in your eyes. But I can't see in there. I can't see. And you say nothing. I say "Miranda." I call your name like that. Miranda. And you're looking at me. Standing at the door. *(Beat)* And then you turn away. *(Beat)* Your back is to me. And you leave me there. *(Beat)* That's when it happens. They put the patches on. And that's when I walk out of my body. *(Beat)* Your father finds you in the yard. I see you there. The two of you. He says, "Your mother died Miranda." Your hair's all knotted. I think, "He won't be able to get them out. The knots. Without me." *(Beat)* And then you ask for something from him. Apple juice, or something. Your face, I see it. It's like an open wound. A flower...
Miranda	Dad...
Sol	You have to forgive me...
Miranda	I...
Sol	You have to forgive me...

Miranda	Dad...
Sol	You have to—
Miranda	Love yourself. *(Beat)* Dad. *(Beat)* Please love yourself. You have to, Dad. Please. You have to do it.

Silence. The light shifts to dark. The GHOST looks up at the sun.

Ghost	This is where totality begins. See. It's not quite as dark as night. We can look up know. We can look at the sun.

MIRANDA looks up at the sun.

Ghost	It only lasts a couple of minutes. Then the moon begins to move again. It becomes dangerous again. When you start to see the light. And with strange shadows caused by scattered light. Look at the horizon. It's still quite light. As if we're in a double time. The whole landscape, listen, it's in a kind of stupor. Birds fly home to trees. Bees burrow in the earth. Flowers close as if it's night. And in the sky the moon hangs slack surrounded by a halo. The opposite of light. A sort of sun that's negative.
Sackiss	Oh. Ha-ha-ha-ha-ha. Ha. Here's a good one. This oughta, this oughta cheer everyone up. *(Beat)* There's this small village in Siberia at the height of the Stalin era. And it's cold there, it's bitter cold. You know what I'm saying? Siberian cold. And it's the dead of the winter. And everybody's fuckin' freezing. And once a week the villagers huddle together and wait for the train to come you know, with the bread. They wait and they wait in the cold. And the train doesn't

come, it doesn't come. It's very late, is what's happening. And finally the stationmaster comes out. *(Beat)* So he says, *(Imitating Russian accent)* "Comrades, I have bad news. The train is going to be three hours late. And I have now further bad news. There is not enough bread to go around. So all of you Jews, *(Beat)* who are waiting, go home! You will have no bread this week." A handful of elderly Jews shuffle off in the cold. *(Beat)* Three hours go by. And these guys have been waiting, all day they've been waiting. And now it's three in the afternoon. And the sun, the sun has started to go down. Slowly to go down. And the temperature has slowly begun to drop. And now it's fucking freezing. It's freezing out there. Finally the stationmaster comes out again. *(Opens his arms)* And he says, "Comrades, I have even worse news than before. The train you all are waiting for will now be six hours late. And even worse than that. There is much less bread the expected. So. Unless you are a veteran. Unless you fought in one of our great wars there will be no bread for you." *(Beat)* So then all the veterans are left waiting. There by the station... All different ages. With their lost limbs. Et cetera. And it just gets colder and colder.

Ghost   This is a long joke. *(Slowly enters the house)*

Sackiss   At nine pm the stationmaster comes out. Again. And he says, *(Imitating Russian accent)* "Comrades, *(Opens his hands)* comrades, there is bad news. The train is even later than we thought. Still worse. Very little bread. Only enough for the veterans of the Great War. Everyone else must go." The people leave. Only two men left standing. Old. Wrinkled. Gray. Footless. One a them's got no foot. The temperature drops to thirty below. And they wait.

And they wait and they wait. Until finally it's midnight. And the stationmaster returns. And his head is lowered. *(Imitating Russian accent)* "Comrades," he says, "I have bad news. There will be no train. And there will be no bread. There is no reason to continue waiting." *(Beat)* And the stationmaster leaves. And the two veterans in silence slowly turn away from the tracks. And one turns to the other and says, *(No accent)* "Fuckin' Jews have all the luck." Ha-ha. Ha-ha. Get it? Get it, Solly? You and me, huh? All the luck. *(Beat)* Yeah. *(Pause)* Yeah. It's just, you know, life isn't like what it is in the movies, is it? No one claps for you in the airport. *(Enters house)*

Miranda   I would watch the sun on the floor, Dad. When we would read together. Shakespeare. *(Beat)* I would watch it move. And I would want it to stop moving. *(Beat)* Because I don't want it to be over. I don't want the reading to be over. I think, oh no, there's the sun on the floor and when it gets to the door, when the floor is covered in shadow, that's when, that's when this will be over. When the sun moves all the way across the floor that's when this will be over. And we won't read anymore. Because it will be night and Mom will come in, and I'll have to sleep and I don't want to sleep, I don't...

Sol   I went back to the theater. I didn't know what else to do. I wasn't... *(Beat)* We're all in this row. All of us. In the mirrors. And where's Sackiss? Who knows where he his? Has anyone seen Sackiss? *(Beat)* I wipe my forehead. And the tissue, the tissue is soaked from it. The sweat. And my hands. They're shaking now. I'm shaking. And my ears. I can hear my heartbeat in my head. *(Beat)* The lights come up on me.

And it's like I'm underwater out there. The other actors, I can see it in their eyes. Everything slow. And heavy. I'm pushing through water. And it's scene four. Miranda. And I'm standing here with Kent. And Kent is in disguise. And this is where the Fool comes in. And I'm waiting for the Fool to enter. Standing here and waiting for the Fool to enter. But where is he? Where's the Fool? *(Beat)* He doesn't come. We're frozen out there. He doesn't come. And the other actors start to leave. And finally I'm left alone out there. I'm all alone. And the light shines in my face. I can't stand to feel it. I can't stand to look in it. The light. I can't stand to look in it. *(Beat)* And then I turn away.

Silence. The sky is dark. The GHOST *emerges from the house.*

Ghost Miranda. *(Beat)* Oh. I didn't mean to interrupt. It's just. I went into the house just now. I had to see it. I had to see it. See it one last time. See the house. Before I go. *(Beat)* I went to the bathroom. And everything was blue in there, Miranda. It was blue. From this light. From this eerie light. *(Beat)* And in that blue light the rooms seem strange to me. The rooms I lived in for twenty years seem suddenly strange. As I walk through. That they contain you and your father. And that I'm not there anymore. That you sleep in those rooms. That your bodies sleep there. *(Beat)* And sleep, too. And sleep seems strange, too, suddenly. The feeling that sleep happens. That the body is tired. Tired from life. And that the body needs to close its eyes and slip into an unconscious state. For hours. Hours out of every day. And I wonder when will they do away with sleep? Altogether? Do you ever wonder that? Because you know they will. Come up with a pill. To do away with sleep. And death, Miranda. They've tried to do away with death. You barely see it. It's hidden from us. And we've built this world on top of it. They'll do away with sleep and death. And all we'll have will be this perpetual state we're in now. This walking. This state that hardly seems real anyway. *(Beat)* Oh and I'm thinking these things as I'm walking down the stairs. And then I see Sackiss asleep there on the couch. Mir. In those awful pants. Those terrible pants. With the pleats. I hate pleats. And that braided belt. And I hate him. And I think. I could kill him right now. You know? Smother his face with a pillow. And I look at him. And I see him there. And I see him as nothing but a body sleeping. A body that needs rest. And then the strangest thing. And then suddenly out of nowhere I feel love for him. I feel, I swear, Miranda, I feel love for him. And I had to tell you. And my heart just opens then. Like a flower. Or something natural. I feel it open. I don't know why. I guess it's just in sleep we look so innocent don't we? Everyone looks so innocent. And we are all innocent. In sleep. I guess it's just that. Lying there. With eyes closed. Needing rest. No matter what we've done. *(Beat)* And in death, too, I guess, Miranda. In death, too. We're all innocent. Aren't we? No matter all the things we've done. At that moment. Aren't we? Just as in birth. At the end we're all innocent. *(Beat)* And Mirand—if we could remember that then maybe we wouldn't be so tired. All the time. We'd feel full of life. *(Beat)* Anyway, I'm just going on and

Sol on. And it seems you're in the middle of something, so... It's just not how I imagined my life. It's just not how I imagined it. *(Beat)* I didn't think I would be here like this. Be in here in this, in this yard. *(Beat)* When I was this age. When I was fifty. *(Beat)* That's all. Not what I pictured. Not what I... *(Beat)* There are these people around you. And there are all these mosquitoes. And there are sprinklers. And you live in this town and it's humid and there are these shrubs. *(Beat)* And I have to send you to school. And... there are... carpools. And kids who play trombone. Instruments like that... and... And you have to hear the wood being cut all the time. And people talking about their weed whackers. About their... Saying, "how much that weed whacker set you back...?" Things like that. And the men. And they talk to you about sports. And their timeshares. And you want something sweet. You know, Mirand? *(Turns and looks at* MIRANDA*)* To take the taste away? *(Beat)* I thought I'd pick up time along the way. *(Beat. He looks front)* 'Cause when you've felt that feeling. When you've been onstage. And the lights come up on you. You know? And I'm the king. And everybody's looking. And I say my first line. *(Beat)* And I don't know what happens. But the weight of the robes. The heaviness of them. And the whiteness of the light. The faces there... The actors' eyes... and the makeup, the sweat beading on the make up like that. The audience, breathing. And the sound of the words. And then the sound becomes the meaning. And it seems that something turns or something. I become then sort of not myself. But something else. And the lights. And we're up here. On stage. And... *(Beat)* I can't talk about it.

(Beat) To talk about it makes it... That's why she says nothing. Cordelia. Isn't it? I understand it now. Right now, Miranda. That's why she says nothing. Mir. Because to say it is to...

Pause.

Ghost   "O! Look upon me, Sir
And hold your hand in... in benediction o'er me."

MIRANDA looks down. Pause.

Miranda   "O...!
Ghost   "O! Look upon me, Sir."
Miranda   "Look... upon me... Sir..." *(Pause)*
And hold your hand in... in benediction o'er me."

Pause. SOL slowly looks up at her.

Ghost   "No, Sir, you must not kneel."

Beat.

Miranda   "No, Sir, you must not kneel."

Pause.

Sol   "Pray... do not mock me: *(Pause)*
I am a very... foolish... fond old man, *(Pause)*
Fourscore and upward... fourscore and upward... not an hour more or less;

And, to... *(Pause)* And to... *(Pause)* To..." *(Pause)*
Miranda...? *(Pause)*
"And, to deal plainly,
I fear... I am not... in my perfect mind. *(Pause)*
Methinks I should know you and know this man; *(Pause)*
Yet I am doubtful: for I am mainly ignorant
What place this is, and all the skill I have
Remembers not these garments; nor I know not
Where I did lodge last night. Do not laugh at me;
For, as I am a man, I think this lady
To be my child Cordelia."

Miranda   "And so I am, I am."

Sol   "Be your tears wet? Yes, faith. I pray, weep not:
If you have poison for me, I will drink it.
I know you do not love me, for your sisters
Have, as I do remember, done me wrong:
You have some cause, they have not."

Miranda   "No cause, no cause."

Sol   "Am I in France?"

Miranda   "In your own kingdom, Sir."

Sol   "Do not abuse me."

Miranda   "Will't please your highness walk?"

Sol   "You must bear with me.
Pray you now, forget and forgive: *(Pause)*
I am old and foolish."

Silence. SACKISS *enters from the house.*

Sackiss   I was going to lunch, you understand, like I always do and
I leave the office... *(Beat)* This one day... *(Beat)* And and

and I open the door. *(Beat)* And the sun it burns my eyes first thing. I remember. *(Beat)* And I raise my arm like this to cover my eyes like this.

Pause. SACKISS *demonstrates and looks around. The other three stand still. Pause.*

Sackiss   And I have my own space, you know, too. I have my own space. So it's not like I have to, I have to wander in some big lot, or some big parking structure. Nah. I have my own, my own space. It has my name on it too. Painted on the cement block or whatever that thing is. And it makes me feel, I don't know... good. To see that. You know? Everyday. I feel good to see my name like that. Feels like I've accomplished something. *(Beat)* Maybe it doesn't sound like much. But it seemed like something. *(Beat)* And to other people I think as well. To see that—my name means certain things have been accomplished in my life certain—my name. That I am somebody. 'Cause people, 'cause in Hollywood—not everybody gets a name on a space. I mean with all those cars, all those cars, it's lawless to think of them circling and circling and searching and limited spaces and swarming the roads and the freeways and all looking for a place, looking for a place to park. And to know everyday my car not only has a place, but my name is on it. My name is on that fucking spot. You know? *(Pause)* That means something for fuck's sake. *(Pause)* Maybe it doesn't mean that much to you out here but... *(Pause)* And other people, other people know it, too —they know it too. 'Cause they have to see it everyday.

"Oh, well, I guess I can't park in that spot," they say to themselves. Because that guy's name's on it. That guy being me. That's his spot, they think. That guy. And he has an important position, and important job in the studio. *(Pause)* So anyway, I'm walking to my car and and and... *(Pause)* And the great vastness of the desert. I never noticed it. And the cars. The noise of them. The cars. *(Pause)* The sky suddenly—the desert *(Pause)*—the vastness of it suddenly. I feel myself walking... How do I...? Uh. Just the, uh, the sky over my head. Just...And I'm suddenly it's like I'm... I feel a pain in my chest. I feel a pounding in my chest... It's that—that elephant on there. A pounding. And I'm leaning on the hood of a car. Ha ha ha—leaning on the hood of a car to catch my breath. And somebody honks a horn and I jump you know? 'Cause somebody's in the car, somebody's in the car I'm leaning on. And I jump and I look up 'cause I thought the car was parked see I thought the car was empty. So I smile at the guy, as I try to catch my breath, but it's hard to see 'cause there's a glare, it burns my eyes it you know... And I look up at him, I look through the window of his car and it's one of those big cars you know it's so big. It's so, so high. That he's, that he's towering above me and it's like I'm looking up at my dad or something. And I can't see his eyes. But through the glare I can feel he hates me, from up there. *(Pause)* And he's behind glass, the glass of his car and he's high up in the air... like a king. *(Pause)* And he hates me. And the pain in my chest—it's the elephant. And the sweat on my head—it's too hot—here suddenly—the sun beats down on me here. And I make a face—like this—like I give him one of these—like I shrug—like what's the big deal—apologetically—*(Pause)* And through the glare his eyes are missing—through the sun reflected on the window—and then he peels out and I fall over. Onto the pavement. On all fours. And like a little kid I skin my knees, through my pants I can feel them. Skinned. And my hands with all the tiny gravels on them. *(Pause)* I skin my knees. And the sweat drops on my hands. From my head. You know? *(Pause)* I don't say this to—I don't want—I want—*(Pause)* So. I go back into my office and the phone rings and it's this girl. I get this call, and I thought it was... I know it sounds... but I thought it was... *(Beat)* But it's from you Miranda. And she wants to know will I help her father. *(Beat)* But I guess... When I heard her voice... I just... I felt... an emptiness. *(Beat)* I guess that's really why I came here. Sol. *(Beat)* I'd like Miranda to be—to come with me. To Hollywood. Is what I'm saying.

Pause.

Sol   What?

Pause.

Sackiss   I'd like Miranda to be in it—my movie.
Miranda   What?
Sackiss   I want her to play the girl. The lead.
Miranda   No...
Sol   Miranda...
Miranda   I don't understand...

Sackiss	There's work out there. There's acting work.
Miranda	Acting.
Sackiss	Yes.
Miranda	I don't act.
Sackiss	Well sure you do.
Miranda	I don't.
Sackiss	You told me that you did. And I heard you. I heard you quoting Shakespeare.
Miranda	My dad's the actor, Mr. Sackiss.
Sackiss	And so are you, you said...
Miranda	But I didn't call you here for me!
Sackiss	Are you sure, Miranda?

Pause.

Sol	Go...
Miranda	What...?
Sol	Go, Miranda...
Miranda	No...
Sol	Leave...
Miranda	I don't want to leave you... *(Slowly turns and looks at the GHOST)* Mom...
Ghost	Miranda...
Miranda	I don't want to go...
Ghost	But that's why I'm here...
Miranda	Why?
Ghost	To say goodbye...

Pause.

Miranda	No...
Ghost	You have to go...
Miranda	I can't...
Ghost	Listen to me.
Miranda	No...
Ghost	Mirand...
Miranda	Mom...
Ghost	No matter what happens, Miranda. No matter what happens. When you're at the place. Are you listening to me? When you're at that place, Miranda. When you're about to die, I mean. Time doesn't, time doesn't do anything for you then. *(Beat)* What do I mean? I mean... well, when you're in a place you just are there. And so everything that came before isn't there anymore. It's just gone now. It's all gone. All you really have is now. Not anything that happened before. And everything just happens so fast. No matter how slowly it really happened. When you felt, "Oh, this will never end, this day," or when you're in pain and you think, "This is unbearable, this pain. This is unbearable, this pain." *(Beat)* Or you watch the sun in the room. And it takes forever. It takes forever for the sun to simply go from here to there. From the corner to the table.
Miranda	Yes... *(Slowly walks upstage to SACKISS)*
Ghost	It's like when you go on a trip. The trip has a beginning and an end. And no matter how long the trip was, no matter how many things you saw and waiting in line and that fight and getting sick, well at the end of it when you're driving back home or flying back home, the whole thing seems really seems fast. Like the ends of time get pinched together. And everything in between gets shortened. All

that is just gone. One day it's just gone. And it seems as if it happened quickly. Like it flew by. No matter what, it happened quickly. Because it all just speeds up to that point. Where you are now.

SOL raises his head up and looks directly at the sun. MIRANDA slowly covers her eyes with one hand.

Ghost   And right before we die, I mean, it all just speeds up to that point, Miranda. And we don't know when that point is. But death will come to us like lights out. Like lights out. On this. On you crying. And my dissatisfaction with you and this. The stale air. The humidity. And I was humiliated by this and that. And where do we go? Anyway? And how did we get here? Anyway? And why here? And why you? And why here? And how did we get here anyway? And lights out.

SOL looks momentarily peaceful. BRILLIANT WHITE LIGHT, then BLACKOUT.

The End

Contributors

Steven Leigh Morris has been theater editor and critic of the *LA Weekly* since 1998. His reviews, commentaries, and articles have been published in *The New York Times, The Los Angeles Times, American Theatre Magazine, DRAMA Magazine* in London, *L.A. Stage,* and *Back Stage West.* He is the recipient of three awards for journalistic excellence from the Los Angeles Press Club. Morris has also been a playwright in residence at the Los Angeles Actors' Theater, Actors' Gang, and Moscow's Theatre on Spartacus Square. His plays have been commissioned by the Mark Taper Forum and presented in New York, Los Angeles, and Edinburgh, as well as at the Lublin International Theatre Festival.

Sarah Koskoff is an actor and playwright living in Los Angeles. Her play *Debt* was produced by Oxblood Theater Collective, directed by Wesley Walker.

Murray Mednick is the founder of the Padua Hills Playwrights Festival and Workshop, where he served as artistic director from 1978 through 1995. Born in Brooklyn, New York, he was for many years a playwright-in-residence at New York's Theatre Genesis, which presented all of his early work, including *The Hawk, The Deer Kill, The Hunter, Sand,* and *Are You Lookin'?.* He was artistic co-director of Genesis from 1970 until 1974, when he emigrated to California. Plays produced since then include *Iowa and Blessings* (for the PBS series "Visions"), *The Coyote Cycle, Taxes, Scar, Heads, Shatter 'n Wade, Fedunn, Switchback, Baby, Jesus!, Dictator,* and *Freeze.* Mednick's plays *Joe and Betty* and *Mrs. Feuerstein* received dual runs in Los Angeles and New York in 2002; *Joe and Betty* received the American Theatre

Critics Association's Best New Play Citation in that year. He is also the recipient of two Rockefeller Foundation grants, a Guggenheim Fellowship, an OBIE, several Bay Area Critics Awards, the 1997 *LA Weekly* Playwriting Award (for *Dictator*) and a 1992 Ovation Lifetime Achievement Award from Theatre L.A. for outstanding contributions to Los Angeles theatre. Most recently, Mednick was awarded the 2002 Margaret Harford Award for Sustained Excellence in Theater by the Los Angeles Drama Critics Circle.

John O'Keefe, who began working with the Padua Playwrights Festival in 1982, has written more than 40 plays and has won three Bay Area Critic's Circle Awards, six Hollywood Drama-Logue Awards, three *LA Weekly* Awards, four Dallas TheaterCritics Circle Awards, the New York Performance Art Award (Bessie), and a citation by the American Theater Critics Association.

John Steppling is an original member of the Padua Festival, and former artistic director of Empire Red Lip in Los Angeles and former co-artistic director of Heliogabalus and Circus Minimus, both in Los Angeles. His plays have been performed in Los Angeles, San Francisco, London, New York, Paris, and soon in Krakow, where he lives with his wife Anna. Steppling is a Rockefeller Fellow, two time NEA recipient, MacDowell Colony Resident, and a PEN-West winner. His plays include *Dream Coast*, *Teenage Wedding*, *Neck*, *Contagion: An American Book of the Dead*, *Dog Mouth*, *Standard of the Breed*, *The Shaper*, and *Pledging My Love*.

Wesley Walker's plays include *The Conception*, *Freak Storm*, *Bloody Mary*, and *Found*. He directed Murray Mednick's *16 Routines* for

Padua last season, as well as Oxblood's productions of *Debt* and *The Definite Child*. Additionally, he wrote and directed parts of *Murdered Sleep: Meditations on Macbeth, Citizen Faust, White Cold Virgin Snow, Conquest Of The New World,* and *Aftershock* for Empire Red Lip, a collective of playwrights headed by John Steppling and Guy Zimmerman. A classically trained singer, Wes has fronted for several L.A. post-punk bands, and music plays an important part in his work.

Guy Zimmerman has been artistic director of Padua Playwrights since 2000, overseeing award-winning productions of new plays in Los Angeles and New York by numerous contemporary playwrights, including Murray Mednick, John Steppling, and John O'Keefe. Under his direction, the company's productions have garnered *LA Weekly,* Garland, LA Drama Critics Circle, and American Theatre Critics Association awards. In addition, he has moved two plays to Off-Broadway stages in New York City to critical acclaim. He recently completed a feature film of Mednick's play *Girl on a Bed* and has also directed short films based on texts by Paul Bowles, Sissy Boyd, and his own plays, *The Wasps* and *HeadTrader.* His own plays include *Splinter, HeadTrader, La Clarita, Hide,* and *The Inside Job.*

ABOUT PADUA

Padua Playwrights is a theater company devoted to extending and deepening the influence of New York's Off-Off Broadway movement in the 1960s, when European theatrical influences merged with a jazz-inspired, American sensibility to produce a new brand of transformative theater. This uniquely modern, uniquely American approach to writing for the stage is exemplified by such writers as Murray Mednick, Sam Shepard, and Maria Irene Fornes. Among its practitioners is a multitude of diverse voices, such as prominent Padua alumni Henry David Hwang, John Steppling, John O'Keefe, Jon Robin Baitz, Marlane Meyer, and Kelly Stuart, as well as more recent graduates such as Guy Zimmerman, Wesley Walker and Sharon Yablon—all cultivated at the Padua Hills Playwrights Festival/Workshop during its eighteen-year run in Southern California.

The Padua Hills Festival/Workshop began in 1978 when Murray Mednick invited five other playwrights, including Shepard and Fornes, to join him on the old Padua Hills estate in the foothills of the San Gabriel Mountains, just east of Los Angeles. The playwrights, as well as playwriting students and actors, were given free reign to re-investigate their creativity, developing writing exercises for the morning, rehearsing in the afternoon, and presenting the results in the evening. Under Mednick's artistic direction, the Festival became a model that, staged annually, had a lasting impact on American theater.

In 2000, Padua Playwrights re-launched as a production company mounting regular seasons of new work. Since then, under the artistic direction of playwright and director Guy Zimmerman, the company has staged seventeen productions, including three in New York City, that have garnered a host of *LA Weekly*, Ovation, Garland, and Los Angeles Drama Critics Circle award nominations, as well as an American Theatre Critics Association citation. The company is in the process of completing a five-volume anthology series, distributed nationally by TCG, as well as an ongoing exploration of ways to expand its audience via digital media productions of original plays. Visit www.paduaplaywrights.net for more information.

PERMISSIONS

Requests for permission to stage plays, in part or in their entirety, should be directed to the following sources:

Times Like These
johnokeefe.org

Baby, Jesus!, G-Nome, 4 Way Mars, Vagrant *and* **The Wasps**
Guy Zimmerman
Padua Playwrights Productions
964 Tularosa Drive
Los Angeles, CA 90026

Dog Mouth, Wilfredo, Temple Dog, Apple Juice Man
info@paduaplaywrights.net

Padua Playwrights Press books are available from your local book-seller or visit www.paduaplaywrights.net.

Other available titles:

Hipsters in Distress by Murray Mednick
Includes *Are You Lookin'?*, *Scar*, *Skinwalkers*, and *Dictator*
"A playwright's playwright... Mednick has spent his career at the forefront of avant-garde theater."—Sandra Ross, *LA Weekly*
458 pages, Paperback, ISBN 0-9630126-7-3
$14.95

Padua: Plays from the Padua Hills Playwrights Festival
Includes plays from the Padua Hills Playwrights Festival by:
Neena Beber, Maria Irene Fornes, Joseph Goodrich, Murray Mednick, Marlane Meyer, Susan Mosakowski, John O'Keefe, John Steppling, Kelly Stuart.
504 pages, Paperback, ISBN 0-9630126-4-9
$18.95

Three Plays by Murray Mednick
16 Routines, *Joe and Betty*, and *Mrs. Feuerstein*
Murray Mednick at his darkly comic best.
300 pages, Paperback, ISBN 0-9630126-3-0
$14.95

Best of the West
Includes plays from the Padua Hills Playwrights Festival by:
Susan Champagne, Martin Epstein, Maria Irene Fornes, Julie Hebert,
Leon Martell, Murray Mednick, Susan Mosakowski, John Steppling,
Kelly Stuart.
312 pages, Paperback, ISBN 0-9630126-2-2
$14.95

The Coyote Cycle
Seven Plays by Murray Mednick
"...it permanently reshaped my vision of what theatre could achieve—
ritual, magic, playfulness, and respect for the playwright-actor bond
entered my creative vocabulary and have been my resources ever since...
in a day when much of the public has come to doubt the power of
theatre, Murray Mednick's *Coyote* is proof that the best of it can still
change lives."—David Henry Hwang
176 pages, Paperback, ISBN 0-9630126-1-4
$15.95